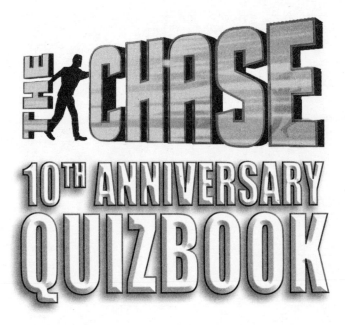

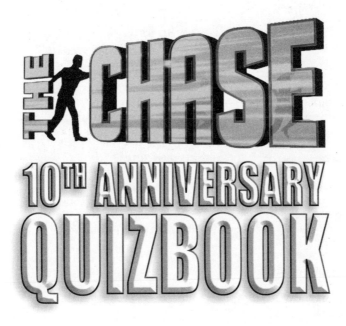

Foreword by Bradley Walsh

hamlyn

An Hachette UK Company
www.hachette.co.uk

First published in Great Britain in 2019 by Hamlyn,
an imprint of Octopus Publishing Group Ltd
Carmelite House
50 Victoria Embankment
London EC4Y 0DZ
www.octopusbooks.co.uk

ISBN 978-0-600-63634-2

A CIP catalogue record for this book is available from the
British Library

Printed and bound in the UK

10 9 8 7 6 5 4 3 2 1

Questions compiled by James Bovington
Factoids written by Ian Cross

Publishing Director Trevor Davies
Editor Sonya Newland
Typesetter Jeremy Tilston
Production Controller Grace O'Byrne

CONTENTS

FOREWORD

Ten years ago, who'd have thought that I'd be sitting here today writing about 10 years of *The Chase*? Well, I did. I knew the instant we started that first show that we had something special going on. It was, and remains, the Holy Grail of television formats, with the best end game you'll ever see.

I love a quiz me – television, newspaper, pub quiz especially – and here was a format where along with learning random facts, you could have enormous fun.

We started with the Dark Destroyer, a man who could kill a joke stone dead from 50 miles, and the Beast, who could sniff out a Victoria sponge cake from the same distance. Next to join us was the Governess, Old Frosty Knickers herself, now a national treasure, loved and feared by all (just feared by me). Then came the Sinnerman, with his terrific fashion sense, and finally the Vixen who, just when you think someone can't get any smarter, whips out her ukulele and strums you into submission.

And who faces the famous five? Well, as you know, four people who have never met before but who, by working as a team, have a chance of winning thousands of pounds. Over the course of 10 years of *The Chase*, I've had the pleasure of meeting and standing alongside over 5,500 contestants wanting to take down a Chaser, amongst them a Red Arrow pilot, dream maker, retired nut tester, film director, cake designer, tugboat navigator, stage hypnotist, cartoonist, quantumologist, pantomime dame, chocolatier, Beefeater, zoo interpreter, town crier, diamond consultant, football agent and one milkman – and they all delivered.

Behind the scenes there is a bunch of people who loosely refer to themselves as television professionals: studio crew, production team, question writers, runners, contestant researchers, producers, editors. We have become family to one another – a strange, dysfunctional family possibly, but we laugh like drains all day, and together I hope we bring you a little laughter and even more general knowledge.

So. Enjoy the book, and here's to another 10 years of *The Chase*!

Bradley Walsh, 2019

INTRODUCTION

Welcome to *The Chase 10th Anniversary Quizbook*.

We wanted to mark the occasion by bringing you a collection of the most infamous moments from over 1,500 shows. This means we can offer you quizzes where there have been solo winners; quizzes where a huge amount of money has been won; the most noteworthy celebrity Chases; the best family quizzes; 'Lazarus' wins; perfect runs and numerous oddities from a decade of shows. There's even a section where you have to guess what connects the answers to give the Chase an added edge.

The variety of quizzes in this book means that you can dip in and choose one that suits your scenario, whether that's a post-meal game with the family or a quick quiz on the daily commute. How you treat the different challenges is up to you, but if you're trying a Final Chase, we suggest you are strict with yourself (or the family member or friend you're pitching the questions to) and stick to the two minutes permitted. If that Final Chase is a perfect run, then you've not only got to keep to the time limit, you also can't get a single question wrong. Tough indeed, but that's why our Chasers are the best at what they do!

There are some real challenges lined up for you in these pages. We've given you a quiz from the Australian version of the show to see if you can cope with some questions from a different cultural perspective. There's also a selection of favourite questions from one of our key question setters, who just happens to be a four-time World Quizzing Champion – so good luck with those!

Of course, there are simpler tasks in this book: those occasions when things didn't go so well for a contestant or a Chaser. And there's more than just questions. We've compiled lots of facts about the show, profiled the Chasers, collected all Brad's classic one-liners as well as those questions that gave him – and you – the giggles.

The Chase 10th Anniversary Quizbook contains all the elements of a show that has entertained millions of viewers for the last 10 years. Enjoy!

TIME CHASE

SOLO WINNERS

THE CHASE

SOLO WINNERS

It's hardly a national secret that Chasers don't like losing. However, it's one thing losing to a full house of four contestants but a whole different kettle of fish losing to a single, solitary, solo player. They *hate* it! To be fair, it doesn't happen that often, but when it does the viewers love it as much as the Chasers don't. So, here's a selection of some solo brainboxes who put one over on a Chaser all by themselves. Oh, and Anne Hegerty asked for it to be made clear that she is the only Chaser *never* to lose to a single player. Actually, she has – in a Lazarus show where she'd already caught the whole team – but she said that didn't count. And you don't argue with the Governess...

Now it's your turn. Could you beat a Chaser all on your own like these people did?

PETE

Pete was a football-loving estate manager from Hertfordshire who went Head to Head with Shaun in Series 4, set him 18 and pocketed £10,000. Pete was training to become a certified referee – he'd have been an unusually popular one with all that cash! He used it to treat his wife to a fabulous holiday for her 40th birthday.

1   What type of creature is a barracuda?

2   *West Is West* is the sequel to what 1999 film?

3   What pop star was born Michael Barratt?

4   What medical condition used to be known as dropsy?

5   How many sides has a hexagon?

6   Arborio rice is from what country?

7   Which Prime Minister became First Earl of Avon?

8   Beatrice and Eugenie are which prince's daughters?

9   Who did Elin Nordegren divorce in 2010?

10   Santa Fe is the capital of what US state?

11   Who directed the TV play *Nuts in May*?

12   What four-letter name is given to iron oxide?

13   The Battle of Agincourt took place during what war?

14   In what Italian city is the Pitti Palace?

15   Humbug sweets have what flavour?

16   Mr Bumble features in what Dickens novel?

17   In Morse code, dot dash represents what vowel?

18   Who directed both *The Pink Panther* and *10*?

19   What's the world's largest ape?

20 King's Lynn is in what county?

21 Oak-apple Day celebrates the restoration of which king?

22 Who won the Booker Prize for *Hotel du Lac*?

23 Evian and Perrier are brands of what?

24 How many legs does a centaur have?

25 Which French chemist pioneered treatment for rabies?

26 Selim the Grim ruled what empire?

27 The ATP and LTA are involved in what sport?

28 A cobbler mends what items?

29 What was the nationality of artist Murillo?

SOLO WINNERS

MAXINE

Maxine worked as a customer advisor in a bank in Bristol when she set Shaun 19 to catch in Series 4. When he didn't make it, she took home £8,000. She'd honed her memory by working as a croupier when she was younger, and the money came in very handy furnishing her first home, which she'd recently bought.

1   The husband of your sister is your what?

2   Sherpas live in what mountain range?

3   'Heart Vacancy' was a 2010 hit for which boy band?

4   What type of creature is a Kissing Gourami?

5   Joe Calzaghe was world champion in what sport?

6   What type of food is Danish Blue?

7   Who did David Tennant replace as the Doctor in *Doctor Who*?

8   What war began with an attack on Fort Sumter?

9   What animal is the children's character Miffy?

10 How many dimes in a dollar?

11 *Breaking Dawn* is the fourth episode in what film series?

12 What volcano on Martinique erupted in 1902?

13 Horseradish sauce is traditionally served with what meat?

14 Who was the long-running host of *Play Your Cards Right*?

15 'I'm Outta Love' was a 2000 hit for which female singer?

16 Queen Victoria had how many children?

17 Bela Lugosi played which vampire in a 1931 film?

18 *The Nutcracker* ballet is set during what holiday?

19 How were TV's *Gilmore Girls* related?

20 Traditionally a chandler made what household items?

21 What country's currency is the Afghani?

22 In what film does Bruce Willis first say 'Yippie-ki-yay'?

23 In Indian cuisine, what is kulfi?

24 Which novelist wrote *The Cement Garden* and *Enduring Love*?

25 What does SW stand for on a radio?

26 Watchmaker Rolex is based in what country?

27 In 2010, what group had a Number One with 'The Club Is Alive'?

28 In legend, who cut the Gordian knot?

29 A Chelsea Pensioner's coat is what colour?

30 What league football team is known as The Canaries?

31 What's the opposite of the nautical term 'leeward'?

32 Who presents *Country House Rescue*?

33 Nick Clegg was leader of what political party?

34 A lexicographer compiles what books?

35 James Degale is an Olympic gold medallist in what sport?

36 What's the longest river in Southeast Asia?

37 'Poire' is the French word for what fruit?

38 A Geiger counter is used to detect what?

39 Which MP was the first woman to take her seat in parliament?

40 Who played Dirk Gently on TV in 2010?

SOLO WINNERS

HELEN

Helen was a retired TV journalist and a founding member of *Channel 4 News* who appeared in Series 5. She set Shaun a score of 14 on a tricky set of questions, and went back to her home in Bedfordshire with £5,000. She'd travelled the world with her job but wanted to use the money for a Christmas trip to see her only sister in Australia, as it had been five years since they last got together.

1   What French term for 'please' is abbreviated to SVP?

2   In the Bible, Saul was the first king of what land?

3   In what century did the Young Pretender live?

4   The pineal gland is in what organ of the body?

5   In 1999 who did singer Victoria Adams marry?

6   In what UK country does UTV broadcast?

7   'Great spotted' and 'green' are species of what bird?

8   What London theatre opened in 1818 as the Royal Coburg?

9   In the Falklands War, what kind of weapon was an 'Exocet'?

10   Who is the famous brother of DJ Janice Long?

11   The US Masters golf tournament lasts for how many days?

12   What colour were Giles Gilbert Scott's K6 phone boxes?

13   Fleet Street was the traditional home of what industry?

14   What ship cuts through a frozen sea?

15   Amarillo is a city in what US state?

16   Who wrote the play *Absurd Person Singular*?

17   Egg-nog is a type of what?

18   The 'brown Swiss' is a breed of what farm animal?

19 Halkidiki is a tourist area in what country?

20 Who is the subject of the *Chandos Portrait*?

21 What organ of the body do you exfoliate?

22 In what year was the Queen's coronation?

23 How many official languages does Switzerland have?

24 Who wrote horror novels *The Dark* and *The Fog*?

25 What part of the body is removed in a tonsillectomy?

26 'Bateau' is French for what form of transport?

27 What flavour is Poire Williams liqueur?

28 What decade was the African Union launched?

29 Gary Sobers competed in what sport?

30 In a chess match, what is the role of the 'arbiter'?

31 Herm belongs to what island group?

32 In maths, what kind of angle is greater than 180 degrees?

33 What dried fruit forms the spots in spotted dick?

34 What dog breed is also known as an Alpine mastiff?

35 What French newspaper is named after the Barber of Seville?

36 What Australian plain takes its name from the Latin for 'no tree'?

37 Someone with 'D. Phil' after their name is a doctor of what?

38 On the road, what shape is the red stop sign?

39 The TV drama *Secret Army* was set during what war?

40 What's the party of Russian President Vladimir Putin?

SOLO WINNERS

JOHN

Appropriately enough for an international fund-raising advisor, John from Buckinghamshire raised himself £5,000 when he set Mark a massive 20 back in Series 5. This was, and still is, a joint record high score for a solo contestant. He was a marathon runner who proved just as much at home during the Final Chase sprint, and wanted to use the money to take on the gruelling three-day 'Rim to Rim' Grand Canyon challenge!

1   In weights and measures, what two letters indicate a pound?

2   What nationality was neurologist Alois Alzheimer?

3   What news agency is known as the AP?

4   *I Should Coco* was a Number One album for which Britpop band?

5   In what sport might you use 'live bait'?

6   What nationality is businessman Mohamed al-Fayed?

7   What type of creature is a goosander?

8   Bell-metal is mainly an alloy of tin and what other metal?

9   What day of the week gets its name from the Roman god Saturn?

10   Cape Colony became part of what African country?

11   Phlebitis is inflammation of what blood vessels?

12   Wyandotte is a breed of what farm animal?

13   Scallion is another name for a spring... what?

14   What's the only Great Lake named after a Canadian province?

15   Rugby player Manu Tuilagi was born in what country?

16   On an aircraft, what's measured using a pitot tube?

17   Ten plus five equals what?

18   Who did Diana Mitford marry in 1936?

19   The Pentland Hills overlook what Scottish city?

20   Which Irish novelist wrote *Anybody Out There*?

21   What film awards are nicknamed 'The Oscars'?

22   People in what profession use an endoscope?

23   TV's Alf Garnett supported what football team?

24   Who was the 35th President of the USA?

25   In a rice pudding, the rice is cooked in what liquid?

26   Which pop star played Deena in the film *Dreamgirls*?

27   Which cardinal is the enemy of the Three Musketeers?

28   What is the medical name for the gullet?

SOLO WINNERS

DAVE

Our resource planning analyst from Liverpool proved very resourceful when he set Shaun a total of 15 back in Series 6. He went home with £5,000 and, appropriately for a man who played in a Beatles covers band, he didn't need any 'Help!'. He used his winnings to complete an 11-foot long dragon tattoo on his body!

1   Which Shakespeare couple are married by Friar Laurence?

2   'Single Ladies' was a Top 10 hit for which singer?

3   The Japanese Tosa is a breed of what animal?

4   How many micrometres make one metre?

5   In Wales, what sport is governed by the WRU?

6   What sign of the zodiac has five syllables in its name?

7   Which Prince of Monaco married Grace Kelly?

8   The mineral azurite is mined as an ore of what metal?

9   At what joint does the femur connect with the pelvis?

10   '501' is the most commonly played version of what sport?

11   Who is supported by his 'Rhythm and Blues Orchestra'?

12   A 30th wedding anniversary is traditionally given what name?

13   The NUT is the National Union of... what?

14   Dai is a Welsh form of what male first name?

15   The Dannebrog is the national flag of what country?

16   *Electric Warrior* was an album by which 1970s band?

17   The army of the Soviet Union was once named after what colour?

18   A tanner works mainly with what material?

19 Michael Schumacher won five Formula One titles with what team?

20 The Irish Grand National takes place at what racecourse?

21 In legend, what is found at the end of a rainbow?

22 What major political party was formed in 1988?

23 A 'flag officer' serves in which of the armed forces?

24 Potting and squopping are techniques in what game?

25 Serum forms part of what bodily fluid?

SOLO WINNERS

PIP

Pip was a mature student of history and archaeology from Conwy in Wales. No great surprise at her victory over Shaun, as she'd been a keen league quizzer for 18 years. She walked away with £7,000 after setting him 17, and was planning to use the cash to pay off her tuition fees.

1 'Verde' is the Italian word for what colour?

2 The sovereign gold coin was worth how many pounds?

3 What is the largest city in the state of Texas?

4 Kuala Lumpur hosted the Commonwealth Games in what year?

5 The Black Watch are members of which of the armed forces?

6 Singer Johnny Cash was a star of what music style?

7 In what city did Judy Garland die?

8 Who wrote the book on which the film *Bambi* is based?

9 In theatre, what stage direction is Latin for 'he goes out'?

10 What TV panel show has a round called 'General Ignorance'?

11 A species of penguin and a type of pasta share what name?

12 In what English city is the Roodee racecourse?

13 In what decade did the punk movement start?

14 The Battle of the Coral Sea was part of what war?

15 What colour is the circle on the flag of Bangladesh?

16 What was Buddy Holly's real first name?

17 Eartha Kitt played Catwoman in what '60s TV show?

18 An apple martini is known by what one-word name?

19 Prior to 1935, Iran was called what?

20 Who directed the film *The Untouchables*?

21 Niger is a country on what continent?

22 What common name is given to the egg of a head louse?

23 In the 80s, what was the name of Bruce Hornsby's backing band?

24 What long-distance path ends at Kirk Yetholm in Scotland?

25 Branston Pickle was first made by Crosse and who?

26 The Gulf of Cadiz is an inlet of what ocean?

27 What is the second animal listed in the OED, after aardvark?

28 Which Welsh composer wrote the musical *Gay's the Word*?

29 The 'big screen' refers to what form of entertainment?

SOLO WINNERS

RENEE

Renee was an air stewardess from Hampshire with a taste for the high life. She took £7,000 off Shaun after setting him a very respectable 19. She was a real petrol-head, passionate about all sorts of motor sport, and planned to use her cash to fund a Champagne-all-the-way trip to the Monaco Grand Prix.

1   In the saying, 'the proof of the pudding is in the...' what?

2   Mount Vesuvius overlooks what Italian city?

3   The game Trivial Pursuit was invented in what country?

4   Which former Olympic medallist founded the Great North Run?

5   A portable two-way radio is known as a 'walkie...' what?

6   Who wrote the novel *Mansfield Park*?

7   Florida softshell is a species of what reptile?

8   What colour are the lion's claws on the coat of arms of England?

9   One Jamaican dollar is made up of 100 what?

10   Who wrote the film *Good Will Hunting* with Matt Damon?

11   Devon's two cities are Plymouth and where?

12   What chemical element is named from the Latin for 'Russia'?

13   To put yourself in danger is to risk 'life and...' what?

14   Pan's People and Legs and Co. were regulars on what TV show?

15   In what decade did Jack the Ripper commit his murders?

16   What's a male hippo called?

17   What Californian city is nicknamed 'Frisco'?

18   Boxer Lennox Lewis was world champion at what weight?

19   So-called 'leap year babies' are born under what star sign?

20 Which English scientist wrote the 1704 work *Opticks*?

21 'Sherbet dab' is rhyming slang for what form of transport?

22 A 'bibliography' literally means a list of what?

23 What island nation is the most southerly member of the EU?

24 *Aqualung* was a '70s hit album for which prog rock group?

25 The term 'equestrianism' means riding what?

26 Operation Overlord took place during what conflict?

27 Boer and Bagot are breeds of what farm animal?

28 What letter is represented by four dots in Morse code?

29 Complete the name of this pop group: KC and the... what?

30 'Trolley dolly' is a nickname for what job?

31 What shape surrounds the Early Learning Centre logo?

SOLO WINNERS

SUSAN

Susan was a wedding photographer from Flintshire who won an enormous £50,000 after setting Paul 17 back in Series 8. Aside from her photography business, she and her husband also ran a tea room – where Susan's lemon drizzle cake was the best-seller. Maybe the thought of that put the Sinnerman off? Susan used her winnings to take a trip to the Galapagos Islands.

1   Eurostar trains go under what stretch of water?

2   In maths, the abbreviation LCD means 'Lowest Common...' what?

3   The Nobel Foundation is based in what Scandinavian city?

4   TV comedy *The Thick of It* was created by which satirist?

5   Bunny Wailer is most associated with what genre of music?

6   Sunset Strip is a section of what longer Los Angeles road?

7   *The Divine Comedy* was originally written in what language?

8   What's the traditional term for a female hare?

9   Who renounced his Greek and Danish royal titles in 1947?

10   What fruit is 'silver' in the rhyme 'I Had a Little Nut Tree'?

11   What Norman Mailer novel is about Gary Gilmore?

12   'Lemon Head' is a round on what ITV2 panel show?

13   Peregrine Cavendish is the 12th Duke of... where?

14   The *Bamboo Annals* tell the history of what country?

15   'Girasol' is an old name for what large flowering plant?

16   Rolex is a famous maker of what items?

17   How many athletes race in an Olympic 100 metres final?

18   The city of Kiev stands on what river?

SOLO WINNERS

19 In 1994 Anthea Turner left what children's TV show?

20 Jane Norman is a chain of what type of shops?

21 If you double a number what do you multiply it by?

22 What card game is scored using pegs on a board?

23 The musical *Kismet* is set in what Middle Eastern city?

24 What type of creature is a bitterling?

25 George VI belonged to what royal house?

26 In what decade was David Beckham born?

27 What two colours make up the logo of Air Canada?

SOLO WINNERS

HUW

A retired RAF navigator from Oxford, Huw really took off against Shaun with an excellent score of 19, which was good enough to earn him £7,000 in Series 10. He was going to use the cash to improve his golf game – although, with a handicap of 18, he was quite a decent player already – and redecorate his daughter's bedroom with new furniture and gadgets.

1 Spain's Costa Blanca lies on what sea?

2 What sort of intelligence is known by the letters AI?

3 Helen Mirren won an Oscar for her lead role in what film?

4 Napoleon fought what country's army at the Battle of Borodino?

5 The court for playing what sport has two free throw lines?

6 The Sherpa people are native to what country?

7 Who sang lead vocals on the Duran Duran hit 'The Reflex'?

8 The name of what airline means 'union' in Arabic?

9 What fast-food chain sells the 'Boneless Banquet' meal?

10 What former rulers of Venice lived in the Palazzo Ducale?

11 Which American wrote the 1843 horror story 'The Black Cat'?

12 Who's the mother of TV presenter Chloe Madeley?

13 How many shillings made up a pre-decimal pound?

14 Camembert cheese comes with skin of what colour?

15 The NFL team The Jaguars are based in what Florida city?

16 On a farm, what sex is a rooster?

17 Q is the standard symbol for what playing card?

18 Who played Georgie Elgin in the '50s film *The Country Girl*?

19 The HQ of what car company is just outside Gothenburg?

20 Who was the leader of the 1979 Iranian Revolution?

21 What Olympic sport is a modern form of jujitsu?

22 In the TV series, 'Casper' was a friendly what?

23 Who is the narrator of *One Thousand and One Nights*?

24 *Anti* is the eighth album by which Barbados-born singer?

25 In what book does Christian journey to the Celestial City?

26 American hero Jim Bowie died at what Texas siege?

27 The island nation of Tuvalu is in what ocean?

28 Dwayne Johnson plays Luke Hobbs in what film franchise?

SOLO WINNERS

CHRIS

A technical account manager from Bolton, Chris proved that the Vixen isn't the only good quizzer from the town when he scored 16 against Shaun and took home £4,000. It wasn't a big surprise – he was a member of Mensa and quizzed every week at his local pub. He planned to use the cash to buy himself a car.

1   A set of nightwear pyjamas consist of how many garments?

2   Suffragettes Emmeline and Christabel shared what surname?

3   *Le Devoir* is a newspaper published in what Canadian city?

4   'Zanni' are stock characters in what Italian form of theatre?

5   What species of ape is the largest living primate?

6   What European language is a form of Arabic mixed with Italian?

7   In America, PBS stations broadcast in what medium?

8   The painter William Hogarth was born in what century?

9   In olden days, what was kept in a powder keg?

10   What value British coin was withdrawn in 1984?

11   The Bluebird Café is a setting in what American TV drama?

12   What's the sport of riding horses over fences in an arena?

13   What Christian festival is called 'Pâques' in French?

14   James Bigglesworth is the full name of which fictional pilot?

15   Dustin Hoffman played 'Ratso' Rizzo in what Oscar-winning film?

16   In the 90s, apartheid fully ended in what country?

17   What's eight times eight?

18   What was the first complete car design by Alec Issigonis?

19   A griffin is a creature typically with the wings of what bird?

20 BRL is the currency code for what country?

21 Tea is poured through what projection of a teapot?

22 What was the first Chanel perfume?

23 In American sports, what does MLB stand for?

24 Nanjing Road is a busy shopping street in what Chinese city?

25 In the recording term 'mag tape', what is 'mag' short for?

26 What type of plants are cultivated in sylviculture?

SOLO WINNERS

JAMES

Shaun came up against another regular quizzer when he faced James, a studio manager from Bedfordshire. James set him 18 and waltzed off with a very tidy £10,000. He attends a pub quiz every week and said his team always wins. He planned to take his girlfriend on a 'proper' summer holiday. With a budget of £10K, that's a proper 'proper' holiday!

1   On what continent is Vietnam?

2   What lager was first brewed in Melbourne in 1888?

3   Greta Garbo played which Dutch spy on film?

4   The French writer Cyrano de Bergerac lived in what century?

5   Steven Berkoff's play *Sink the Belgrano!* is about what war?

6   Liverpool's Maritime Museum is located on what dock?

7   The San Siro stadium is home to Inter Milan and what rival club?

8   How many edges does a cuboid have?

9   Model Edie Sedgwick was the muse of which US pop artist?

10   Ray Daley replaced Terry McCann in what TV series?

11   Jamie Peacock retired from what sport in 2015?

12   Jazzer McCreary is a character in what radio drama?

13   Bobby Moore played Terry Brady in what war film?

14   In the kids' song, which elephant 'said goodbye to the circus'?

15   In 1921, Faisal I became king of what country?

16   In the rhyme 'Rub a Dub Dub', how many men are in the tub?

17   The TV series *Up Pompeii* was set in which empire?

18   Brie Larson plays 'Ma' in what 2016 film?

SOLO WINNERS

19 During what revolution is Dickens' *A Tale of Two Cities* set?

20 The Orange river in South Africa flows into what ocean?

21 What first name links the actresses Lange, Alba and Tandy?

22 In transport, what does the 'H' in HGV stand for?

23 Which author created the fictional Scottish setting of Stonemouth?

24 The word 'antiseptic' comes from what European language?

25 What is returned in the Elvis song 'Return to Sender'?

26 The munchkin man Boq appears in what West End musical?

27 How many bones are in the little toe of a human foot?

28 Who invented the wind-up Eco Media MP3 player?

SOLO WINNERS

ALISON

A company director from Sutton Coldfield, Alison won £5,000 after setting Mark 19 in the Final Chase. She was a real sci-fi nut and once went to a *Star Trek* convention in Las Vegas to get a hug from Captain Kirk himself, William Shatner. She failed on that occasion, but planned to use her winnings to try again when he came to a convention in Birmingham. In the words of Mr Spock – perfectly logical.

1   In what calendar does the horse follow the snake?

2   A heptagonal object has how many sides?

3   Who played Grace in the TV comedy *Will & Grace*?

4   The Propylaea is the entrance gateway to what Athenian hill?

5   The term 'heliacal' relates to what celestial body?

6   Who played Inspector Clouseau in the 2006 *Pink Panther* film?

7   The town of Harlow is in what English county?

8   The first Roman triumvirate was made up of Caesar, Crassus and who?

9   Who wrote the novel *The Mayor of Casterbridge*?

10   'Warwick Avenue' was a 2008 hit for which Welsh singer?

11   Edward Burne-Jones was a member of what artistic group?

12   In what position did footballer Peter Bonetti play?

13   What US TV series was based on books by Laura Ingalls Wilder?

14   Ultrasonic waves are too high for humans to what?

15   *Elektra* and *Der Rosenkavalier* are operas by which composer?

16   Who was the last English king to reign as Henry?

17   The term 'over easy' refers to eggs cooked by what method?

18   In 2010, what Iraq war film won six Oscars?

19 Clive Woodward was knighted for services to what sport?

20 What Christian holy day comes the day after Mardi Gras?

21 In GCSEs and A Levels, what grade is one below an A star?

22 Which of Madonna's children gets her name from a French town?

23 What 1926 Puccini opera is set in China?

24 Bundhosen are a longer version of what German men's garment?

SOLO WINNERS

REBECCA

Rebecca was a teaching assistant from Darlington who loved vintage clothes. She certainly turned in a vintage performance when she set Shaun 17 and walked away with £5,000. Her hobby was playing the drums and she planned to use the money to treat her parents to a 40th wedding anniversary holiday. They deserved it after listening to her drum practice for all those years!

SOLO WINNERS

1   Tiger Woods has won four PGA Championships in what sport?

2   What word can mean 'to feed on grass' or 'to touch lightly'?

3   What nickname is given to Schubert's Eighth Symphony?

4   The word 'epidermal' relates to the outermost layer of what?

5   Made in Dorset, what kind of food is Blue Vinny?

6   What kind of simple boat was Thor Heyerdahl's *Kon-Tiki*?

7   Varaha is an avatar of which Hindu god?

8   What long-running TV gardening show started in 1968?

9   Pierre Darcys is a brand of what French wine?

10 *Dummy* and *Third* were hit albums for which Bristol band?

11 The resort of Whitley Bay lies on what sea?

12 Xanthophobia is an irrational fear of what primary colour?

13 In the 90s, Phil de Glanville captained England in what sport?

14 *Between the Acts* was the last novel by which Englishwoman?

15 What is 32 times two?

16 Fry's Turkish Delight is covered in what confection?

17 The Koh-i-Noor diamond is known as 'the mountain of...' what?

18 Which Welsh actress won an Oscar for the film *Chicago*?

19 What 1919 treaty created the League of Nations?

20 What two letters indicate 'Goal Defence' in netball?

21 'Marzo' is the Italian name for what month?

22 Kevin Spacey voices a grasshopper in what 1998 Disney film?

23 The battleship *Potemkin* was built for what country's navy?

24 Who released the 2006 debut solo album *Jarvis*?

25 A retinoid is a derivative of what vitamin?

26 In Australia, blue gum is a species of what tree?

SOLO WINNERS

KEITH

Keith was an engineer from West Yorkshire with a fascination for TV. He achieved his ambition by appearing on it and winning £6,000 after he set Shaun 13. A rugby league fan for over 50 years, he was going to use the cash for a trip to Australia to watch the 2017 Rugby League World Cup.

1 Darts legend Jocky Wilson was born in which UK country?

2 What musical instrument is a Johnny Marr Jaguar?

3 How many stars were on the first American flag?

4 Who was Culture Secretary during the 2012 London Olympics?

5 Which current UK broadcaster began its service in 1922?

6 'Free the Joy' was a slogan of what chocolate company?

7 Italy's Pelagie Islands are located in what sea?

8 'Sweet Child O' Mine' first appeared on which Guns N' Roses album?

9 The 2016 animation *Spy Squad* stars what doll?

10 Which composer's home can be visited on Vienna's Domgasse?

11 Who was Tsar of Russia from 1881 to 1894?

12 In 2016, which female tennis player was banned for two years?

13 Dr Liz Wilson is the vet of which comic strip cat?

14 A cheroot is a short, thin type of what object?

15 What nature charity runs the annual 'Tree of the Year' contest?

16 The word 'kidult' blends 'kid' with what other word?

17 What relation is actress Emily Head to actor Anthony Head?

18 Elgar was Master of the King's Music for which monarch?

19 The harvested kernel of what cereal grain is known as 'paddy'?

20   What bay do the Spanish call the Golfo de Vizcaya?

21   What type of high street store is Vision Express?

22   Who is the late brother of actor James Belushi?

23   Gary Mabbutt played 16 seasons for what football team?

24   Anne of Austria was the mother of which French king?

25   Fish breathe through what organs?

26   Madonna's hit 'Beautiful Stranger' was used in what film series?

27   A soldier's cleaning duties are known as 'spit and...' what?

28   A croquette is usually cooked by what method?

SOLO WINNERS

PETER

A business owner from Plymouth, Peter set Shaun 15 and went back to the south-west with £5,000 in his pocket in Series 11. A keen musician, he'd been playing the guitar for 30 years and owned six of them. But rather than buying another guitar with his winnings, Peter was being practical: the cash was used to fix the broken fence in his back garden!

1   The Andean or spectacled bear is native to what continent?

2   The name of what football club is abbreviated to PNE?

3   *The Secret Adversary* is a book by which female crime writer?

4   Actor William Mapother is the cousin of which other actor?

5   The royal throne at Westminster Palace is in what chamber?

6   Epsom Downs racecourse is in which UK county?

7   What type of creature is a streaked berrypecker?

8   The Foucault method measures the speed of what?

9   What city became the capital of the United States in 1800?

10   *Stand As One* is a 2016 live album from what music festival?

11   In what sport do women compete for the Espirito Santo Trophy?

12   The Hugli is an arm of what other Indian river?

13   What branch of America's armed forces has the initials USMC?

14   Which part of an ancient Greek settlement meant 'upper city'?

15   What do the J and D stand for in writer J. D. Salinger's name?

16   Windiescricket.com is the website of what cricket team?

17   According to the saying, what does misery love?

18   The Marquess of Rockingham was Prime Minister in what century?

19   In nutrition, an LCD is a 'low-carbohydrate ...' what?

20   'She Bangs' was a hit for which Puerto Rican singer?

21   What birthday is called the 'big five-oh'?

22   Which tennis player was nicknamed 'Ivan the Terrible'?

23   What post was held by William Temple from 1942?

24   How many edges does a 50 pence piece have?

25   Comedian Lenny Henry made his TV debut on what show?

SOLO WINNERS

THE CHASE

TOP 10
BIGGEST PRIZE
WINNERS

TOP 10 BIGGEST PRIZE WINNERS

The Chase has always been unusually generous for a tea-time quiz show when it comes to handing out big cash prizes. Then again, if you've got what it takes to beat a Chaser – some of the finest quizzers on the planet – then you deserve to be well rewarded. And every now and again our contestants walk away with life-changing sums of money. These are the questions our players answered to win the Top 10 highest amounts ever given away on the daytime editions of *The Chase*. Could you have done what they did? Give these questions a try...

JANICE, SARAH, KEVIN AND OVIE

In 10th place, with a meagre £62,000 cash pot, was this full house from Series 9 who took Mark to the cleaners after posting an incredible score of 24 in their Final Chase. They were Janice, a pensions administrator from Alloa, Sarah from Nottingham, an English graduate who wanted to be a teaching assistant, Kevin, an insurance broker from Hartlepool, and Ovie, a sales advisor from Twickenham who used to be a professional dancer. Kevin was the player who went big, bringing back £48,000 in his Head to Head. It was the sort of score that deserves to win – and with a fantastic six pushbacks, Mark could never get close.

1   The sport of figure skating takes place on what surface?

2   Panadol is a trade name for what drug?

3   The Dog in the Pond is a pub in what TV soap?

4   What vegetable is also known as 'turnip-cabbage'?

5   What animal is T. S. Eliot's Old Deuteronomy?

6   At night, what colour light indicates 'starboard' on a ship?

7   Which George Cole character often said 'a nice little earner'?

8   Which royal is patron of the Scout Association?

9   What's 10 per cent of 120?

10 The Indian team Rajasthan Royals plays what sport?

11 *Sweet Baby James* and *Hourglass* are albums by which singer?

12 Brandenburg and Lower Saxony are states in what country?

13 'The infernal serpent' is a phrase in what Milton epic poem?

14 What Football League team is known as the Shrews?

15 What car company makes the B-Max and C-Max models?

16 Singer Ernest Evans was known as 'Chubby...' who?

17 What is the most westerly point of mainland England?

18 What radioactive noble gas is produced by the decay of radium?

19 The vibrations of what part of a bee make a buzzing noise?

20 Who illustrated Roald Dahl's poetry book *Revolting Rhymes*?

21 Swaziland is a country on what continent?

22 Cherry Blossom is a brand of what type of polish?

23 Who played J. J. McClure in the film *The Cannonball Run*?

24 What is the nickname of Bradford's rugby league team?

25 How many milliamps are there in an amp?

26 What surname is shared by film directors Spike and Ang?

27 The River Wye flows through what two countries of the UK?

TOP 10 BIGGEST PRIZE WINNERS

JUDITH

In 9th place is the only solo player in the list. Judith was a charity volunteer from Cambridgeshire who went Head to Head with Jenny, set her a record-equalling solo winning total of 20 and walked off with a life-changing £70,000, which actually makes her the biggest winner on our list as she had no one to share the prize with. It was a perfect storm of a game for Judith, who had sat on seat 4 and watched all her team-mates get caught. She then got home with the big money, set a big total and pushed Jenny back an incredible eight times out of nine! She planned to use her winnings to go on a pottery course. After a win like that, she could build her own kiln!

1   What natural material is harvested as 'lumber'?

2   What company made the 707 plane?

3   Fugitive Rob Donovan returned to what TV soap in 2017?

4   The green pigment verdigris forms naturally on what element?

5   What is the official religion in Yemen?

6   Matt Bomer plays a male stripper in what film series?

7   What large white mammal is known in Dutch as 'ice bear'?

8   Ma Joad is a character in what John Steinbeck novel?

9   The torch of what US statue was replaced in the 1980s?

10   Woden was the earlier form of which Norse god?

11   Which Australian singer wrote Rihanna's hit song 'Diamonds'?

12   What is the largest city of Lebanon?

13   'Pacman' is the autobiography of which Filipino boxer?

14   In the southern hemisphere, what solstice falls in December?

15   Who was Prime Minister at the time of the 1916 Easter Rising?

16   The papal tiara is depicted on the flag of what city state?

17 In 2013, '1D Day' was dedicated to fans of which boy band?

18 'Ithaca' is a section of what James Joyce novel?

19 Who is the hero of the film *Raiders of the Lost Ark*?

20 What strait separates Alaska from Russia?

21 The Artful Dodger appears in what Lionel Bart musical?

22 What medical term means 'stiffness of death' in Latin?

23 What relation is the Countess of Wessex to the Princess Royal?

24 A 'Gearhead' is a fan of what TV show?

25 Dorlcote Mill is the setting for what George Eliot novel?

26 Which Nobel Prize was created most recently?

TOP 10 BIGGEST PRIZE WINNERS

HONEY, DEB AND OLIVER

The first of several teams in joint 8th place next. This threesome from Series 11 played Paul for £75,000 and went home with £25,000 apiece. They were Honey, a voiceover artist from Herefordshire, Deb, a retired recruitment consultant from Newbury, and Oliver, a primary school teacher from London. They set the Sinnerman 17 after Oliver in seat 4 had gone big and brought back £68,000. As so often, the win was all about the pushbacks, with the team getting an excellent seven out of nine, meaning Paul just couldn't catch them. Oliver had wanted to buy a garden shed... presumably he now has a gold-plated one!

1   Monochromatic means using only one what?

2   Sister Winifred is a character in what BBC period drama?

3   In astronomy, what type of object was Shoemaker Levy 9?

4   Which English artist painted six of his servants in the 1750s?

5   Chorizo sausage originated on what European peninsula?

6   Venom is an arch-enemy of what Marvel superhero?

7   The dramatist Euripides wrote in what language?

8   In 1471, which king won the Battle of Tewkesbury?

9   In the comic *Asterix and the Black Gold,* what is black gold?

10   Kids TV show *Bagpuss* was first shown in what decade?

11   What Australian band released the album *Let There Be Rock*?

12   Downpatrick is a town in what country of the UK?

13   'Triple talaq' is a method of divorce in what religion?

14   What American sunglasses brand makes the Clubround model?

15   What strait connects the Andaman and South China seas?

16   What item of cutlery has a handle and a blade?

17 Which British Olympian was born Fatima Vedad?

18 Whitehaven is a port in what county?

19 What type of winged insect is an eastern tiger swallowtail?

20 In Spanish, the word 'tío' refers to which male relation?

21 What city is the Woody Allen film *Manhattan* set in?

22 The title of what *Carry On* film includes a rank in the army?

23 The Birmingham North Relief Road was part of what motorway?

24 What Italian word is used for an individual member of the Mafia?

TOP 10 BIGGEST PRIZE WINNERS

MATTHEW, CALUM AND JAN

Another team in joint 8th place and another £75,000 win. This trio from Series 11 were Matthew, a full-time dad from Essex, Calum, an English student from Bristol, and Jan, a graphologist from Stirling who worked as a Morticia Addams lookalike! It was Morticia herself who did the damage, when Jan went big from seat 4 and brought back £65,000 all on her own. They were playing Mark and set him a catchable 17, but then proceeded to land five pushbacks. Mark got close – but not close enough.

1   What fictional sport was first played on Queerditch Marsh?

2   In what film does Tom Cruise's character fly an F-14 Tomcat?

3   In Egyptian mythology, whose tears were said to flood the Nile?

4   Andrew Bonar Law represented what party as Prime Minister?

5   Bowstring wax is used in which Olympic sport?

6   Which Irishman received an honorary knighthood in 1986?

7   The diplodocus dinosaur walked on how many legs?

8   In 1943, which Mexican painted *Diego on My Mind*?

9   The line 'Play it, Sam' is from what 1942 film?

10 In the UHT treatment of milk what does the 'U' stand for?

11 The Gulf of Mannar is an inlet of what ocean?

12 What animals are Dasher and Dancer in an 1823 poem?

13 The film *Raiders of the Lost Ark* is set in what decade?

14 Thomas Woodrow were the first names of which US President?

15 Chorus girl Peggy Sawyer is the heroine of what musical?

16 The Parti Québécois is a political party in what country?

17 'Tickler' is a mature type of what cheese?

18   What TV sci-fi series featured the ship's computer Zen?

19   Who wrote the novel *Jane Eyre*?

20   Solent University is in what British city?

21   What creature is a little blue heron?

22   What famous ballet features an army of gingerbread soldiers?

23   In what century did the Battle of the Boyne take place?

TOP 10 BIGGEST PRIZE WINNERS

ANTON, EMMA AND BONNY

Another £75,000 win, this time over Shaun in Series 10, means another threesome in joint 8th place. They were Anton, a cabbie from Glasgow, Emma, a training scheme co-ordinator from London, and Bonny, a retired actress from Lincoln with green fingers and two allotments. It was Bonny on seat 4 who brought back the big money, with a £64,000 high offer. They set Shaun a catchable 17 but came up with six pushbacks, which kept him off their tail. It meant that Bonny could buy her beloved allotments instead of renting them.

1 What street did Tony Blair move into in May 1997?

2 Point Reyes Blue is a variety of what dairy product?

3 What is the French word for 'Saturday'?

4 Which Poet Laureate wrote the memoirs *Summoned by Bells*?

5 John Cazale played Fredo Corleone in what film series?

6 In what war was the 'Dickin Medal' for animals first awarded?

7 Hydromania is an excessive craving for what liquid?

8 Which female singer had a hit in the '80s with 'Manchild'?

9 *Doctor, Nurse* and *Matron* are films in what comedy series?

10 In cricket, what part of the body is another name for the 'On' side?

11 What famous stately home is on the banks of the River Derwent?

12 How many zeroes appear on a percent symbol?

13 The name of what vegetable means 'cabbage sprout' in Italian?

14 Princess Jasmine first appeared in what Disney film?

15 What name is given to the dissolved substance in a solution?

16 In 2002, what became the Republic of Ireland's official currency?

17 Who is Britain's second-longest reigning monarch?

18 *Violator* and *Ultra* were albums by what electro band?

19 Which US car manufacturer pioneered factory mass production?

20 Cingula are bundles of nerve fibres in what organ?

21 At a wedding, who is traditionally said to be 'blushing'?

22 What's the smallest US state by area?

23 Ken Clarke was Chancellor under which Prime Minister?

TOP 10 BIGGEST PRIZE WINNERS

MICKEY, HELEN AND ROY

Yet another £75,000 win means another team in joint 8th place. These three players set Paul a very respectable 21 back in Series 9. They were Mickey, an X-ray operative from Hertfordshire, Helen, a singer from London, and Roy, a retired maintenance engineer from Scarborough. Unusually, two players went high in this game: Mickey brought back £22,000 and then Roy chipped in with £49,000! The Sinnerman made a valiant attempt to catch them, but three pushbacks out of three meant he came up short.

1   In Asia, what type of geographical feature is K2?

2   Dankeschön is 'thank you' in what language?

3   What Mel Brooks film features Sheriff Bart?

4   The song 'My Man's Gone Now' is from what Gershwin opera?

5   Which Tory MP was born Theresa Brasier in 1956?

6   What type of creature is an erne?

7   What burger chain took its name from a Popeye character?

8   'Ego' was a 2009 hit for which girl group?

9   In 1967, what country won the Six-Day War?

10   Carrie-Anne Moss played Trinity in what film trilogy?

11   In *The Tempest,* who releases Ariel from a witch's spell?

12   The Caelian is one of what capital city's seven hills?

13   What was Nelson's flagship at the Battle of Trafalgar?

14   Boarding and roughing are offences in what Winter Olympic sport?

15   What gas is the main component of firedamp or mine gas?

16   What organs are chiefly affected by bronchitis?

17   Babies 'R' Us is a division of what retailer?

18   Who was the last French king to live at Versailles?

19   Canadian rye is a form of what alcoholic drink?

20   Who starred as Margaret Tate in the rom-com *The Proposal*?

21   The FIFA series of computer games is based on what sport?

22   The novel *The Brothers Karamazov* is set in what country?

23   *Live SOS* was a 2014 album by which Australian band?

TOP 10 BIGGEST PRIZE WINNERS

THE CHASE

SANDRA, JONATHAN AND EAMMON

Our final £75,000 winners and our final joint 8th place. They were Sandra, a decorator from Sheffield, Jonathan, a marketing assistant from Leeds, and Eamonn from Belfast, a professional storyteller who certainly had a tale to tell after this show! As so often with huge wins, it was seat 4 that went big, with Eamonn bringing back £68,000. They set Jenny 17, a score the Chasers regard as a banana-skin total – one they should catch but it's easy to come a cropper on.

1   South Korea's only land border is with what country?

2   Which Brontë sister shared her first name with a Stuart monarch?

3   Frenchy and Cha-Cha are characters in what Broadway musical?

4   What chemical element has the symbol Ac?

5   The Tien Shan mountain range is on what continent?

6   Who played coughing Bob Fleming on *The Fast Show*?

7   Muscle fatigue is caused by an excess of what acid?

8   What sport is played by the Dallas Mavericks?

9   In the USA in what month does Veterans Day fall?

10   In the early 90s, which US rapper famously wore harem pants?

11   *Any Objections* was a book by which Peruvian photographer?

12   What planet shares its name with a liquid metal?

13   What name is given to the ant that lays eggs in a colony?

14   Redcar and Ripon are venues for what professional sport?

15   *In My Shoes* is the memoir of a co-founder of what shoe brand?

16   What deadly sin is also the name for a group of lions?

17   The Apollo moon missions stopped in what decade?

18   Which artist sold the painting *The Red Vineyard* to Anna Boch?

19 What name is given to a female seal?

20 The song 'I Want to Break Free' features in what stage musical?

21 'Crow's feet' are found around what part of the face?

22 The company Fujifilm is based in what country?

23 Which American hosts the TV show *Man Finds Food*?

DEBBIE AND DERRICK

Third place in our list now, as a duo back in Series 7 took a staggering £80,000 off Shaun. They were Debbie, a landlady from Manchester who wanted to go and see the Moomins in Finland, and Derrick, a police dispatcher from Wrexham. It was Derrick in seat 4 who went big and brought £72,000 back to join Debbie in the Final Chase. They set Shaun 18, which was enough on the day to bag the cash. Let's hope that Debbie and Moomintroll lived happily ever after!

1   Who won the men's singles at Wimbledon in 2013?

2   What part of your hand is greased if you are being bribed?

3   What was Clint Eastwood's occupation in *Play Misty For Me*?

4   Periosteum is the outer surface of what part of the body?

5   'Guten Tag' is a greeting in what European language?

6   A yukata is a light version of what long Japanese robe?

7   *Dieting with the Duchess* is a Weight Watchers book by who?

8   Singer Nana Mouskouri was born on what island?

9   In what sea is the Malta Channel located?

10 'Holiday Rock' was the theme song to what TV sitcom?

11 What bank did William Paterson found in 1694?

12 'White Satin' is an old nickname for what spirit?

13 In 2010, what political party became the Official Opposition?

14 Who played heiress Tracy Lord in the film *High Society*?

15 Trooping the Colour is held annually on what parade ground?

16 What metric unit of mass is a cg?

17 The word 'paternal' refers to what relation?

18 Powhatan was the father of which famous native American woman?

19 Wally Hammond captained England in what sport?

20 Dutch foil consists of zinc and what other metal?

21 A stegosaurus had how many feet?

22 Who played the title role in the film *Yentl*?

23 The Gulf Stream current is named after what gulf?

24 In what century was the composer Franz Schubert born?

CRAIG, RAKESH AND LAUREN

Second place in our list goes to a trio from Series 8 who faced Shaun and took home an incredible £90,000! The plucky threesome was made up of Craig, a military engineer from Essex who wanted to build a 'shed-pub' in his garden to serve his home-brewed beers, Rakesh, a wine salesman from Liverpool who planned to visit the Napa Valley vineyards in California, and Lauren, a full-time mum and regular league quizzer from East Sussex. No surprise when she went big from seat 4 and brought back £77,000 for the team's prize fund. They set Shaun a tricky 20, which was exactly what they needed. Presumably, it was all round to Craig's 'shed-pub' to celebrate, with Rakesh supplying the Champagne!

1   What season is known as 'fall' in America?

2   Aspartame is used as a substitute for what sweet ingredient?

3   Joan is the first name of what *Father Ted* character?

4   In 1970, who became Egyptian President?

5   What's the minimum number of Mondays in any month?

6   *International Velvet* was a Number One album by what Welsh group?

7   In what country was writer Alexandre Dumas born?

8   Food writer Matthew Fort is a judge on what TV cooking show?

9   A muezzin calls people to prayer in what religion?

10   The Birman is a breed of what domestic animal?

11   What 2013 sci-fi film has a hero called Ender Wiggin?

12   The city of Barcelona stands on what sea?

13   Which female humorous poet wrote 'Oh No! I Got a Cold'?

14   Who was the Roman equivalent of the Greek god Zeus?

15   The film *Cold Mountain* is set during what war?

16   What's four times eight?

17 The red light on the rear of a car is called what?

18 *Original Pirate Material* was the debut album by which UK act?

19 Flo-Jo was a famous nickname in what sport?

20 In 2014, which pop star named his third child Amelia?

21 Guinea-Bissau is a country on what continent?

22 What anti-litter campaign group has the initials KBT?

23 In what century was the planet Uranus discovered?

24 Dean Stockwell played Al in what TV time travel show?

25 In what board game might you 'Advance to Mayfair'?

TOP 10 BIGGEST PRIZE WINNERS

GAYNA, TIM, LUCA AND DIANE

First place on our list goes to a full house of four players who faced the Governess and went home with a mouth-watering £100,000 – not bad for a tea-time quiz show! They were Gayna, a laundry assistant from West Yorkshire who was a regular league quizzer, Tim, a retired database administrator from Northamptonshire, Luca, a medical student from Cardiff who wanted enough money for two takeaways a week during his studies, and Diane, a housewife from Lancaster who was an adrenaline junkie with an ambition to go wing-walking. Yet it was wasn't the quizzer on seat 1 who went high, it was fearless Diane in seat 4 who brought back £86,000 to her team. They set Anne 21, a difficult total to catch at any time but impossible when you get pushed back four times. It was the all-time record win for *The Chase* daytime shows, and means Luca can have takeaways every night for the next 10 years!

1   A rhetorical question is one that does not require a what?

2   What ancient republic was founded in Italy in 509 BC?

3   'Endless' is a fragrance by which *Sex and the City* star?

4   Ralf Hütter is the longest-serving member of which German band?

5   What does the 'e' in 'e-cigarette' stand for?

6   The Battle of the Kentish Knock took place in what sea?

7   What metal has the chemical symbol Cu?

8   Bellini painted *The Drunkenness of...* which biblical figure?

9   What type of table condiment is Fleur de Sel?

10 *Alf* is the 1984 solo debut album by which female singer?

11 The Norris Trophy is awarded in what winter sport?

12 In maths, six is the product of two and what other number?

13 What instant coffee brand launched the Dolce Gusto system?

14 A nocturne is usually played on what musical instrument?

15 An Act of Parliament in draft form is called a what?

16 What is an ostrich said to bury in the sand?

17 Complete the title of the Alan Rickman film: *Truly, Madly,...* what?

18 Jollof rice is a dish originally from what continent?

19 GWR.com is the website of what rail company?

20 A thermophobic avoids high levels of what?

21 How many internal angles does a rectangle have?

22 In the game Monopoly, what land vehicle is a playing token?

23 What European capital city comes last alphabetically?

24 The dove and the swan were symbols of which Greek goddess?

TOP 10 BIGGEST PRIZE WINNERS

HIGHEST WINNING SCORES

HIGHEST WINNING SCORES

Sometimes even the Chasers admit that a team's high score deserved to win.
That doesn't stop them trying their hardest to catch it, mind you, but if a team
gets it right and posts a score of 23 plus, a defeat by the Chaser is hard to take.
Here are some of the best-ever Final Chase performances by our teams.
Could you have done as well with their questions? Well, here's your chance
to find out. We'll start with a few teams that managed to score 25 and
work our way up to the really mega-scores...

TOM, MATT AND JOYCE

A trio consisting of Tom, a carpenter and avid quizzer from Kettering, Matt, a statistician from London, and Joyce, a retired office administrator from Lincolnshire blended nicely as a team in Series 9 and set the Beast an excellent 25 to catch. There was £42,000 in the prize fund, largely thanks to quizzer Tom going high and bringing back £36,000 on his own. It was still a very close-run thing in the end though, with Mark getting a tantalisingly-close 24 and just being beaten by the clock.

1   In what sport are dogs raced from traps?

2   What area of Moscow do the French call La Place Rouge?

3   Megan Mullally played Karen Walker in what US sitcom?

4   Carthaginian is another name for what series of wars?

5   In the game 'Rock Paper Scissors' what beats 'Rock'?

6   What Verdi opera was commissioned by the Khedive of Egypt?

7   Stena Line specialises in what sort of shipping?

8   *Allan Quatermain* is the sequel to what H. Rider Haggard novel?

9   W is the symbol for what unit of power?

10   Na'vi is a fictional language in what James Cameron film?

11   Which Austrian was UN Secretary-General in the 70s?

12   A transdermal patch delivers medicine through what organ?

13   Who sang lead vocals on the 1980 Number One 'Brass in Pocket'?

14   'Aardvark' and 'meerkat' are words from what African language?

15   Which rugby league Super League team is based in France?

16   What's the legal process by which a marriage is ended?

17   What surname links pop singer David and TOWIE star Joey?

18   The Kuiper Belt extends beyond the orbit of what planet?

19   What company makes the chocolate bar TimeOut?

20   The Munch Museum is in what European capital?

21   What's three-quarters of 40?

22   The myxoma virus causes what disease in rabbits?

23   Thomas Jefferson was what US President's Secretary of State?

24   Voodoo featured heavily in what '70s James Bond film?

25   Which TV chef owns a restaurant called Fifteen?

HIGHEST WINNING SCORES

PAUL AND GARETH

Paul, a complaints handler from Rotherham, and Gareth, a barman from Derry, formed a perfect pairing when they took £15,000 off Shaun back in Series 4 with a score of 25. Shaun came close, scoring 22 before running out of time, but at the end of the game there were certainly no complaints from Paul, and it was time for Gareth to get the drinks in!

1   How many weekdays begin with 'T'?

2   Rasputin came from what country?

3   'All By Myself' and 'Think Twice' were hits for which singer?

4   The Gulf of Riga is part of what sea?

5   What TV magazine originally listed only ITV programmes?

6   The Lhasa Apso is a breed of what pet?

7   Who won Series 2 of *Pop Idol*?

8   Who's the title character in *The Merchant of Venice*?

9   What is a tartan skirt called?

10   What Australian state is an island?

11   Human Torch and The Thing are half of which superheroes?

12   The *Queen Elizabeth* liner was launched in what decade?

13   How many 'i's in Mississippi?

14   Shiitake is a type of what food?

15   Eilat is a resort in what country?

16   Butterflies and moths belong to what order of insects?

17   In German, what does 'danke' mean?

18   Who played the Prime Minister in *Love, Actually*?

19 Molineux is home to what football team?

20 Who was the first king of the House of Windsor?

21 What nationality was car designer Enzo Ferrari?

22 How many hours in three days?

23 'Speed of Sound' and 'The Scientist' were hits for what British band?

24 Which EastEnders actress also played the Bionic Woman?

25 Which Roman leader was murdered on the Ides of March?

26 In what country is the Aswan High Dam?

27 Which jockey holds the record for most Epsom Derby wins?

28 Who played Alex Owens in *Flashdance*?

29 The Soviet Union's flag had what colour background?

30 Great Britain ruled what country during the Raj?

HIGHEST WINNING SCORES

OLIVIA, GARETH, JO AND CHRIS

A fifth 25, this time from Series 2, was scored against Shaun by a full house super-team consisting of Olivia, a market research interviewer from Bury St Edmunds, Gareth, an international buying manager from Maidstone, Jo, a legal secretary from Bolton, and Chris, a telecoms project manager from Croydon. Gareth was the star, scoring a mammoth 12 in his Cash Builder, but despite the others posting strong scores themselves (9, 8 and 9), they all took the low offer so ended up playing for just £19,000. It was, in the end, a smart move. They needed a full house to post their 25 and anything less might not have been enough, as Shaun came very close to a catch with 23 of his own.

1   Who became the youngest ever Formula One World Champion in 2008?

2   Which circle runs through the North and South Poles at right angles to the Equator?

3   What's the capital of the United Arab Emirates?

4   Which *Friends* character was played by Matthew Perry?

5   What colour is associated with the book of quotations from Chairman Mao?

6   Kevin Keegan left Liverpool for which German club?

7   What's the most populated city in the USA?

8   In fashion, raglan, dolman and short are types of what?

9   Who played Charles in *Four Weddings and a Funeral*?

10   Fenner's is the cricket ground of which university?

11   Which actress and TV presenter is married to the actor Tim Healy?

12   Which Canadian province's name means 'New Scotland' in Latin?

13   Which man's name represents 'V' in the NATO phonetic alphabet?

14   What single was ABBA's final UK Number One?

15   What's the title of Harper Lee's only novel?

16   Which of the Muppets was originally given the surname Lee?

17 Which archangel foretold the birth of Jesus to Mary?

18 Which gangster film starred Ben Kingsley as Don Logan?

19 Singer Norah Jones is the daughter of which Indian musician?

20 'Pomme' is French for which fruit?

21 Which country did Britain defeat in the Falklands War?

22 Who played Blake Carrington in *Dynasty*?

23 Which Norwegian playwright wrote *A Doll's House*?

24 Michael O'Leary became chief executive of which Irish airline in 1994?

25 How many musicians make a quintet?

HIGHEST WINNING SCORES

ANDREW, JOE AND MARIA

Andrew, a copy-editor from London, Joe, a woodworker from Gloucester, and Maria, a doctor's receptionist from Manchester set the doctor and stand-up, Paul Sinha, an enormous 26 in Series 9. Andrew had taken the high offer and brought back £30,000, meaning the team were playing for a prize fund of £41,000. Such a high score as 26 made things tricky for the Sinnerman, and he had to rush his answers to keep up with the clock... That's when Chasers make mistakes – which is exactly what happened to Paul. Five pushbacks killed off his chances, as he only managed 15 in reply.

1   What type of snack is a fig roll?

2   In what '80s Dustin Hoffman film does Michael become Dorothy?

3   Bobcats are native to what continent?

4   Who was the longest-lived man in the Bible?

5   What winter sport uses goals that are four feet by six feet?

6   What is the UK's largest budget airline?

7   The One Ring is a central feature in what trilogy of novels?

8   'One Shot' was a 2010 hit for what boy band?

9   In what century was the Battle of Waterloo?

10 Tierra del Fuego is divided between Argentina and what country?

11 What is the only primate in the Chinese zodiac?

12 What flower is named after horticulturist William Forsyth?

13 The Grange B&B features in what TV soap?

14 Which woman became India's Prime Minister in 1966?

15 Tennis star Monica Seles was born what nationality?

16 What is added to a Pot Noodle prior to eating?

17 How many members were there in the original Sugababes line-up?

18 Which 19th century Pointillist painted *Circus Sideshow*?

19 'Redmayniacs' are fans of which Oscar-winning actor?

20 What bone forms the upper arm in the human body?

21 Choo-choo is a child's term for what form of transport?

22 Which king succeeded Henry VII in 1509?

23 Flora Poste is the heroine of what Stella Gibbons novel?

24 Shakira's hit 'Hips Don't Lie' featured which Fugees rapper?

25 The Celtic Sea is an inlet of what ocean?

26 Who won a Golden Globe for his role in *Doctor Zhivago*?

HIGHEST WINNING SCORES

ROB, GRAHAM AND VERITY

Another threesome setting a 26, this time in Series 5. Shaun found himself up against Rob, an orchard worker and keen quizzer from Somerset, Graham, a retired bank manager from Worcestershire, and Verity, a healthcare assistant from Burton-on-Trent. Unsurprisingly, Rob the quizzer took the high offer and brought £30,000 home, which meant a £39,000 prize fund in their Final Chase. It was closer than they would have liked, and Shaun almost caught them with 24 of his own. Close but not close enough – the team took home £13,000 apiece.

1   'Especially For You' was Number One for Kylie Minogue and who?

2   Graham Onions has played for England in what sport?

3   Which actress married singer Eddie Fisher in 1955?

4   Defenestration means to throw someone out of what?

5   What's 2012 (two thousand and twelve) divided by two?

6   What fish is normally used in a Caesar salad?

7   Who wrote the novel *Far from the Madding Crowd*?

8   What chemical element is named after a US state?

9   What is known as the 'king of beasts'?

10 Colchester is in what county?

11 'The Shoop Shoop Song' was UK Number One for who?

12 What city's at the northern end of the M11?

13 What do the British call a 'diaper'?

14 Calligraphy is the art of what?

15 Publishers Larousse are based in what country?

16 Anthony Ogogo competes in what sport?

17 What's the main language spoken in Uruguay?

18 Pinot noir is a variety of what fruit?

19 In what decade was Marilyn Monroe born?

20 Who has had hits with 'In My Head' and 'Whatcha Say'?

21 'Jam-jar' is rhyming slang for what?

22 What company makes the Air Max trainers?

23 Who played *Cheers* bar owner Sam Malone?

24 Which French king ruled for 72 years?

25 A cygnet is the young of what bird?

26 What unit of weight has the symbol mg?

HIGHEST WINNING SCORES

ANNA, DAVID AND ANGELA

Another trio, this time from Series 4, set the Sinnerman another 26. Anna, a full-time mum from Hertfordshire, David, a fire alarm service manager from Bognor Regis, and Angela, a shopping-centre administrator from Halifax soon set the alarm bells ringing for Paul after Angela on seat 1 scored 11 in her Cash Builder. Clearly, the full-time mum had quiz shows on the TV all day! This was a cautious team, and with each contestant who got back taking the middle amount, they were left with a Final Chase prize fund of £24,000. Once again, the need for speed meant mistakes by the Chaser, and Paul only managed 19 in reply.

1   Eric Clapton famously plays what instrument?

2   *The Archers* is broadcast on what radio station?

3   Who plays Susan Storm in the *Fantastic Four* films?

4   Ferritin is a protein that helps the body to store what?

5   Kung fu originated in what country?

6   Who loses his tail in the Winnie-the-Pooh stories?

7   Nick Carter and Brian Littrell belong to what American boy band?

8   What American city is known as Beantown?

9   On what day of the month is April Fools' Day?

10 What 'tapestry' tells the story of the Battle of Hastings?

11 What nationality was the poet W. B. Yeats?

12 Alecia Moore is the real name of which singer?

13 In cookery, a bap is a type of what?

14 Which of The Goodies co-hosts *Springwatch*?

15 How many *Lethal Weapon* films have there been?

16 Malvolio is a character in what Shakespeare play?

17 DFS is a retail chain selling what?

18 What's the official language of Libya?

19 In what team sport did Jane Sixsmith play for England?

20 Linseed oil comes from what plant?

21 Which Take That member was a judge on *The X Factor*?

22 Lambrusco wine comes from what country?

23 Which actress played Evy in the *The Mummy* films?

24 'How You Remind Me' was a hit for which group?

25 How many novels in a trilogy?

26 American bobtail is a breed of what pet?

27 Who led the *Kon-Tiki* expedition?

28 Heraklion is the capital of what Greek island?

29 What TV soap is set in Albert Square?

30 What are the spines on a porcupine called?

HIGHEST WINNING SCORES

SARAH, KIT AND CLARE

The Beast was also bested by another trio scoring 26 in Series 4. Sarah, a pub cook from Leyburn, Kit, a drama teacher from Hampshire, and Clare, a student nurse from Nottingham played for a Final Chase prize fund of £14,300 after Clare had played it ultra-cautiously and taken the low offer to make sure she got home. It was a wise decision – the more bodies back, the bigger the total. And 26 is a very big total. As always, Mark gave it his all, but could only manage 21 in reply. A tactically perfect game by the team meant victory.

1   Travelling is a foul in what indoor ball sport?

2   Who presented *You Are What You Eat*?

3   Who was Oscar nominated for his role in *A Single Man*?

4   What mythical animal can only be caught by a virgin?

5   On a ship, what's the opposite of starboard?

6   How many sides has a nonagon?

7   Alex Kapranos is lead singer of what band?

8   Vector is a supervillain in what 2010 film?

9   A Moses basket is used to carry what?

10   What's a 'Bath Oliver'?

11   Who plays River Song in *Doctor Who*?

12   'Hot in Herre' and 'Ride wit Me' were hit songs for who?

13   Which of London's Thames bridges can be raised?

14   Don King is a promoter of what sport?

15   Who played 'The Good' in *The Good, The Bad, and The Ugly*?

16   *Green Eggs and Ham* is a best-selling book by who?

17   Arrivederci means 'goodbye' in what language?

18 The Amazon flows into what ocean?

19 What disease is also called scarlatina?

20 Pamela Anderson married which singer and rapper in 2006?

21 The Bishop of Rome is the head of what church?

22 What first name links TV detectives Bergerac and Taggart?

23 What spirit is in a bloody *Maria* cocktail?

24 In what county is Gatcombe Park?

25 Figures of Guy Fawkes are traditionally burnt on what *date*?

26 Who played Archie Leach in *A Fish Called Wanda*?

27 Which singer has been a judge on *American Idol* and US *X Factor*?

28 Clumber, Irish water and Sussex are breeds of what dog?

29 Polska is the local name of what country?

HIGHEST WINNING SCORES

SARAH, VANESSA AND MARTIN

One more 26, this time from a threesome in Series 3, and again the Beast was up against it. Sarah, a clerical officer from Newcastle, Vanessa, a French teacher from County Derry, and Martin, a customer service advisor from Oldham, all played it safe and brought back what they had earned in their Cash Builders, meaning a total in the Final Chase of £17,000. Mark came flying out of the traps and almost caught them, running out of time with a too-close-for-comfort 24.

1 In what quiz show can contestants 'phone a friend'?

2 What's the handle of a sword called?

3 In what year was James Cameron's *Titanic* released?

4 What's 10 degrees Celsius in degrees Fahrenheit?

5 What nocturnal bird is a symbol of wisdom?

6 What's the currency of Malta?

7 The word 'gingival' refers to what part of the body?

8 Pho is a noodle soup from what Asian country?

9 The Dingles feature in what TV soap?

10 Ottawa is the capital of what country?

11 Who wrote the novel *Brave New World*?

12 How many senators sit in the US Senate?

13 In what month is Guy Fawkes Night?

14 What's the official language of Costa Rica?

15 What band founded Apple Records in 1968?

16 Who played Commandant Yamauchi in the TV show *Tenko*?

17 What's the letter E worth in Scrabble?

18 In what city are the Spanish Steps?

19   What's the fourth Gospel of the Bible?

20   Who wrote the anti-slavery novel *Uncle Tom's Cabin*?

21   What tree do acorns come from?

22   What's a dealer at a gambling table called?

23   *Urban Hymns* was a best-selling album for what band?

24   In 1976, Basil Hume became the Archbishop of which diocese?

25   How many bears in the Goldilocks fairy tale?

26   What Cambridgeshire city has the postcode PE?

27   What follows delta in the Greek alphabet?

28   What type of creature is a redstart?

HIGHEST WINNING SCORES

THERESA, GILL AND SHAHAB

Back in Series 3, Shaun came up against a trio who set him a staggering 27 to catch in the Final Chase. They were Theresa, a credit controller from Cheshire, Gill, an HR director from Bolton, and Shahab, a journalist from London. All three took the middle amount and they amassed a prize fund of 24,000 – clearly formidable opponents for Shaun. It was the old story when faced with a huge total for the Chaser; any error means they slip behind the clock and when they try to accelerate, more mistakes happen. That's exactly how it turned out for Shaun, who could only manage a disappointing 15 in reply.

1   In the fairy tale, who said: 'Why granny, what big eyes you have'?

2   Who became editor of *Private Eye* in 1986?

3   Protozoa have how many cells?

4   On what continent is the world's largest wetland, the Pantanal?

5   Whose first Number One was 'I Should Be So Lucky'?

6   What comedian created Theophilus P. Wildebeest?

7   Concorde was retired in what decade?

8   In 1975, Mozambique become independent from what European country?

9   The word 'nasal' refers to what part of the body?

10   What was the currency of Spain before the Euro?

11   Who starred in the films *Double Impact* and *Timecop*?

12   What US state is nicknamed the 'Pelican State'?

13   Who presents *Shooting Stars* with Bob Mortimer?

14   What creatures live in an apiary?

15   Which two Charleses have appeared on the £10 note?

16   What British passenger liner is anchored off Long Beach, California?

17 What type of musical instrument is a bongo?

18 Siberia is mainly in what country?

19 Who founded the Egyptian city of Alexandria?

20 Who wrote the novels *The Woman in White* and *The Moonstone*?

21 In money, what is 10 per cent of six pounds?

22 What salad ingredient is a 'love apple'?

23 Who was the original presenter of *Blankety Blank*?

24 The Eclipse Stakes horse race is run at what course?

25 The River Ganges flows through Bangladesh and what other country?

26 Who wrote *The Satanic Verses*?

27 What New York museum is known as MoMA?

HIGHEST WINNING SCORES

CALLUM, MARILYN, SARAH AND SEAN

Top of the shop for Paul in Series 5 – and almost an unbelievable catch.
A full house of Callum, a radio producer from London, Marilyn, a retired
administration director from Reading, Sarah, a psychology researcher, also from
London, and Sean, a hotel night manager from Blackpool set him an amazing 28
in the Final Chase. A cautious approach of middle amounts and getting all four
back paid dividends... but only just! An incredible chase by Paul saw him almost
catch the team, finishing just short with 27 of his own. A game, probably, that
no one deserved to lose but one that the team were delighted to win, splitting
£24,000 between them.

HIGHEST WINNING SCORES

1   What country awards the Legion d'Honneur?

2   Audrey Fforbes-Hamilton appeared in what sitcom?

3   Who was US President during the Cuban Missile Crisis?

4   What music awards were founded in 1996 by Kanya King?

5   What king of England was known as 'the Conqueror'?

6   Capitol Hill is the political centre of what US city?

7   In finance, what does SVR stand for?

8   Who did Nick Cannon marry in 2008?

9   What's the only day of the week containing the letter O?

10   Dennis Lillee played cricket for what national team?

11   Who was the first female DJ on Radio 1?

12   Who writes the *Warrior of Rome* series of books?

13   Rehab is short for what word?

14   Who was the main host of *That's Life*?

15   The French resort of Biarritz is on what bay?

16   Which German novelist wrote *The Tin Drum*?

17 Neapolitan ice cream normally has how many flavours?

18 Who's the female member of N-Dubz?

19 What does a cartographer draw?

20 Who was the mother of Richard the Lionheart?

21 Sumo wrestling began in what country?

22 What part of the face can be described as 'lantern'?

23 What's the oldest university in the States?

24 Who released the album *Electric Ladyland* in 1968?

25 'Lino' is short for what floor covering?

26 Photosynthesis produces what gas?

27 What was the lioness in *Born Free* called?

HIGHEST WINNING SCORES

SAM, JAMIE AND PHIL

And here's one that didn't get away! Twice in the history of *The Chase*, teams have scored 26 and been beaten, once by the Beast in Series 2 (see page 222), and on this occasion when the Governess found herself facing a threesome back in Series 3. Sam from Bicester, the MD of a market research consultancy with a passion for random information, Jamie, a medical student from London, and Phil, a warehouse operative and regular pub quizzer from Southampton must have thought they had the game in the bag when they set Anne 26 to catch in the Final Chase – but they forgot that the Governess never knows when she's beaten. A brilliant chase saw the team caught with nine seconds to spare and their prize fund of £11,100 (Jamie took the low offer) disappear into thin air.

CONTESTANT SET

1   What's the Spanish for coast?
2   In *Thunderbirds*, who was Lady Penelope's chauffeur?
3   Jim Dixon is the hero of what Kingsley Amis novel?
4   The 1960 Summer Olympics were held in what city?
5   Concertina, razor and barbed are types of what?
6   How many of Henry VIII's wives were beheaded?
7   A 'Deadhead' is a fan of what US rock group?
8   Which London-born comedian wrote the novel *Meltdown*?
9   The PGA is an organisation in what sport?
10 The auditory canal is in what organ of the body?
11 What's cyberphobia the fear of?
12 What's the capital of Nicaragua?
13 What 1865 book features a Mad Hatter's tea party?
14 What planet shares its name with a liquid metal?
15 Which pop singer is nicknamed 'The Peter Pan of Pop'?
16 Jane Couch was world champion in what sport?
17 The phrase Y2K referred to what year?
18 What part of the body does a podiatrist specialise in?
19 What Australian bridge is nicknamed 'The Coathanger'?
20 What was the nationality of poet Ezra Pound?
21 What number is signified by 'octa'?
22 What form of transport was a Zeppelin?
23 The Battle of Britain took place in what year?

HIGHEST WINNING SCORES

24   What US state is known as the 'Green Mountain State'?
25   What type of food is pumpernickel?
26   The initials DVD stand for 'Digital Versatile...' what?

CHASER SET

1   What animal produces gammon?
2   Lakshmi is a popular goddess in what religion?
3   What sitcom was set in the offices of Globelink News?
4   In what English city was Cary Grant born?
5   OTT is an abbreviation of what phrase?
6   How many musicians are in a septet?
7   The Denning Report investigated what 1960s affair?
8   Who refereed the 2010 World Cup final?
9   In Chinese philosophy, what's complemented by yang?
10   Tawny and scops are types of what bird?
11   In what US state is Daytona Beach?
12   Glevum was the Roman name for what city?
13   'Cardiac' relates to what organ?
14   What metal has the chemical symbol Ag?
15   Jack and Meg White form what rock duo?
16   Elizabeth I died at what royal palace?
17   What colour can come before grocer, horn and house?
18   In what UK city is New Street station?
19   White dwarf and supergiant are types of what?
20   Who wrote the play *A Taste of Honey*?
21   Who played Basil Fawlty in *Fawlty Towers*?
22   In the Narnia books, what type of animal is Aslan?
23   Which Egyptian film actor was nicknamed 'Cairo Fred'?
24   Which future king married Caroline of Brunswick?
25   Yoghurt is made from what substance?
26   In what country was Ned Kelly a notorious outlaw?
27   What's the name of Leona Lewis's debut album?
28   What's the currency of Peru?
29   Oscar statuettes are plated with what metal?
30   What Asian country won the cricket World Cup in 1983?

HIGHEST WINNING SCORES

THE CHASE

CELEBRITY CLEVER DICKS: 10 WHO GOT 10

CELEBRITY CLEVER DICKS:
10 WHO GOT 10

The Celebrity Chase is a hugely popular version of the show. All our celebs play for charity, which means the Chasers are a little more generous than usual with their high offers. The real fun is trying to guess in advance which celebrities will crash and burn and which will turn out to be genuine brainboxes.

The following 10 celebrities all fell into the brainbox category, scoring a tremendous 10 in their Cash Builders. Would you have thought these celebs were quiz geniuses? More to the point, could you have done as well as them with their questions? Now's your chance to find out – are you as clever as a Celebrity Clever Dick?

SHAUN WILLIAMSON

Shaun Williamson might have come to the public's attention playing dopey Barry in *EastEnders* but that just shows what a good actor he is. When it comes to a quiz, Shaun is almost Chaser standard! Not only did he score 10 in his Cash Builder, he also took the Beast's high offer of £50,000 – and brought it home –before guiding his team of actor Sally Lindsay, boxer Barry McGuigan and former Atomic Kitten Jenny Frost to a £56,000 win!

1   Who composed the stage musical *Cats*?

2   What is the shiny, colourful lining inside an oyster shell called?

3   Tafari Makonnen took what title as Emperor of Ethiopia?

4   The American company Baskin-Robbins is famed for its 31 flavours of what food?

5   Theophilus P. Wildebeeste was an alter ego of which TV comedian?

6   The flugelhorn belongs to what family of musical instruments?

7   In 2011, Delia Smith left her post as catering manager of what football club?

8   'Up the Junction' and 'Cool for Cats' were Top 10 hits for what group?

9   Helen Mirren played Morgana in what film about King Arthur?

10   What word of German origin was used for the bombing of London in World War Two?

11   What Buckinghamshire stadium hosts the National Wheelchair Championships?

MATTHEW WRIGHT

TV presenter Matthew Wright proved he really did have the 'Wright stuff' when he too scored 10 in his Cash Builder. That led to Anne giving him a high offer of £40,000, but Matthew decided to take the cautious route and stick. He managed to get back, as did team-mates presenter Suzy Perry and *Benidorm*'s Crissy Rock, but Ian Watkins – 'H' from Steps – couldn't step away from the Governess quick enough and went out. They set Anne 18 in the Final Chase but it wasn't enough, and she caught them with 12 seconds to spare.

1   The pub snack 'scratchings' is made from the skin of what animal?

2   Anne Bancroft played what character in *The Graduate*?

3   Which pop superstar headlined the half-time show at the 2012 Super Bowl?

4   What South American country claims sovereignty over the Falklands?

5   What sport was once described by Robin Williams as 'baseball on valium'?

6   Which author's 200th birthday was celebrated in February 2012?

7   What airport was mentioned by Lorraine Chase in a '70s TV advert for Campari?

8   From 2013, what awards ceremony will take place at the Dolby Theatre?

9   In the TV series *Sherlock*, Irish actor Andrew Scott plays which character?

10   The only meat a kangatarian chooses to eat comes from what animal?

ALASTAIR STEWART AND KEITH CHEGWIN

An extraordinary show with not one but two celebrities hitting double figures in their Cash Builders. Newscaster Alastair Stewart and national treasure Keith 'Cheggers' Chegwin both scored 10 before they faced the Governess in their Head to Heads. Despite high offers of £50,000 to Alastair and £61,000 to Cheggers, neither would be tempted and they both made it back safely, as did their team-mates TV personality Kim Woodburn and Atomic Kitten Natasha Hamilton. So, Anne was facing a full house in the Final Chase and they set her a tricky 17. It proved to be enough and they went home with a £29,000 pot to split between their charities.

ALASTAIR STEWART

1 Tartan Day is a celebration of the heritage of what country of the UK?

2 The kissing party game played by teenagers is called 'spin the...' what?

3 In 2013 David Dinsmore became editor of what tabloid newspaper?

4 What trees feature in the name of one of the five classic horse races?

5 In *Doctor Who*, what does the letter 'T' stand for in TARDIS?

6 The astronomer Sosigenes was the advisor of which Roman leader?

7 *Strictly Ann* is an autobiography by which former Conservative MP?

8 In World War Two, which future US President commanded Patrol Torpedo boat 109?

9 Winnie-the-Pooh was indirectly named after what Canadian city?

10 Which of Prince Charles's parents was playing squash when he was born?

11 Gertrude is the mother of which Shakespearean title character?

KEITH CHEGWIN

1 What popular board game allows a maximum of 32 houses and 12 hotels?

2 Treacle, custard and Bakewell are types of what open pastry case dessert?

3 In what '90s film did Arnold Schwarzenegger play a spy called Harry Tasker?

4 Who succeeded John Curry as Olympic skating champion in 1980?

5 The name of what optical instrument comes from the Greek for 'far-seeing'?

6 The annual Cooper's Hill cheese-rolling race takes place in what county?

7 In 1945, Clement Attlee replaced Winston Churchill in what political office?

8 The actor Lee Marvin got to Number One in the UK with what song?

9 Soft and sustain are names used to describe what parts of a grand piano?

10 Maritime Law deals with navigation and commerce that takes place where?

11 Marilyn Monroe converted to what religion when she married Arthur Miller?

JESSICA TAYLOR AND RORY MCGRATH

Another double 10 show as singer and former Liberty X member Jessica Taylor and comedian Rory McGrath both scored high. Add in £8,000 from team-mate and Loose Woman Andrea McLean and £4,000 from football pundit Robbie Savage and it was clear the Beast had a super-team on his hands. What happened in the Head to Heads was unusual to say the least, as Andrea stuck, Robbie went low, Jessica took the high offer of £75,000 and Rory, despite his 10, took the low offer of £3,000. However, these proved the perfect tactics all round as the full house made it back and set Mark 22 in the Final Chase. It was a score that deserved to win – and it did, with the team sharing £87,000 between their charities.

JESSICA TAYLOR

1   In the novel *Treasure Island,* Long John Silver has how many legs?

2   In cricket, which fielder must remain directly behind the stumps as the ball is bowled?

3   Inspector Javert is a character in what stage and film musical?

4   What old term for any meat caught in a hunt is now only used for the meat of the deer?

5   What animated children's TV show is set in the town of Pontypandy?

6   What sign of the zodiac has the longest name?

7   In what film does Richard Gere literally sweep Debra Winger off her feet?

8   In what human organ would you find nerve-cell groups called basal ganglia?

9   In 2002, what group won a BRIT Award for the single 'Don't Stop Movin'?

10 What precious gem gets its name from the Greek word for 'invincible'?

11 The terms 'Thoughtcrime' and 'Memory Hole' feature in what George Orwell novel?

RORY MCGRATH

1   In 'Sing a Song of Sixpence', how many blackbirds were baked in the pie?

2   The original Ashes Trophy is usually kept at what cricket ground?

3   'Jo-Jo left his home in Tucson Arizona' in what Beatles song?

4   Which French explorer popularised scuba diving in his book *The Silent World*?

5   The port of Mahón is thought to have lent its name to what creamy dressing?

6   The Gulf of Aqaba is part of what sea?

7   What was discovered in Bonanza Creek in the Yukon in 1896?

8   Who starred as Will Turner in the *Pirates of the Caribbean* films?

9   Which British scientist received the first Albert Einstein Medal in 1979?

10 Which 18th century French queen was often referred to as 'the baker's wife'?

11 Sir Basil and Lady Rosemary were characters in what kids' TV series of the 60s?

12 The Nikkei average is an index quoted on what Asian city's stock exchange?

13 The footballer Roy Race featured in what comic strip?

JONATHAN ROSS

Jonathan Ross proved he's the master of the quiz show as well as the chat show when he scored 10 in his Cash Builder. It was a show notable for two of our celebrities taking the high offer… and bringing it back. Jonathan was offered £66,000 by Shaun, which he accepted – and then proceeded to nearly wreck the set as he climbed up the table to say hi to the Chaser! His team-mate, comedian Katy Brand, had already banked £46,000 from her Head to Head, and with £7,000 from sports reporter Chris Hollins and a low offer of £1,000 from model and TV personality Jo Wood, Shaun was facing a full house and a staggering pot of £120,000! A terrific score of 22 by the team was more than enough, and their charities could celebrate a real windfall.

1   In the title of novels, what number links Men In A Boat and Musketeers?

2   In the US, Bazooka Joe is the mascot of what kind of confectionery?

3   Benedict Cumberbatch won a 2014 Emmy for his role in what series?

4   Who was the last monarch before the Queen to celebrate a diamond jubilee?

5   What's the more common title for Edvard Munch's painting *The Cry*?

6   Who starred as inventor Cade Yeager in the film *Transformers: Age of Extinction*?

7   What religious ritual is designed to expel bad spirits from the living?

8   Which Eurovision winner modelled for Jean Paul Gaultier in 2014?

9   The name of what Japanese comics means 'aimless pictures'?

10   What country's capital city is Reykjavik?

11   Morrissey and which guitarist were the main songwriters in The Smiths?

STEVE PEMBERTON

The League of Gentlemen's Steve Pemberton proved to be in a league of his own when it comes to quizzing, with a 10 in his Christmas Cash Builder back in 2014. Being a Christmas show, all four Chasers on the show at the time were involved (it was before the Vixen joined) and Steve faced Mark in his Head to Head, bringing back the high offer of £50,000 to the team. *Coronation Street*'s Paula Lane, *Educating Yorkshire*'s Matt Burton and actor and comedian Ben Miller all made it back too. Paul drew the short straw amongst the Chasers for the Final Chase and found himself facing a prize fund of £62,000 and a total of 18. It proved to be enough – the team went home triumphant and it wasn't a very merry Christmas for the Chasers!

1   Which character says to Little Red Riding Hood 'All the better to see you with'?

2   In 2014, Liverpool sold striker Luis Suarez to which Spanish football club?

3   What Billy Joel song begins 'Harry Truman, Doris Day, Red China, Johnny Ray'?

4   Who is the only man to have been married to a British Prime Minister?

5   Meaning 'spirit of the times', the word 'zeitgeist' is from what European language?

6   The musical *The Book of Mormon* was written by the creators of what TV show?

7   When it first opened, what motorway ran from Watford to Crick?

8   Which Jim Carrey Christmas film character says 'It's because I'm green, isn't it?'?

9   What South African mountain is flanked by the Lion's Head and the Devil's Peak?

10   *One Leg Too Few* is a biography of Peter Cook and who else?

11   Which famous diary writer made his last entry on 31 May 1669?

IAN LAVENDER

Comedy legend Ian Lavender proved that while he might have played 'stupid boy' Private Pike in *Dad's Army*, he was actually anything but – collecting a cool 10 in his Cash Builder. Unfortunately for Ian, most of his team couldn't stick with him. TV presenter Angelica Bell and Oritse Williams from JLS both got caught by Shaun, leaving Ian with only actress Leslie Ash for company in the Final Chase. The prize fund was a respectable £14,000 but, unfortunately, nerves got the better of the team and they posted a disappointing 11. Shaun knocked that off with over a minute left!

1   In what type of restaurant are you most likely to eat a naan bread?

2   Henry Blofeld and Jonathan Agnew are best known for commentating on what sport?

3   Which Prime Minister said 'I was the future once' on his last day in office?

4   Which gardener is the Saturday morning DJ on Classic FM?

5   Brecon Beacons National Park is in what country of the UK?

6   The black-and-white film *The Lucky Dog* was the first to feature what comedy duo?

7   What racecourse is roughly seven miles from Windsor Castle?

8   In the rhyme 'Tinker, Tailor, Soldier, Sailor', who follows Beggarman?

9   In the Bible, Jesus fed the five thousand with two fish and how many loaves?

10   Construction began on what California bridge in 1933?

11   In Thai cookery, the word 'gai' refers to what bird?

MATT ALLWRIGHT

A very entertaining show, in which TV presenter Matt Allwright proved he was no Rogue Trader and very much to be trusted when it came to a quiz. However, his Cash Builder 10 was overshadowed by team-mate and TV personality Stacey Solomon going high with a £60,000 offer... and bringing it home. It's fair to say that no one was more surprised at that outcome than Stacey herself! After that, the other players – BBC *Breakfast* presenter Louise Minchin and actor Keith Allen – could both go low and get home. Louise got an unusual offer of £346 from the Governess, based on the fact that she gets up at 3:46 every morning. It meant a Final Chase total of £71,346 and a respectable score of 19. Anne's chase lived up to the excitement of the rest of the show with a final-second catch of the team! Sadly, for Matt, it wasn't Allwright on the night...

1   Complete the *Guys and Dolls* song: 'Sit Down, You're Rockin' the...' what?

2   What flowers share their name with a Cadbury's chocolate assortment?

3   How many of the wives of Henry VIII died while still married to him?

4   What religious book gives its name to a so-called 'Belt' in the southern USA?

5   Which Scot co-organised the Live Aid concerts with Bob Geldof?

6   What director links the films *Jabberwocky* and *Time Bandits*?

7   A difficult situation is said to balance on the edge of what piece of cutlery?

8   In 2016, the Switch House opened as part of what modern art gallery?

9   Which British athlete retained his European long jump title in 2016?

10 Complete the title of the Dead or Alive hit: 'You Spin Me Round (Like a...)' what?

11 In the name of the air travel body IATA, what does the T stand for?

12 What male relative is used as an alternative name for a longcase clock?

THE CHASE

CELEBRITIES GOING BIG

CELEBRITIES GOING BIG

As we've mentioned, the *Celebrity Chase* brings out the generous side of the Chasers, with some very high offers. In fact, it's not really generosity, it's just that they know the celebrities are playing for charity so the chance of winning big money is harder to resist. They also know that accepting a high offer dramatically increases the chance of catching them. They're a sneaky bunch, those Chasers... Here are some of the biggest offers taken by celebrities. How would you have done with their questions? As the saying goes, go big or go home. In some of these cases, the celebrities did both!

TIM VINE

Back in Series 2, the Beast played this team like a stringed instrument. He'd already lured broadcaster Vanessa Feltz on seat 3 into taking a high offer of £60,000 and sent her packing, so surely comedian Tim Vine on seat 4 wouldn't do the same? An offer of £100,000 proved just too much to resist. Sadly for Tim, he suffered the same fate as Vanessa, leaving Mark to face journalist Nicholas Owen and actress Laila Rouass in the Final Chase, where he caught the score of 17 with 35 seconds to spare. The Beast loves it when a plan comes together.

1 In 2012, 95-year-old 'Creeky' entered the *Guinness Book of World Records* as the world's oldest what?

A Skydiver   **B** Performing clown   **C** Male stripper

2 What is the cartoon character Andy Capp known as in Germany?

A Dick Tingeler   **B** Helmut Schmacker   **C** Willi Wakker

3 Which of these foods would an 'ovo-lacto' vegetarian NOT eat?

A Eggs   **B** Milk   **C** Fish

4 Which of these London football clubs has NOT been managed by Harry Redknapp?

A Tottenham Hotspur   **B** Chelsea   **C** West Ham

5 After meeting James Dean, which British actor correctly predicted that he would be dead within a week?

A David Niven   **B** Laurence Olivier   **C** Alec Guinness

6 Something considered to be excellent is referred to as the... what?

A Cat's pyjamas   **B** Dog's nightie   **C** Rabbit's negligée

7 The mouth of which of these north-eastern rivers is furthest south?

A Tees   **B** Wear   **C** Tyne

8 In 2011, which Scandinavian country introduced a tax on fatty foods?

A Denmark   **B** Sweden   **C** Norway

DENISE WELCH

The Sinnerman had clearly been watching when the Beast bamboozled Tim Vine, as he used the same tactic against actress and Loose Woman Denise Welch. He'd already caught the first three members of the team – singer Russell Watson, *EastEnder* Rita Simon and former Goodie Bill Oddie – when he got the £100,000 high offer out for Denise on seat 4. Once again, it proved impossible to resist and, once again, it ended in disaster for our celebrity. With all four team members caught, Paul had a Lazarus game on his hands, where one of the team comes back from the dead, playing for £20,000 to split with the others. Of course, in the daytime Chases, this amount is £4,000 but as it's for charity celebrities play for more. Russell Watson took up the challenge – to no avail. A score of just 10 was dispatched with well over a minute to spare.

1   In 1985, which pop duo became the first Western band to play in Communist China?

   A Wham!   **B** Pet Shop Boys   **C** Simon and Garfunkel

2   Which town in the North West hosts the annual World Pie-Eating Championships?

   A Wigan   **B** Warrington   **C** Widnes

3   In 2011, who said 'I've dated girls and I've dated boys – get over it'?

   A Shakira   **B** Katy Perry   **C** Jessie J

4   Traditionally, which of these academic titles is given to a Punch and Judy performer?

   A Doctor   **B** Master   **C** Professor

5   The Trinidad Moruga Scorpion is a type of what?

   A Jellyfish   **B** Rocket launcher   **C** Chilli pepper

CELEBRITIES GOING BIG

JIMMY CARR

Another masterclass in manipulation from the Beast in this show. Having caught rugby player Matt Dawson on seat 1 after he took the middle amount of £4,000, he proceeded to tease each of the others into taking the high offer. First of all, TV personality and Speaker's wife Sally Bercow took £60,000 and was caught, followed by the same offer to *Coronation Street*'s Jack P. Shepherd... with exactly the same result. Only comedian Jimmy Carr was left – and that favourite £100,000 high offer once again proved impossible to resist. Sadly for Jimmy, he couldn't bring it home. Mark had a Lazarus show. Jimmy stepped up for the team but could only set the Beast 12, which he caught with 46 seconds to spare.

1 Which of the founders of French Impressionism painting had English parents?

A Monet	**B** Renoir	**C** Sisley

2 Which American musician starred alongside George Clooney in the 1999 film *Three Kings*?

A Ice Cube	**B** Ice-T	**C** Vanilla Ice

3 Which of these Christian festivals does NOT take place on the same date each year?

A Epiphany	**B** Christmas Day	**C** Easter Sunday

4 Which of these tennis Grand Slam tournaments is NOT played on hard courts?

A Australian Open	**B** French Open	**C** US Open

5 A cocktail of beer mixed with gin is known as what?

A Dog's nose	**B** Cat's whisker	**C** Badger's bum

JOEY ESSEX

In Series 7, Anne was facing the prospect of a full house after failing to catch writer Mark Billingham, chef Aldo Zilli and *Emmerdale*'s Lucy Pargeter, when *TOWIE*'s Joey Essex got up from seat 4 to face her. Desperate times call for desperate measures, so Anne pulled out the £100,000 high offer. Joey fell for it hook, line and sinker and Anne was able to catch him. Not that it helped her in the end, as the team, with a prize fund of £15,000, set her a taxing 18 in the Final Chase. She ran them close but three pushbacks meant she fell short.

1   Nyotaimori is the Japanese practice of serving sushi laid out on what?

     A A ninja   **B** A woman   **C** A sumo wrestler

2   Which of these is the name of a rapper who featured on Chris Brown's Top 10 hit 'AYO'?

     A Jagwa   **B** Cooga   **C** Tyga

3   In 1792, George III bought what royal house?

     A Frogmore   **B** Balmoral   **C** Osborne House

4   What name is given to a sleeping bag with a hood?

     A Mummy bag   **B** Daddy bag   **C** Baby bag

CELEBRITIES GOING BIG

ADE EDMONSON

In Series 9, Mark was also facing the possibility of a full house in the Final Chase when he produced his favourite high offer of £100,000 to try and tempt comedian Ade Edmonson into coming a step closer. *Strictly Come Dancing*'s Anton Du Beke, impressionist Alistair McGowen and TV presenter Sarah-Jane Crawford had already made it back with £13,000 in the prize fund when Ade decided to go big. It was real gamble, but it paid off as he made it home. Could the team get a share of £113,000 for their charities? A score of 17 and a couple of pushbacks achieved in the Final Chase meant they were in with a shout, but unfortunately not a loud enough one – the Beast caught them with 20 seconds to spare.

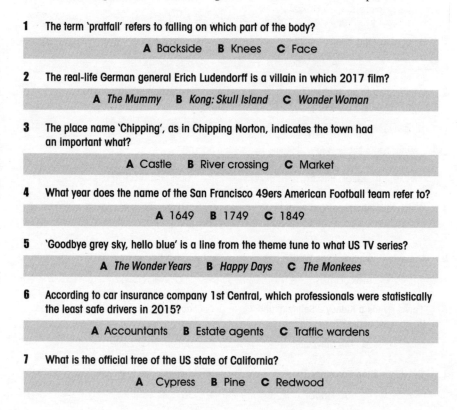

1 The term 'pratfall' refers to falling on which part of the body?

        A Backside   **B** Knees   **C** Face

2 The real-life German general Erich Ludendorff is a villain in which 2017 film?

        A *The Mummy*   **B** *Kong: Skull Island*   **C** *Wonder Woman*

3 The place name 'Chipping', as in Chipping Norton, indicates the town had an important what?

        A Castle   **B** River crossing   **C** Market

4 What year does the name of the San Francisco 49ers American Football team refer to?

        A 1649   **B** 1749   **C** 1849

5 'Goodbye grey sky, hello blue' is a line from the theme tune to what US TV series?

        A *The Wonder Years*   **B** *Happy Days*   **C** *The Monkees*

6 According to car insurance company 1st Central, which professionals were statistically the least safe drivers in 2015?

        A Accountants   **B** Estate agents   **C** Traffic wardens

7 What is the official tree of the US state of California?

        A Cypress   **B** Pine   **C** Redwood

ED BYRNE

Back in Series 3, the Governess was facing a very strong player in comedian Ed Byrne when she produced the biggest high offer *The Celebrity Chase* had ever seen – an amazing £117,000. Ed was on seat 4 and had watched darts player Eric Bristow get back with £3,000 from his Cash Builder. But then Anne caught politician Nadine Dorries and *Emmerdale*'s Sammy Winward. The size of the offer showed how keen Anne was to play just Eric in the Final Chase, but her plan came unstuck when Ed made it home. The prize fund of £120,000 was truly mouth-watering, but a combination of nerves and a tricky set of questions meant they could only set Anne 15 to catch. She made it but, with an equally difficult question set herself, with only 17 seconds to spare.

1   What object did former Cabinet Minister Andrew Mitchell auction on the internet in 2013?

    A Bicycle   **B** Helmet   **C** Backpack

2   When going to an Australian party or barbecue, the instruction 'BYOG' means 'Bring Your Own...' what?

    A Girls   **B** Grog   **C** Grundies

3   Which guitarist is President of the Nude Mountaineering Society?

    A Julian Bream   **B** John Williams   **C** Hank Wangford

4   Which thin, sharp-pointed sword is often used to describe a quick and incisive wit?

    A Curtana   **B** Rapier   **C** Sabre

5   The award-winning Little Wallop cheese is made by which former musician?

    A Alex James   **B** Andrew Ridgeley   **C** Andy Summers

6   'Lewis Needs a Kidney', 'Seinfeld' and 'Larry vs Michael J. Fox' are episode titles in what US comedy series?

    A *The Newsroom*   **B** *Curb Your Enthusiasm*   **C** *Louie*

7   The Edgar Allan Poe story *The Fall of the House of Usher* belongs to which literary genre?

    A Horror   **B** Historical romance   **C** Sci-fi

CELEBRITIES GOING BIG

RACHEL RILEY

It was all about girl power as sports presenter Kirsty Gallacher and *Countdown*'s Rachel Riley faced Shaun in this Soccer Aid special. Kirsty brought back the high offer of £40,000, but then Shaun caught travel writer and actor Charley Boorman and football commentator Clive Tyldsley, leaving Rachel with a high offer of £120,000. She promptly brought it home! In the Final Chase, Shaun made 10 errors and got pushed back four times... and Unicef got a £160,000 donation!

1 What was first advertised as 'the greatest forward step in the baking industry since bread was wrapped'?

A Wholegrain bread   **B** Crustless bread   **C** Sliced bread

2 Most broadcasts of what regular Radio 4 programme are limited to 370 words each?

A *The Archers*   **B** *Just a Minute*   **C** *Shipping Forecast*

3 Who ran the anchor leg when Great Britain won gold at the 2004 Olympics in the men's 4x100 metres relay?

A Darren Campbell   **B** Mark Lewis-Francis   **C** Jason Gardener

4 Medically, alcohol can be used as a what?

A Antihistamine   **B** Antiseptic   **C** Anticoagulant

5 On Instagram, users' 'stories' last for how long before being archived?

A 6 hours   **B** 12 hours   **C** 24 hours

6 Which singer said rock and roll was 'sung, played and written for the most part by cretinous goons'?

A Frank Sinatra   **B** Sammy Davis Jr   **C** Dean Martin

7 Which branch of biology studies the relationship between organisms and their habitats?

A Taxonomy   **B** Physiology   **C** Ecology

8 Which British car company's headquarters are in Crewe in Cheshire?

A Rolls-Royce   **B** Bentley   **C** Morgan

DUNCAN JAMES

The highest offer ever made on *The Celebrity Chase* wasn't taken. Paul offered snooker player Stephen Hendrie £147,000 back in Series 5, but he wouldn't be tempted. So, this is the biggest ever played for. Jenny had already seen TV presenter and property guru Martin Roberts, round-the-world sailor Tracy Edwards and the lovely Debbie McGee make it back with £21,000 when she offered Duncan James from Blue a staggering £139,000. He took the bait and the Vixen had hopes of just three in the Final Chase. Those hopes were dashed as she faced a full house playing for £160,000. Unfortunately, they could only set Jenny 16. She held her nerve and caught them with an easy 25 seconds left on the clock.

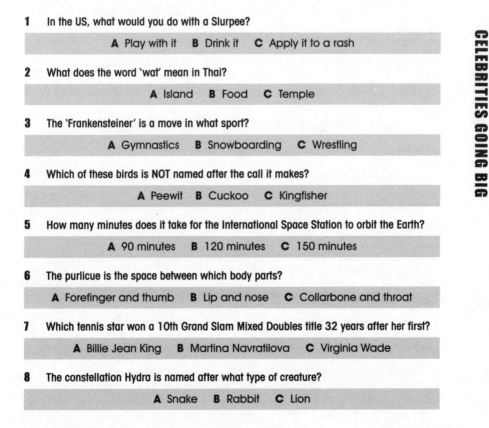

1 In the US, what would you do with a Slurpee?

A Play with it   B Drink it   C Apply it to a rash

2 What does the word 'wat' mean in Thai?

A Island   B Food   C Temple

3 The 'Frankensteiner' is a move in what sport?

A Gymnastics   B Snowboarding   C Wrestling

4 Which of these birds is NOT named after the call it makes?

A Peewit   B Cuckoo   C Kingfisher

5 How many minutes does it take for the International Space Station to orbit the Earth?

A 90 minutes   B 120 minutes   C 150 minutes

6 The purlicue is the space between which body parts?

A Forefinger and thumb   B Lip and nose   C Collarbone and throat

7 Which tennis star won a 10th Grand Slam Mixed Doubles title 32 years after her first?

A Billie Jean King   B Martina Navratilova   C Virginia Wade

8 The constellation Hydra is named after what type of creature?

A Snake   B Rabbit   C Lion

CELEBRITIES GOING BIG

THE CHASE

BRITAIN'S BRAINIEST FAMILY

BRITAIN'S BRAINIEST FAMILY

The Family Chase has clocked up two series already, and we've seen a lot of talented quizzing families. There's a different dynamic to the family shows compared to the daytime *Chase*. After all, those teams are complete strangers so it doesn't matter what happens as they'll never see each other again. Muck it up on a *Family* show, however, and Christmas could become a very frosty affair!

Best of the bunch to date were the French family from Wiltshire, who went home with £20,000 between them back in Series 1. Dad Peter and his children Hattie, Chloe and Ned scored a very impressive combined total of 26 in their Cash Builders. The Chasers regard any combined total over 20 as a 'super-team', which made the French family a 'super-dooper team'! Here are all the questions they used to beat Anne – could you have done the same?

HATTIE (CASH BUILDER)

Seat 1 and therefore designated team captain was Hattie, a website manager and keen quizzer. In fact, she was the captain not just of the family team but also of her pub quiz team. She didn't let the family down, racking up an impressive £8,000 in her Cash Builder.

1   Buzz Aldrin once punched a man who claimed that what 1969 event was faked?

2   'Beyond' and 'Beyond Forever' are fragrances by which British ex-footballer?

3   What novel by J. D. Salinger was first published in 1951?

4   In the New Testament, the Annunciation told of whose forthcoming birth?

5   Who was succeeded by his brother as Cuban President in 2008?

6   The Odin Express is a train ride at what Copenhagen amusement park?

7   After visiting a fruit farm, Steve Jobs came up with the name of what tech company?

8   What boy's name represents a vowel in the NATO phonetic alphabet?

9   What fictional name is given to the holiday destination of *Take Me Out* contestants?

10   What toy company was originated by a Danish carpenter in 1932?

HATTIE (HEAD TO HEAD)

Then it was time for Hattie to face the Chaser. Respecting her excellent Cash Builder, Anne's offers were generous, with a low of £2,000 and a high of £36,000. However, it's hard to go high with £8,000 already earned, so Hattie took the cautious route and stayed in the middle. It was the right decision. She made it back and the family team was up and running.

1 Which of these novels features a prime number in the title?

    A *The Thirty-Nine Steps*   **B** *Fifty Shades of Grey*   **C** *The 101 Dalmatians*

2 Launched in 2016, what is the name of Google's messaging app?

    A Allo   **B** Howdy   **C** What's Up

3 What opera joins *Aida* and *Carmen* in the 'ABCs', said to be the three most-performed operas worldwide?

    A La Bohème   **B** Madam Butterfly   **C** The Barber of Seville

4 In the biblical book of Genesis, who said 'she gave me of the tree, and I did eat'?

    A Adam   **B** Jacob   **C** Noah

5 Which of these is NOT a name for a genuine variety of turkey?

    A Brush-turkey   **B** Scrub-turkey   **C** Wipe-turkey

6 In what decade was Wimbledon first televised?

    A 1930s   **B** 1940s   **C** 1950s

7 Which of these pop groups has NOT had a member join the cast of *Coronation Street*?

    A Boyzone   **B** Girls Aloud   **C** Take That

8 In Roald Dahl's *Matilda*, what relation is Miss Trunchbull to Miss Honey?

    A Aunt   **B** Cousin   **C** Sister

BRITAIN'S BRAINIEST FAMILY

CHLOE (CASH BUILDER)

Next up on seat 2 was sister Chloe, a junior doctor who enjoyed playing really difficult board games with her husband. She kept the pressure up on the Chaser with a commendable £6,000 scored.

1 What piece of furniture can be double, water or four-poster?

2 In 2016, which fantasy TV show broke the record for most Emmys won by a series?

3 'Get back you flea-infested mongrel' is a line from what Baha Men hit?

4 The first wife of Napoleon Bonaparte had what first name?

5 'Young upwardly-mobile professional' is an interpretation of what slang term?

6 What Japanese condiment is usually made of horseradish, mustard and food colouring?

7 The Dixiecrats were a Southern off-shoot of what US political party?

8 *Four Past Midnight* is a collection by which American horror writer?

9 In 1963, Diana Vreeland became editor-in-chief of what fashion magazine?

10 The African country of Angola has a coastline on what ocean?

11 Stefan and a Scottish Granny are characters used by which female ventriloquist?

CHLOE (HEAD TO HEAD)

When it came to her Head to Head game, Anne was determined to make Chloe take the high offer, putting £42,000 on the table alongside a low offer of £1,000. Chloe wouldn't be tempted by the high offer, but maybe she should have considered the low amount – Anne caught her and knocked her out. So, after the first two players, it was one all between Brad and the Chaser.

1 The slow loris releases venom from which part of its body?

    A Elbows   **B** Ankles   **C** Eyeballs

2 Which of these cities is transcontinental?

    A Islamabad   **B** Indianapolis   **C** Istanbul

3 In *The Return of the Jedi,* what word is never spoken in the film, and only appears in the closing credits?

    A Ewok   **B** Lightsaber   **C** Jabba

4 In the nursery rhyme, what did the crooked man buy with the crooked sixpence he found?

    A A crooked cat   **B** A crooked hat   **C** A crooked bat

5 Which of these TV cookery judges is the author of more than 80 cookbooks, with total sales of over six million?

    A Gordon Ramsay   **B** Mary Berry   **C** John Torode

6 At the start of a snooker game, what colour ball lies between the brown and the pink?

    A Blue   **B** Yellow   **C** Green

BRITAIN'S BRAINIEST FAMILY

NED (CASH BUILDER)

Seat 3 was brother Ned, an auditor and cryptic crossword fan. As his sisters will doubtless never tire of reminding him, he didn't score as many as them – but £5,000 was still a very good score.

1   What pub game has a board with a doubles ring and a trebles ring?

2   In 2016, what fast food chain launched a chicken scented sunscreen called 'Extra Crispy'?

3   The Mesozoic era was formed by the Triassic, Cretaceous and what other period?

4   What road surface material patented in 1902 was named after a Scottish inventor?

5   The term 'rain check', meaning to delay something, comes from what American sport?

6   *The Enfield Case* is the subtitle to the sequel of what horror film?

7   In 1936, which future ruler of Spain led an army mutiny in Spanish Morocco?

8   Which Teletubby comes second alphabetically?

9   In 622, the prophet Muhammad left what holy city which had rejected his teachings?

NED (HEAD TO HEAD)

Would Ned be tempted to come a step closer to Anne in his Head to Head? She offered him a huge £50,000, but he was unmoved. He also wouldn't be persuaded by her low offer of £1,000. Sticking with his £5,000 proved to be the correct decision by Ned, as he made it back to his sister Hattie and increased the family prize fund to £13,000.

1 Which of these is a type of mathematical chart?

A Box and paw **B** Box and tail **C** Box and whisker

2 In the 1997 film *Liar Liar*, Jim Carrey's character has what profession?

A Doctor **B** Lawyer **C** Policeman

3 World War Two ended with the final surrender of the Japanese forces on board which American battleship?

A USS *Oklahoma* **B** USS *Mississippi* **C** USS *Missouri*

4 Which of the '5 Ks' of Sikhism is a steel bracelet?

A Kara B Kesh **C** Kirpan

5 In the UK, what scouting group is for the youngest children?

A Cubs **B** Explorers **C** Beavers

6 How many member states of the UN begin with the letter 'J'?

A One **B** Three **C** Five

7 Which of these phrases, frequently used on social media, means 'looking good' or 'perfectly executed'?

A On fleek **B** Lit **C** Fam

PETER (CASH BUILDER)

Finally, on seat 4, it was dad Peter, a primary school teacher and keen pianist. Would he show us where his children got their brains from? He most certainly would, scoring an excellent £7,000 in his Cash Builder.

1   What letter is silent in the name of Dennis the Menace's pet dog Gnasher?

2   Who sang lead vocals on the '80s Number One hit 'Prince Charming'?

3   Which TV physicist co-wrote *Universal: A Guide to the Cosmos* with Jeff Forshaw?

4   What type of animal is Jeremy Corbyn's pet El Gato?

5   What word is in the name of a statue in New York and a bell in Philadelphia?

6   The poet who wrote 'Oh Captain! My Captain!' was Walt who?

7   What's the only Worcestershire sauce that may be called 'Original and Genuine'?

8   What Dylan Thomas play begins with the words 'To begin at the beginning'?

9   Boris Johnson compared Nicola Sturgeon to which Shakespearean character?

10   What annual theatrical gala event is attended by senior royals?

11   Which DC comic book superhero is a fictional Princess of Themyscira?

PETER (HEAD TO HEAD)

By the time it came to Peter's Head to Head, it was clear that the French family had come with a game plan, which was to take the middle amount and get as many players back as possible. Peter dismissed Anne's low offer of minus £1,000 and was equally unmoved by her high offer of £62,000. It proved to be the right move, as he made it back and the team had three in the Final Chase – and £20,000 in the prize fund.

1 Which of these kings was the father of the most English monarchs?

    A Henry III   **B** Henry V   **C** Henry VIII

2 In 2016, the new mayor of Turin pledged to make the city the first of what kind in Italy?

    A Non-smoking   **B** Teetotal   **C** Vegetarian

3 Which of these Cumbrian towns is in the Lake District National Park?

    A Whitehaven   **B** Windermere   **C** Workington

4 Novelists Graham Greene and John Le Carré both worked for which of these organisations?

    A Interpol   **B** SAS   **C** MI6

5 What sort of creature is a 'sea biscuit'?

    A Sea urchin   **B** Sea horse   **C** Sea slug

6 What does the word 'levity' describe?

    A Lightness   **B** Thickness   **C** Heaviness

7 Which of these dances is NOT in triple time?

    A Waltz   **B** Minuet   **C** Foxtrot

BRITAIN'S BRAINIEST FAMILY

THE FINAL CHASE – THE FRENCH FAMILY

With only Chloe missing, could the French family set the Governess enough to really make it difficult for her to catch them? They could! An excellent team performance amassed an impressive 22 in their side of the Final Chase. With their three-step head start they had 19 questions answered correctly across their two minutes – a score high enough to worry any Chaser.

1   Which band replaced drummer Pete Best with Ringo Starr?

2   What's the minimum age of a centenarian?

3   In what country was crime boss Pablo Escobar born?

4   Which American female poet wrote the poem 'And Still I Rise'?

5   About what band did Alan Partridge say: 'Or as they're now known – Sting'?

6   Eristoff and Chopin are brands of what alcoholic spirit?

7   The Egyptian city of Tanta is in what river delta?

8   Who was the first Pope from a Slavic country?

9   On what TV quiz did Henry Kelly often say 'What am I?'

10 The Colosseum is the concert venue of what Las Vegas hotel?

11 Which artist created the cover for the Blur album *Think Tank*?

12 In the night sky, Rigel is the seventh brightest what?

13 Which British peace envoy was kidnapped in Beirut in 1987?

14 Pashto is a language from what continent?

15 Bob Fosse won a Best Director Oscar for what '70s film musical?

16 The Julia Donaldson character Spinderella is what arachnid?

17 The Wagner tuba was built for what opera cycle?

18 Who was appointed the government's 'Enterprise Tsar' in 2016?

19 Which British track cyclist has the nickname 'Trotty'?

20 In what year did Russia officially withdraw from World War One?

21 In the UK, March is usually considered the first month of what season?

22 Which German fashion designer is nicknamed 'King Karl'?

23 Which Queen of Carthage shares her name with a British singer?

THE FINAL CHASE – THE GOVERNESS

Twenty-two is an impressive score and Anne would need an almost flawless performance to catch it. Unfortunately for her, the big total meant she had to answer quickly... and that's when the Chasers start to make errors. Anne got six questions wrong in her Final Chase and, crucially, the team pushed her back on four of them, making it impossible to catch them. It was a very good performance by the French family – one that deserved to win. They went back to Wiltshire with £20,000 and the pride that comes with beating a Chaser. How would you have done in Anne's place? Could you have caught the team?

1 How many wheels does a bicycle with stabilisers have?

2 Shabnam Masood was a character in what TV soap?

3 Trident replaced what former nuclear weapons program?

4 Which of Australia's state capitals has the shortest name?

5 What word follows 'war' in a slang term for make-up?

6 On what photo-sharing app can you 'replay a snap'?

7 What sort of animal are the TV mascots of Andrex and Dulux?

8 In 2013, Nawaz Sharif became Prime Minister of what country?

9 In 2016, Eddie Jordan became a co-host of what TV show?

10 The hepatic plexus is a network of nerves serving what organ?

11 What Royal Navy rank comes between Admiral and Rear Admiral?

12 Donald's Trump's mother was born in what country of the UK?

13 Which jockey-turned writer wrote a biography of Lester Piggott?

14 What company made the drink Tab Clear to rival Crystal Pepsi?

15 Isabella of Gloucester was the first wife of which king?

16 Chelsea and Chiswick are bridges over what river?

17   The Cape Cobras is a cricket team from what country?

18   *Dangerous Lady* is a book by which female crime writer?

19   In fashion, what word can follow 'play', 'jump' and 'three-piece'?

20   What was the last Alfred Hitchcock film shot in black and white?

21   Beefmaster is a breed of what farm animal?

22   What area of Romania is famously associated with vampires?

23   In Greek mythology, who was the god of marriage?

24   Punxsutawney Phil is an animal in what '90s Bill Murray film?

25   In what sport does Newmarket host the Autumn Double?

26   Washington Heights is a neighbourhood in what New York borough?

27   The surname of which Scottish engineer gives a unit of power?

28   Which Latino rapper is nicknamed 'Mr Worldwide'?

BRITAIN'S BRAINIEST FAMILY

THE CHASE

ZERO CASH BUILDERS

ZERO CASH BUILDERS

There's no worse feeling for a contestant on *The Chase* than drawing a blank during the Cash Builder. It's actually quite a rare occurrence, with just over 0.5 per cent of all contestants scoring zero – that's one in 200, or once every 50 shows. There are all sorts of reasons why it happens, from really tough questions to nerves taking over, to what the Chasers call a 'pass spiral' where, after getting a question wrong that they knew the answer to, the contestant is still thinking about the wrong answer when the next question is asked so ends up passing when they probably knew that answer too. Once in a 'pass spiral', it's very difficult to escape.

All the following questions were asked to contestants who scored zero. We won't name any of them – they've suffered enough already – but how would you do? Could you hold your nerve and post an impressive score? Remember that you only have one minute for each set.

CASH BUILDER QUIZ 1

1   *The Social Network* is a film about the founding of what website?

2   The Royal Marines are in which of the armed forces?

3   Who did Roger Federer beat in the final of the 2010 Australian Open?

4   What was the first name of the explorer Shackleton?

5   Sellafield nuclear power station is in what county?

6   Roberta, Peter and Phyllis are the main characters in what book?

7   Who played Dr Mark Sloan in TV's *Diagnosis Murder*?

8   Which comedian had a hit in 1984 with 'Ullo John, Got a New Motor'?

9   What UK agency is officially called the Secret Intelligence Service?

10 Elizabeth I began her reign in what century?

CASH BUILDER QUIZ 2

1   In the traditional saying, what is the opposite of cheese?

2   Which Irish pop twins are 'Let Loose' in an ITV2 show?

3   Whose solo hits include 'Wonderful Christmastime' and 'No More Lonely Nights'?

4   The island of Newfoundland is part of what country?

5   In the *Harry Potter* stories, what relation is Lucius Malfoy to Draco?

6   The painter Georges Seurat is the subject of what Sondheim musical?

7   Which clown is Bart Simpson's idol?

8   What river traditionally divides the 'Men of Kent' and the 'Kentish Men'?

9   Who starred as Jesse in the film comedy *Dude, Where's My Car?*?

10 What type of hat is traditionally worn by the Brigade of Guards?

11 Which Greek shipping tycoon was played by Robert Lindsay in a 2010 play?

ZERO CASH BUILDERS

CASH BUILDER QUIZ 3

1   John Noakes was the longest-serving presenter of what children's TV programme?

2   What Dutch cheese is named after a town just north-east of Rotterdam?

3   The Tyne-Tees football derby is between Newcastle and what other team?

4   Jeremy Renner played a bomb disposal expert in what Oscar-winning film?

5   In gardening, what term means removing flowers when they are dying or dead?

6   In 1991, 'You Could Be Mine' was a hit single for what US rock band?

7   In the 16th century, William Tyndale translated the New Testament into what language?

8   What major mountain range lies between the Black Sea and the Caspian Sea?

9   What term for business failure comes from the Italian for 'broken bench'?

10   What organisation is known for its 'Landranger' and 'Explorer' maps?

CASH BUILDER QUIZ 4

1 Comedians surnamed Brand, Howard and Kane all share what first name?

2 What letter of the Greek alphabet lends its name to the mouth of rivers such as the Nile?

3 Which golfer was the first European to win the US Masters?

4 Candace Bushnell's novel *The Carrie Diaries* is a prequel to what TV show?

5 What two-word rhyming phrase can describe a shady or unscrupulous businessman?

6 Who was the first female Secretary of State for Northern Ireland?

7 In 2012, Trafalgar Square's fourth plinth was topped with a statue of a boy on what toy?

8 'When the Sun Goes Down' was a 2006 Number One for what band?

ZERO CASH BUILDERS

CASH BUILDER QUIZ 5

1 Jock is a common nickname for someone from what country of the UK?

2 The name of what book of the Bible means 'disclosures' or 'visions'?

3 In the 'Charley Says' public information films, what animal was Charley?

4 A miser called John Elwes is said to have inspired what Dickens character?

5 During the '60s and '70s, Katie Boyle presented what TV contest four times?

6 Set in New York, what 1971 thriller starred Jane Fonda and Donald Sutherland?

7 In a proverb about facing your mistakes, what birds 'come home to roost'?

8 In the 1860s, what Tolstoy novel was first published as *Voyna i Mir*?

9 Which *EastEnders* character was played by the late Gretchen Franklin?

10 Fauvism was an art movement originating in what country?

CASH BUILDER QUIZ 6

1 The human body is made up of the torso, the limbs and what?

2 Which Tory Peer was jailed between 2001 and 2003?

3 Which Doncaster-born soprano released the album *I Will Wait for You*?

4 What upholstered seat shares its name with a historical Asian empire?

5 *Continental Drift* is the fourth instalment of what animated film series?

6 What name is given to a horse in a circus that performs without a rider?

7 In what TV comedy did housewife Ria Parkinson frequently ruin the meals?

8 Which male character representing Britain was created in 1712 by John Arbuthnot?

9 Howard Keel played Wild Bill Hickok in what 1953 film musical?

10 What word connects an aircraft landing strip and a model's walkway?

ZERO CASH BUILDERS

CASH BUILDER QUIZ 7

1   The Magician, the Lovers and the Fool feature in a pack of what cards?

2   What name for a type of brown bear means 'sprinkled or streaked with grey'?

3   Which celebrity mum designed the Little Bird clothes range for Mothercare?

4   The Irish festival held in County Kerry each year is called the 'Rose of...' where?

5   In the 1978 film *Death on the Nile*, who played Hercule Poirot?

6   George II was the last reigning occupant of what palace?

7   Kirsty Soames is a character in what TV soap?

8   Lacryma Christi wine is made from grapes grown on the slopes of what volcano?

9   Nathan, Siva, Tom, Jay and Max are the members of what boy band?

CASH BUILDER QUIZ 8

1   'I'm never gonna dance again' is a line from what George Michael song?

2   In 1976, Prince Charles retired from which of the armed forces?

3   What Japanese company introduced the Betamax video recorder?

4   What statue at Giza is known by an Arabic name meaning 'Father of Terror'?

5   Which cyclist rang a giant bell to start the 2012 Olympic opening ceremony?

6   Which English scientist built the world's first reflecting telescope?

7   Who was nicknamed 'The Austrian Oak' when he was a champion body-builder?

8   According to legend, the Greek carpenter Epeius built what famous object?

9   Used in cake decoration, what colour is candied angelica?

ZERO CASH BUILDERS

CASH BUILDER QUIZ 9

1 If tomorrow is Monday, what day was yesterday?

2 Bill Cassidy, the cowboy created by Clarence E. Mulford, has what nickname?

3 Which Cockney stand-up comedian is a former Billingsgate porter?

4 The traditional horn blown by Swiss herdsmen to communicate is called a what?

5 What type of sea shell is used on the logo of Shell Oil?

6 What Lloyd-Webber musical features the songs 'AC/DC' and 'The Race'?

7 The 5:2 Diet involves fasting by limiting calorie intake how many days a week?

8 In 1995 what province narrowly voted against leaving Canada?

9 Russell Brand voices Doctor Nefario in what animated film series?

CASH BUILDER QUIZ 10

1   The Tusk Trust was founded in 1990 to protect wildlife on what continent?

2   Edith Holden wrote *The Country Diary of an Edwardian...* what?

3   Which British actress plays single mum Adele in the 2014 film *Labor Day*?

4   The caldarium was a hot chamber in what type of ancient Roman building?

5   Which Australian Dame has adult children called Kenny, Bruce and Valmai?

6   What cold current, named after a region of Canada, flows south from the Arctic?

7   What language is the subject of Bill Bryson's book *Made In America*?

8   Edmund Tudor, Earl of Richmond, was the father of which king?

9   Which US theatre producer gave his name to annual revue shows known as 'Follies'?

ZERO CASH BUILDERS

CASH BUILDER QUIZ 11

ZERO CASH BUILDERS

1   What Italian sunglasses brand is named after the enforcers of law and order?

2   In 1975, the requirement for arm signals was dropped from what test?

3   In a '90s TV show title, which comedienne was *Through the Cakehole*?

4   What type of American whiskey shares its name with a European royal house?

5   Traditionally, which old male figure is depicted on New Year's Eve with a baby?

6   The title character of what Adolphe Adams ballet dies of a broken heart?

7   Kenny Dalglish won four Scottish League titles playing for what team?

8   What former hunting-ground in Hampshire became a National Park in 2005?

9   What Welsh band's cover of 'Handbags and Gladrags' was a 2001 hit?

CASH BUILDER QUIZ 12

1 What colour is the leather on the Speaker's Chair in the House of Commons?

2 Italian jockey Lanfranco Dettori is commonly known by what first name?

3 Which Greek goddess encouraged the Trojan prince Paris to abduct Helen?

4 What word links the fruit of a wild rose and the thigh and pelvis joint?

5 Shirley Temple and Marlene Dietrich appear on what Beatles album cover?

6 At a christening, the Church of England requires a minimum of how many godparents?

7 In the UK honours system what is the female equivalent of a knight?

8 Which game on *I'm Sorry I Haven't a Clue* has Watling Street and Trumpington's variations?

9 What goes 'swish swish swish' in the song 'The Wheels on the Bus'?

ZERO CASH BUILDERS

CASH BUILDER QUIZ 13

1   What's the only country of Great Britain to have land borders with the other two?

2   According to a long-running ad slogan, what bleach 'kills all known germs'?

3   On '80s TV, William Daniels was the voice of what car?

4   Which Austrian-born woman was executed in Paris in 1793?

5   Noted for its short legs, the Scots Dumpy is a breed of what farmyard bird?

6   Which singer's 2014 album *Paula* is named after his estranged wife?

7   'Simulation' is used by FIFA to describe what type of cheating by footballers?

CASH BUILDER QUIZ 14

1   What horror film series is named after a supposedly unlucky day and date?

2   What name links a chocolate bar and a ship on which a mutiny occurred?

3   What British group's first Grammy win for Best Rock Album was for *Voodoo Lounge*?

4   'Brickipedia' is an online encyclopaedia about what construction toy brand?

5   Whose death prompted the Labour leadership contest won by Tony Blair?

6   The Statham End is a feature of what English cricket ground?

7   Who did Sean Penn marry in Malibu in 1985?

8   What medical term for short-sightedness can also describe a lack of imagination?

CASH BUILDER QUIZ 15

1 In cricket, a batsman out for a golden duck faced how many balls?

2 Rue de la Paix is a fashionable shopping street in what European city?

3 In what comedy show did John Lithgow play an alien posing as a physics professor?

4 A financially successful person is said to have the 'touch' of which legendary king?

5 The Chinese New Year starts in either February or what other month?

6 Who composed the music for the opera *Porgy and Bess*?

7 A Hawaiian sea breeze cocktail includes cranberry and what other fruit juice?

8 In what animated film series do babies called 'dronkeys' appear?

9 The events of what Irish novel take place on 16 June 1904?

CASH BUILDER QUIZ 16

1   Graham Chapman played Brian Cohen in what Monty Python film?

2   What part of a guitar neck is also a word meaning to worry?

3   Former actress Nancy Davis is better known by which married surname?

4   The Bible's Book of Psalms sets a man's lifespan at 'Three score years and...' what?

5   'Spinning Around' and 'Born to Try' were hits for ex-cast members of what soap?

6   Scientist Charles Darwin was the grandson of which famous potter?

7   The Attenborosaurus dinosaur was named in honour of which TV naturalist?

8   Jess is a member of a women's football team in what 2015 West End musical?

ZERO CASH BUILDERS

CASH BUILDER QUIZ 17

1   What dish is a hard-boiled egg wrapped in sausage meat and breadcrumbs?

2   What stage did England reach at the 2015 FIFA Women's World Cup?

3   Which Shakespeare title character is warned about the 15th day of the month?

4   What nickname is given to the film Westerns directed by Sergio Leone?

5   The copper-coloured 'Angel Daffodil' was named after what sculpture?

6   What shipping forecast area lies immediately between Bailey and Shannon?

7   The star Shaula is 'the stinger' in the tail of what constellation?

8   In 2010, Germany finally paid off its debt for what major conflict?

9   Which Irish boy band had a '90s hit with 'Every Day I Love You'?

CASH BUILDER QUIZ 18

1   Lindsay Davenport commentates for the BBC on what sport?

2   'Conan the Republican' is a nickname for which Austrian-born former politician?

3   The Palace of Versailles's Galerie des Glaces is known in English as what?

4   'What Do You Mean' was the first UK Number One for which Canadian pop star?

5   Edward the Black Prince was buried in what important Kent church?

6   Ellie and Carl are childhood sweethearts in what 2009 Pixar animated film?

7   What online retailer runs the Kindle Scout book publishing program?

8   In a famous novel by George Eliot, the Tullivers lived in what type of building?

9   The non-technical name for the lachrimal canal is the 'tear...' what?

CASH BUILDER QUIZ 19

1   The Criminal Investigation Department of the police is known by what abbreviation?

2   How many non-Englishmen have managed the England football team?

3   Which US singer formed a record label called Rhythm Nation in 2015?

4   What trousers share their name with combustible devices that emit bright light?

5   Who is the brother of fictional schoolgirl Bessie Bunter?

6   'Omelette surprise' is an American name for what ice cream dessert?

7   Which TV character had different heads including a turnip, a swede and a mangel-wurzel?

8   West Point Military Academy overlooks what New York State river?

9   Which British boxer advertised cologne with the slogan 'Splash it all over'?

CASH BUILDER QUIZ 20

1   In *Cinderella*, the Fairy Godmother transforms mice into what animals?

2   The 1964 Summer Olympics were the first to be held on what continent?

3   Gala was the wife and muse of which Spanish surrealist painter?

4   What region of Portugal is named after the Arabic for 'the west'?

5   David Guetta's hit 'Hey Mama' features which American female rapper?

6   Which astrologer is the author of *The Real Counties of Britain*?

7   What was the name of Harry Enfield's plasterer character on *Saturday Live*?

CASH BUILDER QUIZ 21

1 Patsy Cline and Tammy Wynette are associated with what type of popular music?

2 Traditionally, what material is waxed to make a Barbour coat?

3 What wartime defensive line was named after a mythical German hero?

4 Which British athlete became the oldest-ever Olympic 100 metres champion in 1992?

5 What did the M stand for in the name of writer Louisa M. Alcott?

6 Who was Oscar-nominated for her role as mum Bobbi in the 2014 film *Wild*?

7 Coley is an edible variety of what creature?

8 A five-clawed form of what mythical beast was a symbol of Chinese imperial power?

CASH BUILDER QUIZ 22

1 The name of what chess piece starts with the letter Q?

2 *Ewoks: The Battle for Endor* was a TV spin-off from what film series?

3 'Dirtee Disco' was a Number One hit for which rapper?

4 What was the first in the series of books about schoolboy William Brown?

5 According to an advertising slogan, what toys 'wobble but they don't fall down'?

6 What branch of maths is named from the Arabic for 'reunion of broken parts'?

7 Which of the solar system's planets has the shortest year?

8 'Twilight of the Gods' is the last part of what Wagner opera cycle?

9 Who played Peter in the 1992 British film *Peter's Friends*?

ZERO CASH BUILDERS

CASH BUILDER QUIZ 23

1 In what word game might a player draw a gallows?

2 In the military, ICBM stands for 'Intercontinental Ballistic...' what?

3 The only Canadian Major League baseball team is based in what city?

4 An 'ovate' object is shaped like what animal product?

5 An alewife is what type of aquatic creature?

6 Reynaldo Bignone replaced which other General as President of Argentina?

7 Walt Disney provided the voice of what cartoon mouse until 1947?

8 Which US travel writer was President of the Campaign to Protect Rural England?

9 'Stone Cold Sober' and 'New York' were hits for which singer?

CASH BUILDER QUIZ 24

1   What country regards the giant panda as a national treasure?

2   What facial feature can be described as 'Roman'?

3   'How Soon is Now' and 'Panic' were singles by what 1980s Manchester band?

4   Which German fashion designer is nicknamed 'Kaiser Karl'?

5   What rank in the police shares its name with a famous English painter?

6   In America, 'hominy' is dried maize kernels used to make what porridge-like meal?

7   In a pack of cards, what suit comes first alphabetically?

8   Who beat Fleur East in the final of *The X Factor* in 2014?

9   Ernest Defarge is a French revolutionary in what Dickens novel?

CASH BUILDER QUIZ 25

1 In what popular board game do players start by drawing seven letter tiles?

2 What word meaning 'poisonous' was the title of a hit song by Britney Spears?

3 The Tate Britain's Clore Gallery holds the work of which British artist?

4 Which US tennis player did Martina Navratilova defeat in five Wimbledon finals?

5 Eccles cakes share their name with a suburb of what northern city?

6 Who was on the British throne at the end of the Spanish Civil War?

7 What Robert Carlyle film was known as *Six Naked Pigs* in China?

CASH BUILDER QUIZ 26

1 Pinga is the younger sister of what fictional penguin?

2 The bony frame formed by the ribs, spine and sternum is called what?

3 Talbot Rothwell wrote several scripts for what series of British comedy films?

4 Robert I secured what country's independence from England?

5 The '60s toy the Easy-Bake is a miniature version of what kitchen appliance?

6 Which manager changed Coventry City's nickname from Bantams to Sky Blues?

7 Which *Only Fools and Horses* character had the catchphrase 'During the war...'?

8 Ecuador and what other South American country have no border with Brazil?

9 In 2015, Prince Charles and Camilla celebrated how many years of marriage?

CASH BUILDER QUIZ 27

1 The name of what London arts venue is abbreviated to 'NT'?

2 What primary colour precedes 'print' to describe a design plan?

3 Who in 1956 said 'We are not at war with Egypt. We are in an armed conflict'?

4 Richmond is a brand of what meat product?

5 England's Euro 2016 squad featured five players from what London club?

6 Who played the title detective in the original TV series *Ironside*?

7 What nursery rhyme features 'a dainty dish to set before the king'?

8 In 1648, Charles I tried to break out of what Isle of Wight castle?

9 What word meaning 'ready' do Italians say when answering the phone?

CASH BUILDER QUIZ 28

1   Swedish vlogger Pewdiepie has over 40 million subscribers on what video website?

2   Which future Iraqi leader nationalised the country's oil industry in 1972?

3   In the 'Doctor Dolittle' stories, what type of farm animal is Gub-Gub?

4   What company makes the Victoria biscuit selection box?

5   Bill Nicholson and Bill Shankly were famous managers in what sport?

6   The fictional Barden University was the setting for what musical film?

7   The Hotel Pennsylvania claims to have the oldest phone number in what US city?

ZERO CASH BUILDERS

CASH BUILDER QUIZ 29

1 If your bank account is 'overdrawn', what value has it dropped below?

2 The extinct Carolina Parakeet was native to what continent?

3 Former BBC Chairman Michael Grade represents what party in the House of Lords?

4 Peter Lodge was the original voice of what London Underground announcement?

5 What Swedish high-street clothing chain sells the 'Divided' fashion range?

6 In 2016, who became the most decorated American gymnast in history?

7 What was the second-highest prize available on *Who Wants to Be a Millionaire*?

8 The source of the Brahmaputra river is in what major mountain range?

9 What Italian currency was used in occupied Ethiopia in the late '30s?

CASH BUILDER QUIZ 30

1   In 2016, what toy doll came in a range of four body shapes?

2   'Feel the Bubbles' appears on the packaging of what brand of chocolate?

3   Which humorous poet wrote 'They Should Have Asked My Husband'?

4   The 'Hand of God' incident was during an England football game against what team?

5   What '70s sitcom centred on a couple trying to become self-sufficient?

6   Associated with Picasso, what art movement had analytical and synthetic phases?

7   The building of what famous Athenian temple began in 447 BC?

8   Which musician set up the film production company Rocket Pictures?

9   Whose famous 1963 speech began 'I am happy to join with you today'?

ZERO CASH BUILDERS

CASH BUILDER QUIZ 31

1 Who was the only British queen regnant crowned in the 19th century?

2 The Ibiza is the best-selling model produced by what Spanish car maker?

3 Humboldt's Sea and Smyth's Sea are on what celestial body?

4 What was the only side to beat West Germany at the 1966 FIFA World Cup?

5 Which Iceland-born broadcaster received an honorary knighthood in 1989?

6 In the Book of Genesis, who left Haran and travelled to found a new nation?

7 What Scottish royal residence has a nine-hole golf course within its grounds?

8 Magyars are most closely associated with what country?

9 In architecture, what name is given to the square slab at the base of a column?

10 In 2016, a near-complete skeleton of what extinct bird sold for £280,000?

CASH BUILDER QUIZ 32

1   What word for 'an out of the way corner' is often paired with a cranny?

2   Laila Morse played which character in *EastEnders*?

3   What Madrid football team plays home games at the Vicente Calderon Stadium?

4   Which *This Morning* host wrote the book *Truly Happy Baby. It Worked for Me*?

5   What famous liner sailed from Queenstown, Ireland on 11 April 1912?

6   In 2017, what was called 'the best day care centre for the elderly in London'?

7   What word follows 'Space' and 'Big Thunder' in the names of two Disney rides?

8   In what film did Danny Devito star as Mr Wormwood, the heroine's father?

9   Which Thomas Hardy title character gives birth to a baby called Sorrow?

ZERO CASH BUILDERS

CASH BUILDER QUIZ 33

1 The island of Eigg is part of what country of the UK?

2 What is the name for the control panel located beneath a car's windscreen?

3 Who's the hero of the Tom Clancy novel *The Cardinal of the Kremlin*?

4 Golf and Pyramid are variations of what card game for one player?

5 What sticky fluid circulates in the vascular system of trees and plants?

6 The mother of which Prime Minister was born Jeanette Jerome in Brooklyn in 1854?

7 The date May the Fourth is observed by fans of what film series?

8 'Lennox Lewis, I'm coming for you' is a quote from which heavyweight boxing star?

CASH BUILDER QUIZ 34

1 What colossal sculpture in Giza measures 240 feet from paw to tail?

2 'Addicted to Spuds' was Weird Al Jankovic's parody of what Robert Palmer song?

3 In what mythology do two goats pull the chariot of the god of thunder?

4 Who is the only US President to have been married three times?

5 On a regular clock face, what number lies directly opposite four?

6 Which former *EastEnders* actress starred in the TV hotel drama *The Halcyon*?

7 In 2017, which British tennis player was a singles semi-finalist at Wimbledon?

8 What cereal ingredient is pieces of grain husk separated from flour after milling?

CASH BUILDER QUIZ 35

1 The name of what cosmetic beauty treatment is often shortened to 'mani'?

2 Michael J. Fox voiced what fictional mouse in a series of films?

3 Which French scientist proved that beer was fermented by living yeast?

4 What gender were people who worked as 'clippies' and 'nippies'?

5 The Wimbledon tennis championships logo is white, green and what other colour?

6 Jack and Frankie Osborne are long-serving characters in what TV soap?

7 According to the proverb, what type of wind blows nobody any good?

8 'The future's not ours to see' is a line from what Doris Day hit?

9 In 2017, what underwear company opened a museum in New York?

ZERO CASH BUILDERS

THE CHASE

LAZARUS WINS

LAZARUS WINS

One thing that makes a Chaser very happy is catching all four members of a team – but there's a downside to taking them all out that the Chasers aren't so pleased with. If the entire team is caught, they get a chance to come back from the dead and make one last attempt to win some money in what the Chasers call a 'Lazarus' show. They can select one of the team to take on the Chaser for a team prize fund of £4,000. If they win (and it doesn't happen often) they go home with £1,000 each. Of course, they choose the strongest player, and that's what cheeses the Chasers off. The Chasers can be really grumpy at times, and grumpiest of all when it comes to Lazarus shows is Paul Sinha. There have only been five Lazarus wins in the history of *The Chase*, and Paul has suffered three of them! Here are the questions... could you have beaten a Chaser on your own?

JOHN VS. PAUL

The first Lazarus team win was against Paul back in Series 6. Caz was a retired primary school teacher from Lowestoft who wanted to win enough money to buy David Beckham to play for her beloved Luton Town. Despite her lofty ambitions, she took the low offer from Paul and still got caught. Next up was John, a police property officer from Malvern, who scored £6,000 in his Cash Builder and took the high offer of £30,000. Unfortunately, he suffered the same fate as Caz – as did Natalie, a probation officer from Stamford, and Andrew, a warehouse assistant from Colchester. So, the Sinnerman had a Lazarus on his hands. Unsurprisingly, it was John the team chose to face him and he set Paul a commendable 16 to catch. It's a pretty good score for a single player and it proved to be enough to keep Paul at bay.

JOHN

1   What kind of animal is a bream?

2   The *Brighton Belle* train travelled from Brighton to what city?

3   The Pillars of Hercules link the Atlantic to what sea?

4   What 1994 film was Natalie Portman's big-screen debut?

5   The sports star born Cassius Clay competed in what sport?

6   'Chien' is the French word for what animal?

7   Before going into comedy, what was Jackie Mason's job?

8   The Irish Oaks horse race is run at what course?

9   What percentage of a metre is a centimetre?

10   Manicotti is a variety of what food?

11   What Chinese dynasty ended in 1644?

12   What subspecies of tiger was declared extinct in 1994?

13   What causes a burn known as a 'scald'?

14   Which fictional Belgian detective had a valet called Georges?

15 Who designed the Güell Park in Barcelona?

16 Kurt Russell played Wyatt Earp in what Western film?

17 What Asian country hosts football's J. league?

18 A famous breed of draught horse is a 'Suffolk...' what?

19 Microbiology is the study of what tiny organisms?

20 Which Ancient Greek wrote the play *Antigone*?

21 Bookmaker Paddy Power was founded in what country?

22 Who wrote the novel *Persuasion*?

23 Austin is the capital of what US state?

24 Cricketer Viv Richards was born on what island?

25 The Moon orbits what planet?

26 Who wrote the novel *A Room with a View*?

27 The first Disneyland theme park opened in what decade?

28 Pima is a superior variety of what fabric?

LAZARUS WINS

PAUL

1   What type of creature is a Shih Tzu?

2   What Canadian province is abbreviated to NS?

3   The Rutherglen wine region is in what country?

4   Who was appointed BBC Director General in 2004?

5   Roger Federer is a famous name in what sport?

6   What car manufacturer produces the Freelander?

7   Who created 'Rumpole of the Bailey'?

8   The model daughters of Annie Lennox are Lola and... who?

9   A gilt frame is the colour of what metal?

10 What London library holds Captain Scott's last polar diary?

11 Lusty Glaze Beach is in what Cornish resort?

12 Who wrote the 2011 novel *The Fear Index*?

13 Which American singer released the '90s album *Janet*?

14 In what country is Kraków?

15 What kind of fish is a bonnethead?

16 Bobby Gillespie is the lead singer of what Scottish band?

17 The Radio 4 programme *Excess Baggage* covered what topic?

18 What continent has the internet domain .aq?

19 Nescafé coffee was first sold in what country?

20 John Loveday is the title character in what Thomas Hardy novel?

21 What's the only British mammal to have spines?

22 Watford and Potters Bar are in what English county?

23 A traditional seed cake is made using what seed?

24 The Iron Guard was a fascist movement in what country?

25 What colour is the edible pulp of a watermelon?

26 Which comedian played Richie in the sitcom *Bottom*?

27 The spectacled bear is native to what continent?

28 In the 1976 film *Robin and Marian,* who played Robin Hood?

29 What type of meat is Aberdeen Angus topside?

LAZARUS WINS

PHIL VS. PAUL

Just a little later in Series 6 Paul came up against another Lazarus game – and again it was a case of facing by far the strongest player in the Final Chase, despite having caught him in the Head to Head. He was Phil, an emergency ambulance control officer from Shropshire, who scored an excellent £8,000 in his Cash Builder before taking the high offer of £40,000. This tactic certainly made it easier for Paul to catch him, but he didn't need any help to catch the rest of the team, who all took the middle amount. They were Sheila, a health visitor from Berkshire, Pam, a dental records manager from Sutton Coldfield, and Paul, a military history editor from Cheltenham. Phil's quizzing pedigree showed as he set Paul a very good 19. It gave the Chaser very little room for error, and a couple of mistakes meant he was beaten by the clock.

PHIL

1   What capital city was called Londinium by the Romans?

2   Which rapper made *The Doggfather* album?

3   Complete the name of the Nobel Prize: 'Physiology or...' what?

4   What's the last word in the New Testament?

5   Fifty years is how many decades?

6   In golf, OB stands for 'out of...' what?

7   Who did Clementine Hozier marry in 1908?

8   Wellingborough and Daventry are in what English county?

9   Hydrodynamics studies the movement of what?

10   The Bee Gees song 'Stayin' Alive' is from what 1977 film?

11   What type of pet is a grimalkin?

12   Clive Hamilton was the pseudonym of which writer?

13   In football, what word is abbreviated to 'sub'?

14   The frontal bone is in what part of the body?

15 What's the only US state with the letter Z in its name?

16 What country has the international registration code HKJ?

17 Anni-Frid Lyngstad famously sang in what Swedish group?

18 In the Bible, the Annunciation was a message to who?

19 Alex Garland's novel *The Beach* is set in what country?

20 What sport is nicknamed 'the sweet science'?

21 What spring month is traditionally said to be windy?

22 A caliper splint is a support for what part of the body?

23 American David Duval is a famous name in what sport?

24 In January 2012, which banker was stripped of his knighthood?

25 Atlantis was a legendary island in what ocean?

26 In what conflict were the Mooner and Eder dams destroyed?

27 What animals did an 'ostler' look after?

28 John Fowles' novel *The Magus* is mainly set in what country?

LAZARUS WINS

PAUL

1 What TV soap features Mitchell's Autos in The Arches?

2 Which satirical magazine features poems by E. J. Thribb?

3 Scottish Lorne sausage is famously what shape?

4 The name of the city of Bordeaux ends in what letter?

5 In 1993, who won the Nobel Peace Prize with F. W. de Klerk?

6 Dian Fossey famously worked with what animals?

7 Bodybuilder Charles Atlas was born in what country?

8 Which actor played James Bond in *Skyfall*?

9 'Abierto' means 'open' in what European language?

10 Tetroxide compounds contain four atoms of what element?

11 Which TV detective owned a basset hound called Fang?

12 What famous stadium is in the London Borough of Brent?

13 What Enid Blyton character is known as 'Oui Oui' in French?

14 The Doctor in *Doctor Who* has how many hearts?

15 What annual music festival was co-founded by Peter Gabriel?

16 'Fair Isle' sweaters are normally made with what material?

17 Baghdad is the capital of what country?

18 Aibileen and Minny are maids in what best-selling novel?

19 What sport was '80s kids show *Jossy's Giants* based around?

20 What species of bird lays the world's largest egg?

21 Annie Walker was the first landlady of what TV pub?

22 Stanley Baldwin led what political party?

23 Who is the only American First Lady to win an Emmy Award?

24 Where on a chicken would you find the 'comb'?

25 The novel *Doctor Zhivago* was written in what century?

26 The BBC Home Service was replaced by what radio station?

27 By what nickname was London criminal Jack McVitie better known?

28 Francis Scott Key wrote the lyrics for what country's national anthem?

LAZARUS WINS

MATT VS. ANNE

In Series 7, Anne joined Paul in the losing Lazarus club. The team was Matt, a freelance journalist from Newark, James, an A&E nurse from Devon, Laura, a travel consultant from Glasgow, and Tony, a retired singer from Surrey. This was an unusual show, as it was Matt who faced the Governess in the Final Chase despite the fact that both James and Laura had outscored him in the Cash Builders, with £7,000 apiece to Matt's £5,000. Once again, Anne's chances of catching them all were enhanced when both Matt and Tony took the high offer. However, Matt proved an inspired choice at the end, as he powered through his Final Chase to rack up an excellent 19. That sort of score is what the Chasers call 'in the fun zone', but Anne wasn't having much fun as the clock ticked to zero before she could catch Matt. The freelance journalist was certainly making headlines that day!

MATT

1   If someone succeeds, they are said to 'cut the...' what?

2   'Howling Laud' Hope is the leader of what political party?

3   In what country did the Beckhams wed in 1999?

4   How many troy ounces of gold do original Krugerrands contain?

5   The lower set of teeth are fixed into what bone?

6   What colour wine is Chablis?

7   Sharon Stone played Catherine Tramell in what film series?

8   Novi Sad is the second-largest city in what European country?

9   What's the three-letter abbreviation for an electrocardiogram?

10   What is the lower house of the UK Parliament called?

11   Bert Weedon was famous as a teacher of what instrument?

12   What insect is a Mazarine blue?

13   What area of London shares its name with a tied ribbon?

14 Which musician was known as 'the quiet Beatle'?

15 What famous building was moved to Sydenham in 1854?

16 Much of the body's cholesterol is made in what organ?

17 How many years in three millennia?

18 Bob Hoskins played which FBI boss in the film *Nixon*?

19 Which Peanuts character does Peppermint Patty call 'Chuck'?

20 What hotel in Las Vegas is named after a town on Lake Como?

21 Russia covers parts of Europe and what other continent?

22 Karl.com is the website of what fashion designer?

23 In 1828, Dingaan became king of what South African people?

24 In what American state is Syracuse University?

25 Both 'gnaw' and 'gnome' begin with what silent letter?

LAZARUS WINS

ANNE

1 Complete the phrase: 'A new broom sweeps...' what ?

2 The Welsh Assembly sits in what city?

3 *The Recluse* is an unfinished volume by which of the Lake poets?

4 Who played Lancelot in the 1995 film *First Knight*?

5 The name of what floor covering is a nickname for a wig?

6 In what US state is Venice Beach?

7 In food, 'umami' is one of the five basic what?

8 Maarivim are evening prayers in what religion?

9 A detached retina, if left untreated, causes the loss of what sense?

10 What French seaport is 22 miles from Dover?

11 Which of Peter Kay's alter-egos sang 'Wind Beneath my Wheels'?

12 In what county is Southwell racecourse?

13 Ethiopian and Mali were empires on what continent?

14 Switzerland is called Svizzera in what language?

15 Who read the story 'The Old Man of Lochnagar' on *Jackanory*?

16 The 3rd Earl Russell was known by what first name?

17 How many people go on a double date?

18 What primary colour gives its name to a species of shark?

19 Which Hanoverian monarch reigned the longest?

20 Major Bagstock is in what Dickens novel?

21 What citrus fruit is often served with fish?

22 In a manual car what pedal do you press when changing gear?

LAZARUS WINS

23 Syon Park is an estate in what capital city?

24 What was the first name of fashion designer Burberry?

25 The Lord High Admiral governed which of the armed services?

26 Pork, mince and apple are all types of what bakery product?

LAZARUS WINS

SCOTT VS. JENNY

In Series 9, it was the Vixen's turn to lose to a Lazarus team when she faced Scott, a bar manager from Hampshire, Samira, a French tutor originally from Mauritius, Richard, a magician from Chelmsford, and Jo, a sales executive from Lincoln. It was a show full of tough questions and relatively low scores in the Cash Builders, and the team didn't help their chances with their tactics. After Jenny had caught Scott and Samira with the middle amount, both Richard and Jo went high and ended up in the same boat as their team-mates. They selected Scott, who had top-scored in the Cash Builders with £4,000, to face Jenny in the Final Chase, but the difficulty of the questions and the low scoring continued, and he could only set 12. It shouldn't have been enough, but this wasn't one of the Vixen's vintage performances. Seven errors – four of which Scott pushed her back on – meant she became the third Chaser to lose a Lazarus.

SCOTT

1   'Potterheads' are fans of what J. K. Rowling franchise?

2   The sauce called a coulis gets its name from what language?

3   Laila Rouass played WAG Amber Gates in what TV drama?

4   Habichtsburg Castle was the ancestral seat of which dynasty?

5   1978 is known as the year of how many Popes?

6   Which *Twilight* actress played Lydia in the film *Still Alice*?

7   Bayer Leverkusen is a top football team in what country?

8   Which Italian composed the opera *La Forza del Destino*?

9   In publishing, what does the 'B' in ISBN stand for?

10 Leucoderma is a condition of what part of the body?

11 'When I was a Youngster' was a 2011 hit for what duo?

12 Who was first re-elected as Russian President in 2004?

13 What's the English title held by Tarzan?

14 What are the two on-pitch officials in a game of cricket called?

15 The play *Peer Gynt* is based on a folk hero from what country?

16 What colour is the fruit produced by cranberry plants?

17 'Civitas' was the status of citizenship in what ancient empire?

18 Cobie Smulders played Robin Scherbatsky in what US sitcom?

19 On what continent is the Malay Peninsula?

20 Which singer and actress played Kira in the film *Xanadu*?

21 Kingsmill is a major brand of what staple foodstuff?

22 Whose abdication did Queen Mary call 'a pretty kettle of fish'?

LAZARUS WINS

JENNY

1   In Spain, what type of shop is a supermercado?

2   Mushrooms and toadstools are types of what organism?

3   Which actor played Jack Taylor in the film *One Fine Day*?

4   What German car company makes the Fayton and Jetta models?

5   What shape is the slot on a Phillips screw?

6   Santiago Cabrera played Sir Lancelot in what TV drama?

7   What name is given to a calculus formed in the gall bladder?

8   What relation was King Henry I to William I?

9   Billie Jean King won 20 titles at what tennis Grand Slam?

10 The town of Schwyz gave its name to what country?

11 'For the First Time' was a hit for what Irish pop rock band?

12 In total, there are how many dots and dashes in the SOS signal?

13 Native to Australia, what creature is a plains-wanderer?

14 Sally Lunn's Historic Eating House is in what Somerset city?

15 Which author created the heroine Lyra Belacqua?

16 A hajjah is a female pilgrim to Mecca in what religion?

17 The flag of the Red Cross movement has what colour background?

18 What US TV comedy stars Jon Cryer as dad Alan Harper?

19 In October 1940, which Spanish dictator first met Hitler?

20 Which actor played James Bond in one 1969 film?

21 The netball position Wing Defence is known by what two letters?

22 In what organ of the body is the preoccipital notch?

23 'Cry Me Out' was a hit for which British pop star?

LAZARUS WINS

CHRIS VS. PAUL

Series 12 saw Paul complete his losing Lazarus hat-trick. Peter, an economist from Warwickshire, Kathryn, a solicitor from Leeds, Zoe, a technology analyst from London, and Chris, a retired maths teacher from Glasgow were a super-team, scoring £23,000 between them in their Cash Builders. It was a real achievement by the Sinnerman to catch four such good players, especially as only Chris, the top-scorer with £7,000, took the high offer. He was the obvious choice to face Paul in the Final Chase and he didn't let his team-mates down, setting an excellent 18. It's the sort of score that requires the Chaser to be on their very best form, but Paul couldn't quite match his Head to Head achievements. He made five errors and Chris took advantage, pushing him back three times. It was a close finish, but not close enough – and the super-team were super-satisfied at the end!

CHRIS

1   In a common joke, what bird crosses the road?

2   The city of Paphos lies on what sea?

3   In TV's *Game of Thrones*, what mythical creature is Viserion?

4   'Ice Man' is a nickname for which Finnish Formula One driver?

5   Oban is a brand of what spirit?

6   Bond girl Tatiana Romanova appeared in what film?

7   What primary colour is the mineral lazurite?

8   Since 1971, Syria has been ruled by men with what surname?

9   What London museum has a 'Mammal Hall'?

10 Girl band Eternal originally had how many members?

11 Who killed the heir to the Austro-Hungarian throne in 1914?

12 What type of domestic appliance is a halogen candle?

13 Poppy Pomfrey is the matron at what fictional school?

14   Which Hollywood A-lister is nicknamed 'Gwynnie'?

15   What Picasso painting depicts the bombing of a Basque town?

16   What suspension bridge near Hull is over 2,000 metres long?

17   How many pounds are there in two stone?

18   Which actress won an Oscar for the film *The Accidental Tourist*?

19   In what book would you find the 'Pauline Epistles'?

20   What animal indicates a zoo on brown UK road signs?

21   Bill Sikes is a villain in what Lionel Bart musical?

22   In 2017, what hit by Aqua was re-released on pink vinyl?

23   William Holman Hunt was a founder of what art movement?

24   Mary, Queen of Scots belonged to which royal house?

25   What part of a plant can also mean to flick through a book?

26   In what American city is the Hooters Casino Hotel?

LAZARUS WINS

PAUL

1 What form of transport is the Airbus super jumbo?

2 In the nursery rhyme, the first 'little piggy' went where?

3 In *Star Wars*, Shyriiwook was a language of what species?

4 Which king was the father of Edward II?

5 What kind of hot drink is a 'lungo'?

6 Chris, Stewie and Meg are siblings in what TV cartoon?

7 *The Big Four* is a novel featuring which Belgian detective?

8 Which Bulgarian tennis player was nicknamed 'Baby Fed'?

9 A 'phial' bottle is usually made from what material?

10 What Freddie Mercury duet was partly sung in Spanish?

11 In 1709, Woodes Rogers rescued which Scottish castaway?

12 A low-pressure sodium lamp shines what primary colour?

13 Nelson's bighorn is a breed of what farm animal?

14 The actors Naomie and Neil Patrick share what surname?

15 What ancient Inca city contains over 100 flights of stairs?

16 Raine Spencer was the stepmother of which royal woman?

17 What is 9 times 12?

18 What Mel Gibson film featured the villain Toecutter?

19 Honorius was an emperor in what ancient civilisation?

20 Who wrote the Jack Reacher anthology *No Middle Name*?

21 What type of male facial feature is a soul patch?

22 The band Franz Ferdinand was formed in what Scottish city?

23 Acetylene contains carbon and what other element?

24 The ITV teletext service originally had what name?

25 Breezers are rum-based drinks made by what company?

LAZARUS WINS

THE CHASE

BIGGEST CELEBRITIY WINS

BIGGEST CELEBRITY WINS

Everybody loves to see the Chasers lose – except the Chasers, of course –
and the only thing better than seeing them lose is seeing them lose BIG.
Because the Chasers get more generous with their high offers in the *Celebrity
Chase* shows, there are more massive team wins than we see in the daytime series.
Here are some of the biggest. Could you have done what these teams did?

CAROL VORDERMAN, PAUL ROSS, SUE CLEAVER AND JOHN THOMSON

Back in the very first *Celebrity Chase* series, a full house took the Beast for £100,000. Maths whizz Carol Vorderman, TV presenter Paul Ross, actress Sue Cleaver and *Cold Feet* star John Thomson all got back with that huge prize fund. It was the lads who did the damage by bringing back their high offers – £40,000 for Paul and £51,000 for John. However, it's no good accruing a big prize fund if you can't back it up with a high score in the Final Chase. This team certainly did that, setting Mark an excellent 22. He gave it his all but it was just too many to catch.

1   What game show is based on the US format *Family Feud*?

2   Mike Tindall plays for England in what sport?

3   'No Regrets' was a 2011 Number One for which artist?

4   The 2011 film *Troll Hunter* is set in what country?

5   What's 25 per cent of 500?

6   In the US, what type of meat product is a 'wiener'?

7   Which *Corrie* character shares his first name with a Northern Irish county?

8   What musical features the song 'The Impossible Dream'?

9   In what sport did Robin Cousins compete?

10 The yak is native to what continent?

11 Whose films include *The Proposal* and *The Change-Up*?

12 Botticelli's *Birth of Venus* is in what gallery?

13 In the nursery rhyme, what bridge 'is falling down'?

14 Hereford brisket and skirt are cuts of what meat?

15 In what city is the Wailing Wall?

16 Mr Memory is a character in what Hitchcock film?

17 Millwall Football Club is based in what city?

18 What's the smallest breed of domestic dog?

19 Which Rat Pack member was born Dino Paul Crocetti?

20 What parts of the body are examined by an optometrist?

21 What's the only US state that begins with D?

22 In slang, how many pounds is a 'monkey'?

23 In the novel *Little Women,* who's the youngest March sister?

BIGGEST CELEBRITIV WINS

HILARY JONES, TINA MALONE, CHARLOTTE JACKSON AND JON CULSHAW

In Series 3, the Sinnerman found himself in the same situation as the Beast, facing another full house with a £100,000 prize fund. TV doctor Hilary Jones, actress Tina Malone, sports presenter Charlotte Jackson and impressionist Jon Culshaw were the team in question, with Jon doing a passable impression of a *Mastermind* Champion by bringing back a huge high offer of £83,000 – this after Charlotte had taken a generous low offer of £3,000. It seemed the team's tactics paid off better than Paul's. A tough set of questions meant they could only set a total of 16, but an equally tough set for the Sinnerman meant it was just enough for a team win.

1   What company was the top global drinks brand in 2011?

2   What word is used to describe a snake discarding its old skin?

3   What furry animals were the interval act at *Eurovision* 1974?

4   What Jane Austen novel is about a resident of Highbury?

5   Softball is a variant of what American sport?

6   Which of the armed forces took part in the Battle of Britain?

7   *Showtime* is a 2012 DVD by which English comedian?

8   Matthew Eager is a big name in what field?

9   What should you put into a steam iron prior to use?

10 Calor is a major supplier of liquefied petroleum... what?

11 Who plays the title character in *Judge John Deed*?

12 What medical name is given to loss of the sense of smell?

13 What name is given to a row of decorative flags?

14 How many Summer Olympics were cancelled due to World War Two?

15 What name is given to a ship's first voyage?

16 Who wrote the sitcoms *Just Good Friends* and *Dear John*?

17 Sneakers are worn on what part of the body?

18 What's the only city in Britain beginning with O?

19 What German football team is sometimes called FC Hollywood?

20 Vincent Cassel played which French gangster in a 2008 film?

21 Gaelic coffee is served with cream and what spirit?

22 'Sunflowers' is a perfume by Elizabeth... who?

23 Which politician married Pauline Tilston in 1961?

24 Salome asked for the head of which biblical character?

25 In Japan, what soft-pink blossoms are known as 'sakura'?

26 What did Islamabad replace as permanent capital of Pakistan?

BIGGEST CELEBRITY WINS

SAMIA GHADIE, ALEX BROOKER, ANNABEL GILES AND JULIAN CLARY

In Series 4, Shaun found himself facing a perfect storm of a full house and a £100,000 jackpot. *Coronation Street*'s Samia Ghadie, Alex Brooker from *The Last Leg*, former model and presenter Annabel Giles and comedian Julian Clary got to that massive total after Annabel and Julian had both gone big with £38,000 and £50,000 high offers respectively. Once again, a tricky question set meant they could only set 16 – and their win hung in the balance. Thankfully for the team, Shaun's set was equally difficult and 16 proved to be a £100,000 winning score.

1 'Faux pas' means 'false step' in what language?

2 Jason Donovan played Mitzi in what West End stage musical?

3 Luis Suarez joined Liverpool from what Dutch football club?

4 What was the name of Tony's wife in *The Sopranos*?

5 Gentle treatment is known as 'handling with kid...' what?

6 What's the full name of the magazine known as *GQ*?

7 What Asian country is home to the Great Wild Goose Pagoda?

8 David Bowie played the Goblin King in what film?

9 The Bosphorus Bridges link Asia to what other continent?

10 In medicine, 'ENT' refers to 'ear, nose and...' what?

11 Ballater is a spa town close to what royal residence?

12 Radio 1 DJ Zane Lowe was born in what country?

13 What first name is shared by the singers Bieber and Timberlake?

14 Luton is a town in what traditional English county?

15 'The Great Asparagus' was a nickname of which French leader?

16 Who played Colonel Ryan in the war film *Von Ryan's Express*?

17 Which British queen married her cousin in 1840?

18 What American bell was once called the State House Bell?

19 What video gaming company created the character Yoshi?

20 King George V was born in what decade of the 19th century?

21 Players start games of Monopoly on what square?

22 What country lies on the western coast of Scandinavia?

23 What British city is known as the 'capital of the Highlands'?

BIGGEST CELEBRITY WINS

FIONA BRUCE, RICK EDWARDS, KATE HUMBLE AND JOE SWASH

There was another £120,000 win in Series 5 when journalist Fiona Bruce, presenter Rick Edwards, wildlife expert Kate Humble and actor Joe Swash took on the Beast. Fiona and Kate played it safe and brought home their Cash Builder earnings, but both lads went for it. Rick brought back £60,000 and Joe £47,000 – with Joe baiting Mark every step of the way. Whether it was Joe's taunts that put him off his game or not, a total of 18 was enough to escape the Beast's clutches, and the team's charities got £30,000 each.

1   Rodin's sculpture *The Thinker* features how many people?

2   The sphynx is a breed of what pet animal?

3   Who played Daniel Cleaver in the *Bridget Jones* films?

4   In 2015, who became MP for Uxbridge and South Ruislip?

5   Margarine is used as an alternative to what dairy spread?

6   Who is the mother of fashion designer Jasper Conran?

7   'Cleanin' Out My Closet' was a 2002 hit for which rapper?

8   Which South African wrote the acclaimed novel *Disgrace*?

9   What musician leads in the haggis on Burns Night?

10 What name links actors MacFadyen and McConaughey?

11 In Italian cookery, the name of what sauce means 'hunter'?

12 Who played Sergeant Odelle Ballard in the TV drama *Odyssey*?

13 What household item is also known as a Hoover?

14 US tycoon Donald Trump is a member of what political party?

15 Holbein painted several famous portraits of which Tudor king?

16 What is tennis player Stan Wawrinka's full first name?

17   On a French school timetable what subject is 'histoire'?

18   In 2015, Alexis Tsipras became Prime Minister of what country?

19   Saponified fats and oils have been turned into what?

20   'Gravel Pit' was a UK Top 10 hit for which US hip-hop group?

21   How are the legs positioned in the yoga 'lotus' position?

22   What Swedish store sells the 'Groggy' corkscrew?

23   Konishiki was a star of what form of wrestling?

24   What type of creature is an orfe?

BIGGEST CELEBRITY WINS

NADIA SAWALHA, JAMES COSMO, GEMMA ATKINSON AND JIMI MISTRY

The £100,000 barrier was first broken back in Series 4 when chat-show host Jonathan Ross and his team won an amazing £120,000 (questions you can find in our 'Celebrity Clever Dicks' section). However, in Series 5 it was broken again when Shaun found himself facing yet another full house, with a prize fund of £105,500. A team full of actors – Nadia Sawalha, James Cosmo, Gemma Atkinson and Jimi Mistri – got to that fantastic total after a solid start, with middle amounts taken by Nadia and James, a low offer of £500 accepted by Gemma and then an amazing high offer of £92,000 brought home by Jimi. A decent 18 set by the team in the Final Chase was just enough, as they outran the Chaser and split that massive prize fund between their charities.

1   Calais is a port in what country?

2   On a snooker table, how many pockets are behind the baulk line?

3   Which former Chinese leader appears on the 100 yuan note?

4   Who plays the title character in the TV drama *Doctor Foster*?

5   Belgian chocolate is a shade of what colour?

6   In Islam, women wear a hijab on what part of the body?

7   What's the married surname of Saturdays singer Rochelle Wiseman?

8   The heroine of what trilogy of novels lives in District 12?

9   What country launched the Mariner space probe programme?

10   What sauce was produced by John Lea and William Perrins?

11   What Welsh venue hosted the FA Cup final six times?

12   'I Can't Dance' and 'Follow You Follow Me' were hits for which band?

13   In what craft might you throw clay onto a revolving wheel?

14   What colour 'stripe' is the name of a famous Jamaican lager?

15 Who was the first female judge on *The X Factor*?

16 What Greater Manchester football club is nicknamed The Shakers?

17 The 14th century bubonic plague is known as the 'Black...' what?

18 What country is immediately west of Sweden?

19 How many of Henry VIII's wives were English?

20 What novel by Ron Rash was made into a Jennifer Lawrence film?

21 What is dipped in egg and milk in the dish French toast?

BIGGEST CELEBRITY WINS

NIGEL HAVERS, MELINDA MESSENGER, MICHELLE HARDWICK AND DAVE GORMAN

There's nothing more difficult for the Chasers than a full house, and in Series 6 it was Anne's turn to face one, once again packing a £100,000 prize fund. She was up against actor Nigel Havers, presenter Melinda Messenger, *Emmerdale*'s Michelle Hardwick and comedian Dave Gorman. It was Dave on seat 4 who had gone big, bringing home a high offer of £86,000. The team managed to set the Governess a reasonable – but catchable – total of 19. But it wasn't to be, as Anne got pushed back five times and just couldn't get close enough to the team.

1   What transport is the *Venice Simplon-Orient-Express*?

2   The dish 'chilli' is known by what longer Spanish name?

3   How many times has Angelina Jolie been married?

4   Which darts player beat Dennis Priestley in four world finals?

5   What part of the body does a 'coiffeur' attend to?

6   What is the name of the fifth film in the Bourne series?

7   Who wrote the play *A Streetcar Named Desire*?

8   In 2009, which band had its first hit with 'Little Lion Man'?

9   What pie topping consists of criss-cross strips of pastry?

10   Which Roman general was elected consul in 59 BC?

11   Which 2012 Disney princess is Scottish?

12   Actress Ruth Jones stars in adverts for what supermarket?

13   Hacking and field are types of what garment?

14   'Insta' is short for what photo sharing app?

15   Who is the lead singer with the band The Specials?

16   In what calendar does the snake follow the dragon?

17   What 1982 conflict is also called the South Atlantic War?

18   James Norton plays villain Tommy Lee Royce in what TV drama?

19   What type of sports academy is run by Chris Evert?

20   Who was the first potter to win the Turner Prize?

21   Ringo Starr Drive is a road in what English city?

22   In April 1917, the USA entered what war?

JAY RAYNER, LUCY PORTER, KRISHNAN GURU-MURTHY AND STEVE DAVIS

The biggest *Celebrity Chase* win ever was £160,000 by *Countdown*'s Rachel Riley and sports presenter Kirsty Gallacher in the Series 9 Soccer Aid special (see the 'Celebrities Going Big' section), but this win from Series 6 runs it close. The Governess found herself up against a real celebrity super-team of food writer Jay Rayner, comedian Lucy Porter, news presenter Krishnan Guru-Murthy and snooker player Steve Davis. In an extraordinary game, the first three players all took the high offer: Jay with £35,000, Lucy with £50,000 and Krishnan with £65,000. It meant that Steve could take an eminently sensible decision and bring back a £2,000 low offer. The full house was in place with a potential win of £152,000! A prize fund that big deserved a big total in the Final Chase – and it got it. The super-team set Anne a very tricky 21 and then proceeded to punish almost every mistake she made, with four pushbacks out of five completed. It was a brilliant performance... good enough to defeat the Governess and ensure what was, at the time, a record high win.

1   Water that has frozen and become solid is called what?

2   Neufchatel cheese comes from what country?

3   Who was top scorer for Wales at Euro 2016?

4   Who was Australia's first female Prime Minister?

5   John Travolta is a famous follower of what religious movement?

6   In the Disney film *The Lion King*, who is Simba's uncle?

7   What is three-fifths of 40?

8   'Amarelle' is a type of what small stone fruit?

9   Which politician was born Shirley Brittain in 1930?

10   In Greek myth, Charon was the ferryman on what hellish river?

11   Doris Day plays singer Ruth Etting in which 1955 film musical?

12   Homo sapiens means 'wise man' in what ancient language?

13 The slang term 'FOMO' means 'fear of' what?

14 The quinton is a violin-type instrument with how many strings?

15 Who wrote the sci-fi novel *The Many-Colored Land*?

16 In the saying, 'there's light at the end of the...' what?

17 In Greek myth, Apollo turned Cycnus into what water bird?

18 Peggy Ashcroft won an Oscar for what David Lean film?

19 Atropine is used in medicine to dilate what part of the eye?

20 In 1769, James Watt patented a modification to what type of engine?

21 Golden Gate Avenue is in what American city?

BIGGEST CELEBRITIY WINS

ANN WIDDECOMBE, SAM NIXON, MARK RHODES AND JIMMY CARR

It was Jenny's turn to come up against a £100,000 full house in Series 9. Politician Ann Widdecombe, children's TV presenters Sam Nixon and Mark Rhodes, and returning comedian Jimmy Carr made up the team. Jimmy had faced a Chaser before, back in Series 2, when he took a £100,000 high offer against the Beast and got caught. Not this time, though, as he managed to bring home the high offer of £82,000 against the Vixen. The team set her a competitive 19 and, when they pulled out three pushbacks from six opportunities, managed to just keep her from catching them.

1 A cardiac MRI is used to visualise what organ?

2 Photoluminescent materials are known as 'glow in the...' what?

3 What sort of reptile is an Asian pipe?

4 The granting of Royal Warrants was re-established by which king?

5 'Bicicleta' is the Spanish word for what form of transport?

6 What type of fruit are casabas and cantaloupes?

7 Which guitarist is lead vocalist on the U2 song 'Numb'?

8 Lord Deben is the title adopted by which former Tory minister?

9 In the Bible, who says 'Let the earth bring forth grass'?

10 What word for a housing loan has a silent 'Y' in the middle?

11 Which former jockey wrote the novel *Second Wind*?

12 What Westminster Square features a statue of Jan Smuts?

13 What mode of transport was the SS *Great Eastern*?

14 What kind of bags can be pyramid, 'one cup' or 'hard water'?

15 Aleph is the first letter of what alphabet?

16 Meryl Streep sang 'Stay with Me' in what film musical?

17 The organisation Transport for London is often abbreviated to what three letters?

18 'Synth' in the music term 'synth-pop' is short for what?

19 What type of pastry is used to make chouquettes?

20 Folly Bridge crosses the River Thames in what city?

21 What football position is nicknamed 'goalie'?

22 *Parky's People* is a memoir by which chat show host?

23 What fresh herb is used in a traditional caprese salad?

BIGGEST CELEBRITY WINS

THE CHASE

CHASER PERFECT RUNS

CHASER PERFECT RUNS

There's no more impressive sight on *The Chase* than a Chaser on a roll, hunting down a team of contestants. Chasers work best when they can get in a rhythm – getting questions wrong and being pushed back can disrupt that rhythm, which is when the teams are in with a chance of winning. So, it's hardly surprising that what makes the Chasers happiest is pulling off what they refer to as a 'perfect run' in the Final Chase, catching the contestants without getting a single question wrong. It makes for depressing viewing for our teams though, as they watch their – often sizeable – totals being whittled away by a relentless stream of correct answers.

Here are a few of the Chaser's finest perfect runs. Can you match their achievements and not make a single mistake?

ANDREW, EMMA, CHRISTINA AND DAVE VS. MARK

The finest perfect run on *The Chase* took place way back in Series 2, and it belonged to the Beast. He was facing one of the strongest teams ever seen, who scored a staggering £36,000 in their Cash Builders. Mark managed to take out Andrew and Emma on seats 1 and 4, even though Andrew had put together a £10,000 Cash Builder and Emma, disappointed that she'd only scored £4,000 in hers, had taken a high offer of £26,000. But he was still facing two fine contestants in the Final Chase. Christine was a baker and caterer from County Londonderry and David was a subtitler from Edinburgh. £12,000 and £10,000 respectively in their Cash Builders showed their pedigree, and they scored an amazing 26 in their Final Chase. Surely the Beast couldn't catch that? Yes, he could. He put in one of the greatest performances of his *Chase* career, with a perfect run of 26 and a dramatic last-second catch. You had to feel for Christine and David. If the Beast hadn't been on top form, they would surely have taken the money home. Mark hasn't stopped reminding everyone about it ever since!

1   Born in 1911, what did American playwright Thomas Williams change his first name to?

2   Daniel, William, Stephen and Alec are the first names of which actor brothers?

3   In English, what country comes first in the alphabetical list of UN member states?

4   How many times has Brazil won the World Cup?

5   What does A stand for in the acronym NATO?

6   By what three letters is monosodium glutamate known?

7   Complete the title of the computer animated film: *Cloudy with a Chance of...* what?

8   Famed for her comic monologues, who wrote the autobiography *George, Don't Do That*?

9   What is the name of the chief temple of Athena, built on top of the Acropolis?

10   Which *Britain's Got Talent* judge played Mia Bevan in the TV show *Cutting It*?

11   The Dumbarton Oaks conference led to the founding of which world organisation?

12 What was the stage name of *Frankenstein* actor William Pratt?

13 Which British boxer became undisputed Heavyweight World Champion in 1999?

14 What type of fruit is a Cox's orange pippin?

15 Meaning 'very soft', what musical term is represented by the letters 'pp'?

16 Which gangster was played by Johnny Depp in the film *Public Enemies*?

17 In the game chess, what piece is sometimes known as a castle?

18 Edna Birch is a character in which soap opera?

19 What central African country became the 54th member of the Commonwealth in 2009?

20 What country won the football World Cup in 1990?

21 The Wash, on the east coast of England, is an inlet of which sea?

22 Complete the title of the book: *Men Are from Mars, Women Are from...* where?

23 While on a visit to England, the painter Rubens was knighted by which king?

24 What term refers to a word that is formed from the first letters of other words?

25 To which island group does Ibiza belong?

26 What breed of dog with a white coat and black spots is named after a region in Croatia?

CHASER PERFECT RUNS

THE CHASE

ALAN, DAVE, KATE AND GILL VS. PAUL

The Sinnerman put in an even more impressive performance back in Series 9, when a full house with a £60,000 prize fund scored 20 in their Final Chase. They were Alan, a zoology graduate from Stirling, Dave, a retired civil servant and regular quizzer from Blackpool, Kate, a full-time mum from Maidenhead, and Gill, a language-school director from Cardiff. Gill was also a self-confessed gambler, so it was to be expected that she took the high offer of £33,000, just as quizzer Dave had with his £20,000. That score of 20 must have given them hope of victory, but the Chasers often say that 20 plus is a 'free go'. That is, no one really expects them to catch it so the pressure is off and they can relax and do what they do best – quiz. That's exactly what Paul did, a perfect run winning the game with 25 seconds to spare. At that pace, he could have caught a 27!

1   A bungalow usually has how many stories?

2   What relation is Zara Phillips to Princess Eugenie?

3   Which actress played Wonder Woman in the '70s TV series?

4   What Herman Melville novel features boat owner Captain Bildad?

5   What empire appointed Herod the Great as King of Judaea?

6   What are made in a cooperage?

7   British actor Anthony Daniels played what robot in *Star Wars*?

8   What nationality was the composer Anton Bruckner?

9   What meal comes after 'English' in the name of a variety of tea?

10 How many dozens are there in half a gross?

11 Nirvana sold 30 million copies of what 1991 album?

12 The Ligurian Riviera is in what Mediterranean country?

13 What alternative name for deadly nightshade means 'fair lady'?

14 What's the first digit of a person's forelimb called?

15 In what film did Peter Sellers play President Merkin Muffley?

16 What material is normally used to write on a slate board?

17 Which is the only Welsh club to play in an FA Cup final?

18 In what century was the painter Canaletto born?

19 What breed of domestic pet is the Smoke Persian?

20 Who is the French mother of actress Lily-Rose Depp?

CHASER PERFECT RUNS

REGGIE, GRAHAM, LUCY AND PAULINE VS. SHAUN

This was a very strange encounter for Shaun Wallace in Series 10. He was up against a super-team: £23,000 between them in their Cash Builders and a star player on seat 1. Reggie scored £9,000 in his Cash Builder, refused to be tempted by Shaun's high offer of £36,000, yet still got caught! It put the rest of the team – Graham, a scheduling manager from Hertfordshire, Lucy, a health visitor from East London, and Pauline, a retired secretary from Manchester – on the back foot. Nonetheless, they recovered quickly and the remaining three all made it home with £14,000 in the prize fund. They then proceeded to put in a terrific performance in the Final Chase, setting Shaun 21. It should have been enough to win – but it wasn't. Shaun was completely in the zone for this chase, firing out correct answers with relentless rhythm. He caught the team with a staggering 25 seconds to spare.

1   In the northern hemisphere, what season begins in June?

2   TV's *The Two Ronnies* were Ronnie Barker and who?

3   British boxer Tyson Fury fights at what weight division?

4   Who was the eldest son of George III and Queen Charlotte?

5   What flower can have the words 'of the valley' after its name?

6   The Ugandan city Kampala is just north of what lake?

7   Which singer has had Number Ones with Blue and Kiki Dee?

8   Cyrus the Great was a leader of what empire?

9   In Greek myth, a centaur is part man and part what animal?

10   Who played scientist Robert Neville in the film *I Am Legend*?

11   Who was the youngest daughter of author Mary Wollstonecraft?

12   What's the currency of Norway?

13   The Bayeux Tapestry depicts events from what century?

14 Genever is an old name for what alcoholic spirit?

15 In the '50s and '60s, Jo Grimond led what political party?

16 What relation to you is your mother's mother?

17 In *Star Trek,* Sybok was whose half-brother?

18 Which West Indian fast bowler was nicknamed 'Big Bird'?

19 What flavour is the liqueur ouzo?

20 Felipe Rose dressed as a Native American in what disco band?

21 Hydrogen sulphide contains hydrogen and what other element?

CHASER PERFECT RUNS

PHILIP AND GAYNOR VS. PAUL

Paul was up against another duo back in Series 10 when Philip, a retired postman from Llanelli, and Gaynor, a software developer from Poole, played for a huge £50,000 after Gaynor had brought home Paul's high offer of £44,000 from seat 4. Their Final Chase total of 17 was a tricky score for Paul to catch, especially when playing for such a large sum of money. Not that the Chasers let the size of the prize fund affect them, of course – they try to play exactly the same way whether they're chasing £100 or £100,000, keeping focused on the questions. Sometimes the trick is not to chase a total, but simply to accumulate correct answers and see how close they get. In this case, Paul's perfect run saw the team's dreams, and £50,000, disappear with 46 seconds left on the clock. A classy performance by the Sinnerman.

1   In legend, everything touched by King Midas turned to what?

2   What is the capital city of Austria?

3   Complete the film title: *Fried Green Tomatoes at the...* what?

4   What Plantagenet king was usurped by Henry IV?

5   Who created the fictional train the *Hogwarts Express*?

6   'Uterus' is the scientific name for what part of the body?

7   What Middle-Eastern country is known as the UAE?

8   In what 1969 film does Charlie Croker speak the last line?

9   What Greek god shares a name with a cooking vessel?

10   The novel *The Great Gatsby* is set during what decade?

11   Which Frenchman created the 1951 artwork *Bicycle Wheel*?

12   The Otterhound is a breed of what animal?

13   What South African city is nicknamed 'The Mother City'?

14   The El Escorial palace is in what country?

15   The Lambdoid suture is found in what part of the skeleton?

16 If you fool someone, what are you said to 'pull over their eyes'?

17 What measurement for the height of a horse is 10.2 centimetres?

18 Qof and Yod are letters in what alphabet?

SHAUNA AND MATT VS. ANNE

It was the Governess who was practically perfect in every way in this Final Chase from Series 11. She'd taken out seats 1 and 4, leaving Shauna, an HR manager from Argyll, and Matt, a salesman from Teeside, attempting to win their £10,000 prize fund. They performed well, scoring 17 on their side of the Final Chase – a score that's been a winning total on many occasions. Sadly, not this one. Anne was in scintillating form as her perfect run demolished the team's total with 41 seconds to go. As she said afterwards, they can't push her back if she isn't getting any wrong!

1   A bicycle has how many more wheels than a unicycle?

2   In what form of tennis are you not allowed to volley?

3   In *The Sound of Music,* which character is 16 years old?

4   Who was assassinated in the Ambassador Hotel in 1968?

5   The crura cerebri are nerve fibres in what organ?

6   Who played Doctor Who companion Clara Oswald?

7   The farad SI unit is named after which scientist?

8   Which Greek writer is known as the 'father of history'?

9   Chutney originated on what continent?

10   What dismissive French phrase means 'that's war'?

11   'Be-Bop-A-Lula' was a 1956 hit for which singer?

12   What nationality was ballet impresario Sergei Diaghilev?

13   What word follows hummingbird hawk in the name of an insect?

14   Superman was born on what planet?

15   Which Dickens title character lodges with Mr Wickfield?

16   What animals feature at the annual Cheltenham Festival?

17   What element is named after the ancient goddess Selene?

JOHN, CAIA AND DAVID VS. ANNE

Anne Hegerty faced three members of a super-team in Series 11. John, a cheese production manager from Dorset, Caia, a gap-year student from Cumbria, and David, a librarian and keen quizzer from London were three-quarters of a team that scored £23,000 in their Cash Builders. Anne had managed to catch Michelle on seat 3, but still found herself facing a prize fund of £18,000 and a team total of 20. It was a 'free go' for Anne, with no pressure to win. No pressure and no problems either! She cruised home with an enormous 30 seconds left on the clock. Super disappointment for the super-team.

1   The daughter of a queen is usually known by what title?

2   A cetologist studies what large marine mammals?

3   Kyle, Eric and Stan are friends in what TV animation?

4   What moon of Pluto is named after a mythical river in Hades?

5   Pantelleria is an Italian island in what sea?

6   Which Australian actress stars in the film *Lion*?

7   What type of shop is known in America as a drugstore?

8   What African kingdom is ruled by the Muslim Alawite dynasty?

9   Chinese mitten is a species of what crustacean?

10   Lovetown and Zoo TV were tours by what Irish band?

11   The Tudor dynasty lasted how many generations?

12   What train service links London to Lille?

13   Which former US First Lady set up an addiction recovery clinic?

14   The drug Propecia is used to treat male pattern what?

15   Gale Mon-feece is a star of what sport?

16   What colour is Milkybar chocolate?

17 In what US state was every NASA space shuttle launched?

18 Who played Sonny in the film *Dog Day Afternoon*?

19 In what war was HMS *Hood* sunk by the *Bismarck*?

20 What Don McLean hit is over eight and half minutes long?

CHASER PERFECT RUNS

NICK AND JOSEPH VS. PAUL

In Series 11, Paul Sinha found himself facing a pair in the Final Chase. He'd taken out the two female players, leaving Nick, a website engineer from London, and Joseph, a door salesman from St Albans, to play. They were both decent contestants, having scored £6,000 each in their Cash Builders, and set Paul a real banana-skin of 16 – the sort of score the Chasers expect to catch, but which will set them down the wrong path if they make just a few mistakes. Not on this occasion, however, as Paul put together a perfect run, winning with 49 seconds to spare. Joseph's dream of buying a life-sized model of Batman had ended with the Sinnerman robbin' his cash!

1   What is the most spoken language in New Zealand?

2   A 'porteur' is a male dancer's role in what dance form?

3   Who presents the TV show *For the Love of Animals*?

4   *Rule Britannia* was the last novel by which Cornwall-based writer?

5   What do the letters RHD stand for when describing a car?

6   Who launched the website 'thefacebook.com' in 2004?

7   Born in 1755, Thomas Lord was a famous name in what sport?

8   Ted Levine played serial killer Buffalo Bill in what film?

9   A 'frosecco' is an alcoholic slushy made with what Italian wine?

10 What painting by Edward Hopper is based on a New York diner?

11 Who wrote the novel *Ross Poldark*?

12 John Tracy was a character in what Gerry Anderson TV series?

13 Which Spanish artist painted *Seated Woman* in 1937?

14   A 'lep-on' is a cross between a lioness and what other big cat?

15   What vegetable is the Edzell Blue?

16   A rhyming term for counterfeit currency is 'funny...' what?

CHASER PERFECT RUNS

KAREN, GARETH AND MIKE VS. JENNY

It was Jenny Ryan's turn to chase down a 17 in Series 12. She was facing a very strong team, with a combined total of £27,000 in their Cash Builders. She'd done well to take one of them out, but when Karen, a musician from Lancashire, brought home the high offer of £47,000, the Vixen was trying to stand in the way of a £60,000 prize fund. It was no surprise that Karen chanced her arm, as she was a regular pub quizzer. The team was completed by Gareth, a sports programme manager from Middlesex, and Mike, a warehouse worker from Moray. They were probably slightly disappointed to post 17, as they'd looked like a team with 20 plus in them. Still, with 17 on the board, they had a right to expect the chase to be closer than it was. The Vixen powered to a perfect run and it was all over with 40 seconds to spare.

1   What cartoon cat famously chases Jerry the mouse?

2   Flint Castle is located in what country of the UK?

3   Which *Star Wars* character is the son of Jango Fett?

4   In a theatre, what arch separates the stage from the auditorium?

5   The name of what baseball team is shortened to 'Bosox'?

6   What bird appears on the Mexican coat of arms?

7   Datterini is a type of what salad fruit?

8   Craig Charles played what role in the comedy *Red Dwarf*?

9   The 1969 film *Battle of Britain* is set during what conflict?

10   Postcodes for Bristol start with what two letters?

11   The Hellas Basin is a huge impact crater on what planet?

12   Which broadcaster produces the *Good Food* magazine?

13   The food company Dole originally sold what tropical fruit?

14   In British law, DPP stands for 'Director of Public...' what?

15 The Foss is a tributary of what North Yorkshire river?

16 Something polychromatic has multiple what?

17 How were the musicians Duane and Gregg Allman related?

THE CHASE

CHASE ODDITIES

CHASE ODDITIES

Many record holders have featured on *The Chase* over the past 10 years, although some of them might be completely unaware that they hold these titles! In this section we salute those gallant *Chase* contestants who can lay claim to some of our oddest honours, giving you the questions they used to win Chase immortality. Could you do as well – or in some cases, as badly – as them and earn your place as a *Chase* oddity?

HIGHEST SCORE IN A CASH BUILDER

Way back in Series 2, Les, a retired company director, set the record for the highest score in a Cash Builder with a staggering £14,000! So, how much did such a talented quizzer win in the Final Chase, you ask? Well, nothing. He didn't even make it back. Despite spurning Shaun's high offer of £29,000 – which, to be fair, wasn't the most generous offer he'd ever made – Les got caught during his Head to Head. The rest of his team made it to the Final Chase (playing for £16,000), set Shaun 19 and got caught with 17 seconds to spare. Still, at least Les had his moment in the sun and set a record that may never be broken.

1   Harpy, bald and golden are species of what bird?

2   What type of pastry is traditionally used to make éclairs and profiteroles?

3   Madonna divorced which film director in 2008?

4   Salisbury is in which English county?

5   Which late BBC DJ was born John Ravenscroft?

6   What's the chemical symbol for tin?

7   'Satnav' is an abbreviation of what two words?

8   Which US President gave the Gettysburg Address?

9   What film features Terry Jones saying: 'He's not the Messiah, he's a very naughty boy'?

10   Which diarist ended many of his entries with 'and so to bed'?

11   What country won the 2010 Six Nations rugby tournament?

12   What Tennessee Williams play features the character Blanche Du Bois?

13   What planet is known as the 'sister planet of Earth'?

14   Who played Rowdy Yates in the 1960s TV show *Rawhide*?

HIGHEST SCORE IN A CASH BUILDER BY A TEENAGER

Brad loves having young players on the show, but it's not always easy for them. It can be tough to answer questions about TV shows that stopped airing before you were even born! But every now and then a really talented young quizzer comes along. One of those was Matthew, a creative-writing student from Sunderland, who set the record for highest score in a Cash Builder by a teenager when he scored £9,000 in Series 9. He was just 18 years old. Unfortunately, he failed to get home with his cash after coming up against Shaun in his Head to Head. What is it about record breakers that Mr Wallace doesn't like?

1 What implements are used in Asia as an alternative to cutlery?

2 What 1972 Marlon Brando film was based on a novel by Mario Puzo?

3 How many countries have representatives in the Benelux Parliament?

4 What word can mean both to indicate with your finger and a tiny dot?

5 Which escapologist was married to his stage assistant Wilhelmina Rahner?

6 What satirical magazine created fictional Tory politician Sir Bufton Tufton?

7 In 2000, which football manager was given the freedom of the City of Manchester?

8 What country shares its name with the third longest river in Africa?

9 Bletchley Park is the main setting for what 2014 wartime film?

10 A police DSU provides what sort of animal support?

11 The character Billy Flynn sings 'Razzle Dazzle' in what stage musical?

BIGGEST LOW OFFER EVER ACCEPTED

Next up is a record holder who shall remain nameless – for reasons that will become apparent. People at home seem to take against contestants who accept a minus low offer, even if it's exactly the right tactical decision according to the Chasers. The biggest low offer ever accepted was by a player in Series 10, who accepted minus £15,000. They were on seat 4 and, at the time, there were two players back with £54,000 in the prize fund. So, if you're of the opinion that a third of £39,000 is better than half of nothing, and that three players have a better chance than two in the Final Chase, it was the sensible option. It worked – at least as far as getting the player back. But sadly it didn't pay off in the long run. The trio set Paul 17 and almost got away with the cash, the Sinnerman catching them with just five seconds to spare!

1 In their hit, which of these did Right Said Fred NOT say they were 'too sexy for'?

          A My cat   **B** This song   **C** Your dad

2 Which of these Italian islands is the smallest in area?

          A Sardinia   **B** Sicily   **C** Stromboli

3 The Leadenhall Building, the London skyscraper that opened in 2014, has what nickname?

          A Walkie Talkie   **B** Cheese Grater   **C** Gherkin

4 Which Greek deity lived in the underworld rather than on Mount Olympus?

          A Hades   **B** Hermes   **C** Hera

CHASE ODDITIES

BIGGEST COMBINED HIGH OFFERS

From low offers to high offers. Sometimes the Chasers like to flash the cash to try and get the team to take a step closer and increase their chances of catching them. None more so than the Beast, who's always ready to put his money where his mouth is. In Series 11, he really pushed the boat out, making the biggest combined high offers ever seen on *The Chase*. The team of Jonathan, a maintenance assistant from South Yorkshire, Iona, a music student from Bristol, Steph, a plastering company owner from Liverpool and Michael, a courier from Essex were offered a combined total of £300,000. The Beast started with fellow Sheffield United fan Jonathan, who scored £2,000 in his Cash Builder and was given an offer of 10 times what he brought to the table. He turned it down but was still caught. The high offers kept coming – £80,000 for Iona and £100,000 each for Steph and Michael – but none would take them. In fact, Iona went low so the three played for £10,000 not £280,000... and got caught.

JONATHAN

1   What does the Caribbean company Sandals specialise in?

        A Shoes   **B** Cocktails   **C** Holidays

2   Which of these countries is NOT a member of the G7 group?

        A Italy   **B** France   **C** Spain

3   Which English king succeeded his grandfather?

        A Richard I   **B** Richard II   **C** Richard III

4   The Tengwar is a writing system created by which author for use in his books?

        A Terry Pratchett   **B** Arthur Conan Doyle   **C** J. R. R. Tolkien

5   What does the Maritime Heritage Trust look after?

        A Lighthouses   **B** Harbours   **C** Ships

6   Which of these elements does NOT exist naturally as a diatomic molecule?

        A Hydrogen   **B** Helium   **C** Nitrogen

CHASE ODDITIES

IONA

1   What South American country was named after the large amount of a type of wood that was found there?

> **A** Brazil   **B** Ecuador   **C** Paraguay

2   Which of these totals is least likely to be rolled with two regular six-sided dice?

> **A** Two   **B** Three   **C** Four

3   In 2017, Wikipedia editors banned using what UK newspaper as a source, calling it 'generally unreliable'?

> **A** *Daily Star*   **B** *Daily Mirror*   **C** *Daily Mail*

4   What animal does Peter Griffin repeatedly fight in the TV series *Family Guy*?

> **A** Donkey   **B** Chicken   **C** Pig

5   Before becoming the first British woman to win an Olympic hammer medal in 2016 Sophie Hitchon had trained as what?

> **A** A nail technician   **B** A plumber   **C** A ballet dancer

6   Which of these words does NOT appear in the Oxford Dictionary?

> **A** Dumbfuggle   **B** Boondoggle   **C** Hornswoggle

7   Kim Kardashian released a pool inflatable shaped like what?

> **A** Her bum   **B** Her husband   **C** Her dog

8   In the mid-90s, which veteran rocker embarked on his Retirement Sucks Tour?

> **A** Eric Clapton   **B** Ozzy Osbourne   **C** Cliff Richard

10ᵀᴴ ANNIVERSARY QUIZBOOK

STEPH

1 In the 18th century, which of these was a name for an extravagantly fashionable man?

A Spaghetti **B** Tortellini **C** Macaroni

2 Which of these is a Trinidadian footballer who played for Birmingham City in the Premier League?

A Strict Dave **B** Stern John **C** Stubborn Tim

3 Named for its yellow-white head, *Neopalpa donaldtrumpi* is a newly discovered species of what creature?

A Macaw **B** Moth **C** Monkey

4 Which of these words appears in the titles of books in both *The Hunger Games* and *Harry Potter* series?

A Stone **B** Prince **C** Fire

5 At the Battle of Waterloo, Lord Uxbridge reputedly said to the Duke of Wellington, 'By God, sir, I've lost my...' what?

A Hat **B** Leg **C** Mojo

6 Which painter designed a logo for Chupa Chups lollipops?

A Salvador Dalí **B** David Hockney **C** Andy Warhol

7 According to *Forbes* magazine, which of these brands is the most valuable?

A Facebook **B** Disney **C** Toyota

CHASE ODDITIES

MICHAEL

1 In what TV show was Charlotte called 'the brunette', Miranda 'the redhead' and Samantha just 'trouble'?

   A *Desperate Housewives* **B** *Grey's Anatomy* **C** *Sex and the City*

2 The 2017 Six Nations rugby tournament saw the introduction of a bonus point for scoring how many tries in a match?

   A Four **B** Five **C** Six

3 Which literary character was described by her creator as an 'American geisha'?

   A Holly Golightly **B** Sally Bowles **C** Blanche DuBois

4 Which of these is a type of illegal business where participants must recruit new members to pay earlier investors?

   A Cylinder scheme **B** Pyramid scheme **C** Spherical scheme

5 What series of video games features teams of garden creatures doing battle with a variety of unusual weapons?

   A Worms **B** Snails **C** Hedgehogs

6 Which of these planets is named after a Greek rather than a Roman god?

   A Saturn **B** Uranus **C** Neptune

7 Where would you most likely see a bottle of the blue liquid 'Barbicide'?

   A Gymnasium **B** Hair salon **C** Pub

HIGHEST SCORE BY A SOLO PLAYER IN A FINAL CHASE THAT DIDN'T WIN

Sometimes a team puts together a score in the Final Chase that you think simply can't lose. On a very few occasions a solo player does the same. However, it doesn't always turn out the way you expect it to. Two players share the record for the highest score by a solo player in a Final Chase that didn't win: Pat, a retired cost clerk from Lancashire, and Tim, an air cabin crew member from Luton, who both scored an incredible 23 all on their own. Unfortunately for them, they came up against Anne and Mark respectively and went home without a penny. This was especially painful for Tim, who'd brought back the high offer and was playing for £45,000.

PAT

1 'Sushi' and 'kimono' come from what language?

2 Which US state is furthest south?

3 Mike Leigh's film *Topsy Turvy* is about what musical duo?

4 Who lost the 1993 Wimbledon singles final to Steffi Graf?

5 What branch of the armed forces was formed in 1918?

6 Who became Mayor of London in 2008?

7 Funchal is the capital of what Portuguese region?

8 What rate of interest is known as the MLR?

9 Mills & Boon specialise in what genre of fiction?

10 With what hobby is Airfix associated?

11 For what film was Mickey Rourke Oscar-nominated?

12 Which of the Great Lakes is entirely within the US?

13 How many days in a leap year?

14 What does the MI in MI6 stand for?

15 What type of fruit is a Worcester Pearmain?

16 Stalin was born in what modern-day country?

17 What were the first names of Morecambe and Wise?

18 What Asian country used to be known as Siam?

19 'Love Changes Everything' is a song from what musical?

20 What aquatic mammal secretes the substance castor?

21 Doctor Robotnik is the enemy of what video-game hedgehog?

22 'Depilation' is the removal of what from the body?

23 Bella Swan is the heroine in what series of novels?

24 Stellenbosch is a wine region in what country?

25 Iraq is on what continent?

26 In radio transmission what does FM stand for?

27 In what year was the General Strike?

28 Which yachtswoman wrote the novels *Wolf Winter* and *Night Sky*?

29 What Australian soap is set in Summer Bay?

30 What was the currency of Italy before the Euro?

ANNE

1 What European island is known as the 'Emerald Isle'?

2 What's the common name for iron oxide?

3 Who wrote *The Old Man and the Sea*?

4 Car makers Hyundai and Kia are from what country?

5 How many days in March?

6 What religion celebrates the festival Hanukkah?

7 Don McLean's song 'American Pie' is about the death of who?

8 Deer and sheep are what type of cud-chewing, hoofed mammals?

9 In the NATO phonetic alphabet, what dance represents T?

10 Who played Jack Dawson in *Titanic*?

11 At what Texas Fort was Davy Crockett killed?

CHASE ODDITIES

12 The inventor of Bakelite was born in what country?

13 In the story, what wooden puppet was created by Geppetto?

14 What do the Americans call a billfold?

15 What hero of Greek myth killed the Hydra?

16 The painter Mondrian was born in what country?

17 What's the currency of France?

18 What sea is linked to the Mediterranean by the Suez Canal?

19 *Desert Island Discs* was first broadcast in what decade?

20 What musical instrument is Pete Seeger mostly linked with?

21 In computing, 'IT' stands for 'Information… what'?

22 Which Scottish queen was beheaded in 1587?

23 What word means 'bread and butter table' in Swedish?

24 Which jockey won the 1986 and 1994 Grand Nationals?

25 The emu is native to what country?

26 What element has the symbol H?

TIM

1 In Cyndi Lauper's hit, what do girls just want to have?

2 How many inches in a yard?

3 What 'shore' is the subject of a US reality TV show?

4 What leather seat is used when riding a horse?

5 Blackburn and Preston are in what county?

6 In *The Lord of the Rings,* what land is ruled by Sauron?

7 The Jarrow March took place in what year?

8 Monterey Jack is a type of what?

9 Who is Jamie Redknapp's football coach father?

10 'One Time' was the first UK hit for which teen idol?

CHASE ODDITIES

11   What De Havilland plane was the first commercial jet airliner?

12   The optic nerve links what organ to the brain?

13   Which *Friends* character had the catchphrase 'How you doin''?

14   Crazy Horse was a chief of what Native American tribe?

15   The okapi is an animal native to what continent?

16   How many numbers are needed to win the jackpot in the Lotto draw?

17   The word 'yodel' comes from what language?

18   What TV drama is set in Seattle Grace Hospital?

19   What's the only US state with a one syllable name?

20   What organisation is known as the UN?

21   Porcini are a type of what?

22   Who did Gabby Yorath marry in 2001?

23   Mrs Moneypenny is a columnist in what newspaper?

24   What would you use to play the game Snap?

25   The source of the Ganges is in what mountain range?

26   *Rockferry* was the debut album of which singer?

27   Nostradamus lived in what century?

28   Bertie Ahern was Prime Minister of what country?

29   In the proverb what is 'next to godliness'?

30   What alpine flower is on Austrian two-cent coins?

31   In what religion are forbidden foods called 'terefah'?

32   Who led the Norman Conquest of England?

33   Which American dramatist wrote *The Iceman Cometh*?

MARK

1   Online magazine *Shoot* is dedicated to what sport?

2   How much do you pay for something that is 'gratis'?

CHASE ODDITIES

3 Who plays Jackson's mother Hazel in *Emmerdale*?

4 Who directed *Cathy Come Home* and *Kes*?

5 How many pounds in two stone?

6 In what ocean is Tahiti?

7 Who had hits with 'Babylon' and 'This Year's Love'?

8 Which German dramatist wrote *The Caucasian Chalk Circle*?

9 What animal is Winnie-the-Pooh?

10 In what month is Epiphany?

11 'Joanie Loves Chachi' was a spin-off from what US sitcom?

12 What British island group includes Muckle Flugga?

13 A sextet is a group of how many musicians?

14 What animals were London Zoo's Chi Chi and An-an?

15 Manuka is a variety of what food?

16 Who played astronaut Tony Nelson in *I Dream of Jeannie*?

17 Oporto is the second-largest city in what country?

18 Former MP Elliot Morley was a member of what party?

19 Which female singer released the album *Killer Love*?

20 The Boeing 747 took its maiden flight in what decade?

21 'Yabba-dabba-do!' is what cartoon character's catchphrase?

22 Ivan IV of Russia is known by what nickname?

23 A vespiary is a colony of what insects?

24 Maria Callas was born in what country?

25 The Year of the Dragon features in what calendar?

26 Who played Marjorie Dawes in *Little Britain*?

27 What year of the '70s was the title of a James Blunt hit?

28 What dinosaur's name means 'arm lizard'?

29 What reality TV show did Stacey Solomon win?

CHASE ODDITIES

HIGHEST AMOUNT EVER PLAYED FOR IN A FINAL CHASE

The Beast has form when it comes to putting really big money on the table, so it's no surprise that he is responsible for the highest amount ever played for in a Final Chase. Mark had already caught the first three players when Ronnie, a juvenile justice worker from Belfast, got up from seat 4. Understandably, nerves got the better of him and he scored a disappointing £1,000 in his Cash Builder. The Beast was determined to catch the entire team so put down a high offer of £101,000. It was too much for Ronnie to refuse and, with a combination of luck and skill, he brought it home. Could he still hang on to it after the Final Chase? Sadly not. The nerves returned and Ronnie could only set nine, which the Beast demolished in just 45 seconds.

RONNIE

1 A professional masseuse provides what type of therapy?

2 Used in soups, grattoni is a type of what staple food?

3 What three vowels are the title of an '80s hit for Freeez?

4 What colour's the top stripe on the Dutch flag?

5 Rupert Sanderson designs what fashion items?

6 Which so-called 'mad monk' was born in Siberia around 1869?

7 Alan Bennett won a 2006 Tony award for writing what play?

8 Kinder Surprise Eggs were first made by Ferrero in what country?

9 What type of creature is a brown thrasher?

10 Who played Wilhelmina Slater in the TV series *Ugly Betty*?

11 The Manhugger giant features in what Roald Dahl book?

12 Which US inventor said 'I start where the last man left off'?

13 What 1965 film starred Christopher Plummer and Julie Andrews?

14   'Gumshoe' is slang for someone who does what job?

15   What type of media publication is *Marie Claire*?

16   The medical abbreviation IVF stands for 'In vitro...' what?

17   Who directed the 2012 film *Moonrise Kingdom*?

18   In the Bible, who cleansed Mary Magdalene of seven demons?

19   Which Spanish painter declared 'I do not seek. I find.'?

20   Persian and sphynx are breeds of what pet?

21   The Caledonian Sleeper departs from what London railway terminal?

MARK

1   A work by which Italian artist inspired the opera *Mona Lisa*?

2   What is the minimum age you can join the British Army?

3   What children's book by E. B. White is about an arachnid?

4   The Altai Mountains are on what continent?

5   In 2003, Monty's Pass won what Aintree steeplechase?

6   Graciano is a red variety of what fruit?

7   *Pitches to Riches* is a spin-off from what business TV show?

8   Cydonia is a region of what planet?

9   Which *Star Trek* actor directed 'The Search for Spock'

CHASE ODDITIES

LOWEST EVER SCORE IN A FINAL CHASE

Another nameless record holder now – and it's not a record any *Chase* contestant would want to hold. Nerves can seriously affect performance, and on this occasion a contestant in Series 10 was so paralysed by them that they managed to set the record for the lowest ever score in a Final Chase, giving the Beast just three to catch. It took him 12 seconds and he was annoyed that he hadn't done it in less than 10. But he did set another record, for the fastest ever catch in a Final Chase!

CONTESTANT

1   'Glasto' is a nickname of what music festival?

2   What book and film series is sometimes abbreviated to LOTR?

3   October Revolution Island belongs to what country?

4   What moon of Jupiter is larger than the planet Mercury?

5   In what famous musical does Maria marry Georg?

6   In what sport can a penalty corner be awarded?

7   How many years does a silver jubilee celebrate?

8   In the Bible, who was the brother of Moses?

9   In *Harry Potter*, what type of bird is Ron's pet Pigwidgeon?

10   Who wrote the script for the 1976 film *Rocky*?

11   In 2007, who became President of South Africa's ANC party?

12   What playing-card is called 'le roi' in French?

13   On what continent are the Carpathian Mountains?

14   What unit of distance can be nautical, statute and Roman?

15   In *Twelfth Night*, who disguises herself as the male Cesario?

16   Diddy Kong is a sidekick of what Nintendo character?

17   Blake Harrison played Private Pike in what 2016 film?

18   What SI derived unit has the symbol N?

19   How many letter Ps are there in 'Mississippi'?

20   Which Chinese leader famously swam in the Yangtze in 1966?

CHASER

1   What is the second letter of the word 'chameleon'?

2   What was the capital of Russia immediately before Moscow?

3   What American sport is played by the Cincinnati Reds?

CHASE ODDITIES

MOST PUSHBACKS IN A FINAL CHASE

As we've said, 16 is what the Chasers call a 'banana-skin score' – a total they should catch but which, with a few pushbacks, can turn into a slip-up. In Series 11, Shaun Wallace came across a whole box of bananas and enabled the team facing him to set the record for the most pushbacks in a Final Chase. Rhidian on seat 1 had gone high for £27,000 and got caught, so things had started well for the Chaser. Unfortunately, it was all downhill from there. Beverley, a business owner from Bradford, Whitney, a student midwife from West Sussex, and Marvin, a financial analyst from Essex all got back with their middle amounts and were playing for £13,000 in the Final Chase. Their score of 16 was one that Shaun expected to catch, but the wheels came off completely in his Final Chase. An astonishing 11 mistakes were punished by a team on fire as they pushed him back a record nine times. Shaun would like to point out that the record belongs to the team and not him…

CHASE ODDITIES

1   Black mamba is a species of what reptile?

2   Michael Flatley is a professional in what style of dance?

3   What Berlin prison was demolished in 1987?

4   Who played Costas in the film *Shirley Valentine*?

5   Bluetick coonhound is a breed of what pet?

6   'Shaktism' is a subdivision of what religion?

7   In taxation, NIC stands for 'National Insurance...' what?

8   Don Bradman scored most of his Test runs in what decade?

9   Which Australian pop star released the album *Enjoy Yourself*?

10   Deal Castle was built by Henry VIII in what English county?

11   In what New Testament book does Death ride a pale horse?

12   Shio Ramen is a noodle soup in what national cuisine?

13   What holiday is 55 days after Halloween?

14 In music, vinyl replaced shellac in the manufacture of what?

15 George Kranky is a character in what Roald Dahl book?

16 What forename links a Bonnie Prince and a son of the Queen?

17 'Dealer's Choice' is a variant of what card game?

18 'Changes' was a 1999 hit for which late American rapper?

19 King Arthur's round table was kept in what castle?

20 What website runs the Prime Music service?

21 A soldier who breaks military law is tried at a 'court...' what?

22 What Leicester company first began making crisps in 1948?

23 What song from the film *8 Mile* won an Oscar?

24 *Ordeal by Innocence* is a '50s crime novel by which woman?

25 What type of light source is made by the company Price's?

CHASE ODDITIES

OLDEST MALE CONTESTANT

As well as the youngsters, Brad loves chatting to our more mature players. In Series 12, Terence became our oldest male contestant at the age of 85. He had served as an engineer in the RAF for 22 years, giving him and Bradley, an ex-engineer himself, plenty to talk about. Terence is still very active, volunteering as an ambulance car driver, ferrying old people about (as he put it)! He played Shaun and was very disappointed in himself when he only scored £2,000 in his Cash Builder. So when a high offer of £48,000 came along, he decided to redeem himself and go high. It was a brave decision but, ultimately, a foolhardy one, as Shaun caught him and he missed out on a place in the Final Chase. Here are his Cash Builder questions for you to try yourself.

1   What type of pet precedes 'tired' to describe someone who is exhausted?

2   'Take my hand, we'll make it I swear' is a line in what Bon Jovi hit?

3   Who convinced Mark Antony to have her younger sister Arsinoe executed?

4   Two main characters in what US sitcom were named after producer Sheldon Leonard?

5   What's the maximum possible number of Wednesdays in a calendar month?

6   In 2017, what football club made goalkeeper Jordan Pickford its record signing?

7   Navelina is a variety of what citrus fruit?

8   'Hansel, he's so hot right now' is a line from what Ben Stiller film?

OLDEST CONTESTANT EVER

Our final *Chase* oddity holds not one but two records. In Series 12, Jean, a retired teacher from Coventry, was not only the oldest female contestant, but also the oldest contestant ever on *The Chase* at the grand old age of 91. She had a fascinating tale to tell, having taught all over the world and gathered four university degrees. She had even dined with Elizabeth Taylor! Jean found herself up against the Vixen, but it turned out her quizzing wasn't quite as impressive as her life story. Nerves got the better of her and she could only manage £1,000 in her Cash Builder. Things didn't improve in her Head to Head, and Jenny caught her – which was a shame because the rest of her team went on to beat the Chaser and take home a share of £16,000. So, no cash for Jean but she's still a *Chase* double record holder. Here are her Cash Builder questions for you to try.

1   How many candidates can a person vote for in a UK General Election?

2   Bernard Montgomery was appointed commander of the Eighth Army during what conflict?

3   What form of transport inspired Karl Dahlman to invent the Flymo?

4   What short name is often given to the fruit of a hawthorn?

5   On TV, how is the villain Oroku Saki known in *Teenage Mutant Ninja Turtles*?

6   Which feline character is described as 'unbounced' in *The House at Pooh Corner*?

CHASE ODDITIES

THE CHASE

GUESS THE CONNECTION

GUESS THE CONNECTION

The Chase question-writing team are an odd bunch. The only thing that pleases them more than writing a cheeky question and making Bradley crack up is writing a question that no one can answer. Sometimes you'd think they don't quite get the point of the show – which is for people to get questions right and win money! So, when we asked them for the next section of questions, they were as happy as Larry. That's because these ones are doubly difficult. The team have taken some tricky questions and put them together in themed groups. Not only do you have to answer the questions, you also have to work out what links the answers. And knowing how devilishly the minds of those question writers work, that could be easier said than done. One thing's for sure, it's not always going to be immediately obvious. Good luck with these!

CONNECTIONS QUIZ 1

1   Which future Prime Minister introduced a 1911 Bill that made tea-breaks a legal requirement?

  A David Lloyd George   **B** Stanley Baldwin   **C** Winston Churchill

2   Which 18th-century economist wrote *The Wealth of Nations*?

3   Which author broke her engagement with Harris Bigg-Wither the day after she accepted his marriage proposal?

  A Jane Austen   **B** Charlotte Brontë   **C** George Eliot

4   Which British painter said 'Light is therefore colour'?

5   Which senior royal was once gifted a fake hand-waving machine?

6   Which British mathematician ran the World War Two code-breaking group Ultra?

CONNECTIONS QUIZ 2

1   Which famous ship began a five-month stay in Tahiti in October 1788?

2   In the US, what coin is worth 10 cents?

3   In 2013, a NASA rover detected a methane 'burp' on what planet?

4   Halley's Comet orbits a solar system in what galaxy?

5   What name is given to a two-storey bus?

CONNECTIONS QUIZ 3

1 What is the capital of Bermuda?

2 What company runs the National Lottery?

3 Deep Thought was a computer designed to play what game?

4 A hirsute person has a lot of what?

5 What city in Illinois is home to nearly three million people?

CONNECTIONS QUIZ 4

1 What charity runs 'The World's Biggest Coffee Morning'?

2 Who produced the West End musical *Cats*?

3 Which of these was the name of five 12th-century kings of Jerusalem?

A Baldwin **B** Barlow **C** Battersby

4 Carnie, Wendy and China formed what US girl group?

5 In the Book of Genesis, the Land of Nod was east of what garden?

6 TV ads for what insurance company feature a nodding dog saying 'Oh yes'?

GUESS THE CONNECTION

267

CONNECTIONS QUIZ 5

1   What vessel gets its name from the Latin for 'under the sea'?

2   Iris Law is the daughter of Sadie Frost and which British actor?

3   The 'morse' is an old name for what large, seal-like creature?

4   In 1867, what precious stones were discovered in Cape Colony, South Africa?

5   What nationality is singer Morten Harket?

CONNECTIONS QUIZ 6

1   Archers schnapps is flavoured with what fruit?

2   In the proverb meaning it's often wise to say nothing, 'silence is...' what?

3   Morecambe and Wise's theme song was 'Bring Me ...' what?

4   In 2019, what large amphibious rodents became a protected species in Scotland?

5   What kind of hard stone is used in Olympic curling?

CONNECTIONS QUIZ 7

1   Who did Frank Muir call 'the thinking man's crumpet'?

2   The river Irwell separates Salford from which other city?

3   The song 'Everything's Coming Up Roses' is originally from what musical?

4   'Crème Anglaise' is the French name for what dessert sauce?

5   What company launched the Macintosh computer in 1984?

GUESS THE CONNECTION

CONNECTIONS QUIZ 8

1   In 1959, which Soviet probe became the first craft to leave Earth's gravity?

A Luna 1   **B** Sputnik 1   **C** Voskhod 1

2   What West Midlands town has the postcode DY?

3   What is Minnie Mouse's full first name?

A Minette   **B** Wilhelmina   **C** Minerva

4   The term 'draconian' comes from what ancient Greek lawgiver?

5   Who is Queen of Sicilia in Shakespeare's *The Winter's Tale*?

6   What star is also called Alpha Canis Majoris?

CONNECTIONS QUIZ 9

1   In 2007, which media mogul bought the *Wall Street Journal*?

2   Who wrote *The Female Eunuch*?

3   Which actor won a posthumous Oscar for *The Dark Knight*?

4   Which cricketer bowled Mike Gatting in 1993 with the so-called 'ball of the century'?

5   Who had her first UK Number One with 'I Should Be So Lucky'?

GUESS THE CONNECTION

269

CONNECTIONS QUIZ 10

1 Amy Winehouse famously wore what '60s hairstyle?

2 What is the common rhyming name for a hand-held two-way radio?

3 'Big hairy' and 'screaming hairy' are species of what animal?

A Armadillo	**B** Yak	**C** Gorilla

4 What small green cucumber used for pickling gets its name from Dutch?

5 Which of these was NOT one of Andy Warhol's *32 Campbell's Soup Cans* in his famous 1962 artwork?

A Chicken Gumbo	**B** Bird's-Nest	**C** Clam Chowder

CONNECTIONS QUIZ 11

1 Fashion designer Lucinda Guinness is known by what first name?

2 What is the exact opposite of dysphoria?

3 What hurricane devastated New Orleans in 2005?

4 What London station was the original Eurostar terminus?

5 How is a Mimosa cocktail more commonly known in the UK?

GUESS THE CONNECTION

CONNECTIONS QUIZ 12

1 Which of these artists was born closest to the National Gallery?

A Caravaggio　**B** Cézanne　**C** Constable

2 What nursing position takes its name from the Latin for 'wife'?

3 What's the capital of Ohio?

4 In the nursery rhyme who went up the hill with Jill?

5 What comes before 'habdabs' in a phrase that means 'to give someone nervous anxiety'?

A Screaming　**B** Wailing　**C** Hooting

6 What old American occupation is used to describe a dishonest tradesman?

GUESS THE CONNECTION

CONNECTIONS QUIZ 13

1. What jewel is the birthstone for July?

2. What's the surname of Scottish tennis-playing brothers Andy and Jamie?

3. On Monopoly's 'Go to Jail' square, what item is in the policeman's mouth?

4. What instrument represents the bird in Prokofiev's *Peter and the Wolf*?

5. What fruit is most associated with 'scrumping'?

6. *A Child's World* was the original title of a painting used to advertise what soap?

7. Barbie's pet Taffy is what animal?

8. In the human body, the iskium and ilium are types of what?

9. Made by Taylors of Harrogate, Malty Biscuit Brew is a variety of what drink?

10. What part of a plant can also mean to flick through a book?

11. What type of animal is Beatrix Potter's Jeremy Fisher?

12. In the dish of sausages baked in batter, what animal is said to be 'in the hole'?

CONNECTIONS QUIZ 14

1 In 2019, a first edition of a book about which boy sold for $90,000?

2 Which 18th-century female ruler of Russia was born in Prussia?

3 'Lips are Movin'' was a 2015 hit for which American pop star?

4 What was the first in the series of books about schoolboy William Brown?

5 On the TV show *Rainbow*, what was the name of the pink hippo character?

CONNECTIONS QUIZ 15

1 The absence of body hair led which zoologist to call humans 'naked apes'?

2 What yoga position is also known as padmasana?

3 After the tiger and lion, what is the third largest living feline species?

4 What Japanese company makes the Piagerro digital piano?

5 Who was a major star of both the *Star Wars* and *Indiana Jones* movies?

GUESS THE CONNECTION

THE CHASE

THE CHASE
DOWN UNDER

THE CHASE DOWN UNDER

The Australian version of *The Chase* began in 2015 and has proved to be a big hit for the Seven Network. It's presented by former lawyer Andrew O'Keefe, who had previously fronted the Australian version of *Deal or No Deal,* and it features, along with the Australian Chasers, our very own Anne Hegerty and Mark Labbett. Their Australian co-chasers are Matt Parkinson, a comedian and actor as well as a top quizzer, known on the show as 'Goliath', Brydon Coverdale, nicknamed 'the Shark', who is a journalist, blogger and veteran of many Australian TV quizzes, and Issa Schultz, 'the Super-Nerd', who is originally from Cornwall but moved to Oz when he was 11 and who has won the Australian Quizzing Championship on numerous occasions. In addition, Shaun Wallace went out to make a few guest appearances on the show in 2018 and Cheryl Toh, an Australian lawyer and widely respected quizzer known as 'the Tiger Mum', appeared as a Chaser in 2019. The format of the show is very similar to the British version but the contestants play for $2,000 per question in the Cash Builder – just over £1,100.

So, how would you cope with *The Chase* Down Under? Here are a few questions from the Australian series to test yourself with…

CASH BUILDER

1   Which famous Australian bushranger died on 11 November 1880?

2   In the comic strip, what is the name of the dog that lives with Garfield?

3   What colour are competitors at Wimbledon tennis championships required to wear?

4   In Norse mythology, what is the traditional weapon of the god Thor?

5   In which Tom Hanks film is life compared to a box of chocolates?

6   Which country is bordered by Honduras to the north and Costa Rica to the south?

7   Released in 2009, iSnack 2.0 was a spin-off of which iconic food spread?

8   What word for a jug also means a person who throws a baseball?

9   Sterling silver is commonly an alloy of silver and which other metal?

10 What is the official Sydney residence of the Prime Minister of Australia?

11 What is the capital of the Philippines?

12 What is the name of the iPhone's voice-activated personal assistant?

13 Which African animal is the tallest land mammal in the world?

14 Which TV series has the tagline 'The truth is out there'?

15 In the novel *Moby-Dick*, what is the name of Captain Ahab's ship?

FINAL CHASE

1   What iconic toy was invented by Erno Rubik in the 1970s?

2   Encephalitis is the inflammation of which major organ?

3   'Bula' is the national greeting in which Pacific country?

4   Which character is the villain in Shakespeare's *Othello*?

5   Australia's national rugby union team has what nickname?

6   Which planet is orbited by the moon Ganymede?

7   What was the name of the woodworker who created Pinocchio?

8   Which Perth psychedelic rock band is fronted by Kevin Parker?

9   Who created and starred in the TV Show *30 Rock*?

10 Orecchiette pasta is named after what body part?

11 Which James Bond film was the first to star Roger Moore?

12 What domestic pet is said to be 'man's best friend'?

13 Which king did Queen Elizabeth II succeed?

14 Australia's current Parliament House is located on which hill?

15 Which ancient Egyptian deity is depicted with the head of a jackal?

THE CHASE DOWN UNDER

MULTIPLE CHOICE

1 A pH value of 7 indicates that a solution is what?

    A Acidic   **B** Neutral   **C** Alkaline

2 What was the duration of the Anglo-Zanzibar War of 1896, the shortest recorded war in history?

    A 5 weeks   **B** 12 days   **C** 38 minutes

3 In 1949, which car manufacturer introduced a van commonly referred to as a 'Kombi'?

    A Bus   **B** Telephone   **C** Glasses

4 A site to rank the attractiveness of fellow Harvard students, what did Mark Zuckerberg name the predecessor to Facebook?

    A Facerub   **B** Facepick   **C** Facemash

5 In a game of chess, which piece begins on each corner square of the board?

    A Knight   **B** Rook   **C** Bishop

6 In Greek mythology, Argus was a giant with a body covered in a hundred what?

    A Eyes   **B** Ears   **C** Arms

7 The Central Coast Mariners play in which Australian sporting competition?

    A A-League   **B** Sheffield Shield   **C** NBL

8 Which Australian comedian wrote music and lyrics for the musical based on Roald Dahl's book *Matilda*?

    A Frank Woodley   **B** Tim Minchin   **C** Paul McDermott

9 Used to describe an aerial attack in World War Two, what does the Japanese word 'kamikaze' mean?

    A Imperial glory   **B** Sacred sacrifice   **C** Divine wind

10 The trademark claim by illusionist Uri Geller was that he could use the power of telekinesis to bend what?

A Matchsticks   **B** Spoons   **C** Time

11 What letters following a name indicate that a person is a Knight of the Order of Australia?

A KA   **B** AK   **C** KOA

12 By what name is Ronald Reagan's 1983 'Strategic Defense Initiative' better known?

A Enterprise   **B** Space Odyssey   **C** Star Wars

13 In his early music career in New Zealand, Russell Crowe used what stage name?

A Rusty Crow   **B** Rockin' Russ   **C** Russ Le Roq

14 Which region of the Pacific Ocean covers the largest area?

A Polynesia   **B** Micronesia   **C** Melanesia

15 In the original 'Yo-ho-ho, and a bottle of rum', how many men were on the dead man's chest?

A 13   **B** 15   **C** 8

16 Which legendary footwear company was established in Tasmania?

A Blundstone   **B** R. M. Williams   **C** Bossi Boots

17 What is the name of a tiny bone in the middle ear?

A Incus   **B** Icarus   **C** Isthmus

18 What caused the biblical character Samson to lose his strength?

A Lie   **B** Kiss   **C** Haircut

19 What is a traditional French toasted sandwich with ham and cheese, topped with béchamel sauce and a fried egg?

A Croque garçon   **B** Croque madame   **C** Croque monsieur

THE CHASE DOWN UNDER

THE CHASE

QUESTIONS CHASERS COULDN'T GET

QUESTIONS CHASERS COULDN'T GET

When it comes to a quiz, the Chasers are a fearsome bunch – you certainly wouldn't be happy if they turned up at your local on quiz night. After all, they include a *Mastermind* Champion, a man who finished 11th last time he entered the World Quizzing Championship, someone who has been ranked the second best female quizzer on the planet, one of the best pop-culture specialists in the UK and a big bloke guaranteed to give anyone the heebie-jeebies in a pub quiz. But they don't know everything, and *The Chase* question-writing team spend their days trying to come up with questions to stump them. It doesn't always work... but sometimes it does. Here's a selection of questions that had our Chasers bamboozled. How about you?

1 Jimmy Tarbuck's game show *Full Swing* was based on what sport?

2 Which medieval king of England was born in Northamptonshire and died in Leicestershire?

A William I   **B** Richard III   **C** Henry II

3 The Imagine Peace Tower in Iceland is a memorial to who?

4 What is the name of the last stone played in an end of curling?

A Chisel   **B** Hammer   **C** Saw

5 Which J. K. Rowling character marries Ginny Weasley?

6 Forget-me-not flowers are most commonly what colour?

7 Traditionally, sailors would get a tattoo of what bird after travelling over 5,000 nautical miles?

A Swan   **B** Seagull   **C** Swallow

8 In 1937, William G. Frazier patented a device for collecting what substance, said to be a hangover remedy?

A Snake venom   **B** Clam juice   **C** Bat spit

9 In 1986, what colour balls were introduced at Wimbledon?

10 What lubricant was originally called 'Wonder Jelly'?

11 What generic name is given to the victim of a con-artist?

A Mark   **B** Matt   **C** Mike

12 What nickname is given to roofless spectator stands in a baseball stadium?

A The bleachers **B** The faders **C** The whiteners

13 The book *Penicillin Man* is about which British scientist?

14 Rose Royce had a 1978 hit with 'Wishing on a...' what?

15 In what activity might you perform a 'fleckerl'?

A Ballroom dancing **B** Billiards **C** Bull-fighting

16 Which group had the most UK Number One singles in the 1970s?

A Mud **B** Slade **C** Abba

17 'Flammable air' was an early name for what gas?

18 Running through Devon and Cornwall, the A39 has what nickname?

A Atlantic Highway **B** Road to Hell **C** Electric Avenue

19 What is the next bank holiday after Christmas Day?

20 How many players take part in a game of Chinese chess?

21 What would you be most likely to do with a Bedford Rascal?

A Drive it **B** Eat it **C** Wear it

22 What relation to you is the daughter of your nephew?

23 Which of these sportsmen would be most likely to make a play called an alley-oop?

A LeBron James **B** Lee Westwood **C** Lionel Messi

QUESTIONS CHASERS COULDN'T GET

24 Which of these is an advocaat-based cocktail?

        A Fluffy duck   **B** Fluffy dice   **C** Fluffy duster

25 What TV cartoon featured the cowardly pet tiger Cringer?

26 In American slang, 'homie' is short for what?

27 Which TV personality writes the *How to Garden* book series?

28 The Specsavers logo is what bright colour?

29 Which magic double act was known for its use of white tigers and lions?

        A Penn and Teller   **B** Siegfried and Roy   **C** Barry and Stuart

30 A media sensation in the 1930s, what creature was 'Gef' who was said to live at a farmhouse on the Isle of Man?

        A Singing spider   **B** Talking mongoose   **C** Yodelling beaver

31 Which of these was a real New York physiologist who gave his name to a type of exercise movement?

        A King Plank   **B** Royal Burpee   **C** Sovereign Starjump

32 'We Never Sleep' is the motto of what US detective agency?

33 In what city is Puccini's *La Bohème* set?

34 A reinforced covering for the toe of a boot is called what?

35 The 'Frietmuseum' in Bruges is dedicated to what foodstuff?

QUESTIONS CHASERS COULDN'T GET

36 The Ugly Duckling in the Hans Christian Andersen story is actually what type of bird?

A Cygnet   **B** Gosling   **C** Peachick

37 The name of what army rank means 'not public'?

38 In which of these sports do races start with a sequence of five red lights?

A Rowing   **B** Sailing   **C** Formula One

39 Which retailer's loyalty scheme is called 'Sparks'?

40 Bred by farmers living under Prussian occupation, what did the 'Danish Protest Pig' look like?

A The Danish flag   **B** A Danish pastry   **C** The Danish king

41 'We'll all have tea' is a line from what nursery rhyme?

42 Maxim and Gatling were inventors of what sort of gun?

43 Tetratomic describes a molecule with how many atoms?

44 Singer Stephanie Nicks is better known by what name?

45 A quilt is usually a covering for what item of furniture?

46 'Old Ned' and 'Old Harry' are nicknames for what figure?

47 What insects live in a termitary?

48 What nature conservation charity launched 'Operation Lapwing'?

49 What did Andy Murray start tying to his tennis shoes in 2015?

A Front door key   **B** Wedding ring   **C** Piece of haggis

50 Which author was played by Ian Hart in the film *Finding Neverland*?

A Arthur Conan Doyle   **B** Rudyard Kipling   **C** Anton Chekhov

51 Which of these is NOT a character from *Under Milk Wood*?

A Willy Nilly   **B** Organ Morgan   **C** Dickie Brickie

52 What part of the body can go before 'mark', 'muff' and 'ring'?

53 What common name is given to marker pens with fluorescent ink?

54 Which of these planets does NOT have rings around it?

A Saturn   **B** Venus   **C** Uranus

55 'Nanu nanu' was a greeting in what Robin Williams sitcom?

56 In what BBC soap is there a hair salon called Blades?

57 Danny Zuko is leader of what gang in the musical *Grease*?

58 What number 'out of ten' is said to be a complete success?

59 What Argentinian dance appears in the NATO alphabet?

60 Which London royal residence has 775 rooms?

61 What game features a double-blank and a double-six tile?

62 British road signs that give information are all what shape?

> **A** Triangular   **B** Circular   **C** Rectangular

63 In 2013, what clothing item was banned in male elite amateur boxing?

> **A** Head guards   **B** Vests   **C** Underwear

64 British actor Edward Hardy uses what first name professionally?

65 Opera legend Placido Domingo was born in what country?

66 Which Spice Girl designed the VB Rocks jean collection?

67 The splenic pulp is the tissue of what organ?

68 What term describes funds that are provided to start a new business?

> **A** Seed money   **B** Root payments   **C** Stem cash

69 Butterkist is the UK's biggest seller of what snack food?

70 What type of alcoholic drink is Laurent-Perrier?

71 On what part of a building is a fresco usually painted?

72 Plus twos are a variety of what kind of clothing?

73 What Roman god gives his name to the 'bow' above the upper lip?

74 In what popular kids' game can you put a cowboy hat on a mule?

75 Leonardo Da Vinci's *Last Supper* is painted onto the wall of what type of building in Milan?

A Convent   **B** Castle   **C** Restaurant

76 'Vassermann' is the German name for what sign of the zodiac?

77 What colour are the seeds of a red poppy flower?

78 The name of what Asian currency is a word for a yearning?

79 What type of accessory is an Omega Speedmaster?

80 Actually made from parts of a monkey and a fish, which of these is an exhibit at the British Museum?

A Unicorn   **B** Merman   **C** Dragon

81 If a car is travelling at 60 miles per hour, what distance is covered in a minute?

A Half a mile   **B** A mile   **C** Two miles

82 In a typical round of golf, which club is used most frequently?

A Driver   **B** Putter   **C** Sand wedge

83 World darts champion Bob Anderson was picked for the 1968 British Olympic team for what event?

A Discus   **B** Shot put   **C** Javelin

84 In a standard UK plug, what terminal is connected to the fuse?

A Live   **B** Neutral   **C** Earth

85 What word appears in the titles of over 200 novels by romantic novelist Barbara Cartland?

A Love **B** Pink **C** Desire

86 Who plays the title character in the TV detective drama *Vera*?

A Brenda Blethyn **B** Pauline Quirke **C** Caroline Quentin

87 Which royal house provided the first kings of the United Kingdom?

A York **B** Stuart **C** Tudor

88 Peter Phillips' wife shares her name with what season?

89 Which of these dishes is a flaming dessert?

A Baked Alaska **B** Crêpe Suzette **C** Rum Baba

90 Jelly is a slang name for what explosive substance?

91 Which of these amphibians does NOT have a tail?

A Newt **B** Salamander **C** Toad

92 What colour are TV's The Simpsons?

93 What do you normally do with samphire?

A Burn it **B** Eat it **C** Wear it

94 'Going for an English' was a famous sketch in what TV comedy series?

A *The Fast Show* **B** *Goodness Gracious Me* **C** *Monty Python's Flying Circus*

95 The acnestis is the difficult-to-scratch place between what parts of the human body?

A Toes   **B** Shoulder blades   **C** Ribs

96 Vera Wang, Ángel Sánchez and Jenny Packham are all well-known for designing what?

A Wedding dresses   **B** Home interiors   **C** Handbags

97 Which of these conditions is treated in alternative medicine by using the stings of honey bees?

A Rheumatism   **B** Heartburn   **C** Athlete's foot

98 Which of these gems consists mainly of calcium carbonate?

A Amethyst   **B** Diamond   **C** Pearl

99 Which of these is a children's toy that asks players to 'twist me', 'stretch me', 'poke me', 'shake me' and 'dip me'?

A Crazy Cucumber   **B** Bonkers Banana   **C** Silly Sausage

100 Rose Pouchong is a blend of what drink?

101 Which of these is NOT a type of savoury vegetable pie?

A Homity pie   **B** Gala pie   **C** Woolton pie

102 In TV's *Dallas* who was the youngest of the Ewing brothers?

103 How many 'G's are in the word 'luggage'?

104 Which of these songs was a hit for Fleetwood Mac?

A 'Everywhere'   **B** 'Nowhere'   **C** 'Somewhere'

105 In real-life Quidditch, what is used to replace the magical golden snitch?

    A Marble in a balloon   **B** Tennis ball in a sock   **C** Orange in a hanky

106 In 2016, Blur's Alex James revealed that for 10 years he hadn't washed what?

    A His feet   **B** His hair   **C** His underpants

107 What colour shade was used by NASA for its space shuttle suits?

    A Worldwide white   **B** International orange   **C** Black hole blue

QUESTIONS CHASERS COULDN'T GET

THE CHASE

OLAV'S
FAVOURITE
QUESTIONS

OLAV'S FAVOURITE QUESTIONS

The Chase question-writing team is a hot-bed of quizzing talent, dedicated to producing the finest questions ever seen on a tea-time quiz show. But one member has a slightly better quizzing CV than his fellow writers. Olav Bjortomt is a four-time World Quizzing Champion, the youngest ever World Champion, four-time European Champion, a Quiz Olympics champion and an international quizzer for England. The lad can quiz a bit! He started his TV quiz career as a 17-year-old contestant on *Fifteen to One*, but even though he's appeared on many different programmes he says the sum total of his TV winnings is £50 and he's happier behind the camera. International quizzing is a different kettle of fish, however. Olav claims he knows more about Soviet rock music and Mongolian painters than he does about the Grand National and British pub names, and that's the sort of knowledge it takes to be World Champ. Aside from *The Chase*, he also writes the fiendishly difficult quiz in *The Times* every day and general knowledge questions for *University Challenge*, as well as competing weekly in the Quiz League of London. He is, without doubt, a world-class quizzer whom *The Chase* is happy to have on board!

How would you get on with Olav's questions? Here are some of his favourites.

1 Which quiz show host played James Bond in a 1956 radio adaptation of Ian Fleming's novel *Moonraker*?

    A Bob Holness   **B** Bamber Gascoigne   **C** Ted Rogers

2 What did George Bernard Shaw say the English people had invented 'to give them some idea of eternity'?

    A Cricket   **B** Bird-watching   **C** Knitting

3 The philosopher Albert Camus said 'Everything I know about morality and the obligations of men, I owe to...' what?

    A Football   **B** Being French   **C** Tintin

4 'No no, no no no no, no no no no, no' are lyrics from which '90s pop hit?

    A 'No Limit'   **B** 'No No No'   **C** 'Yes'

5 In which children's game can you play with bumboozers, commies and peewees?

    A Marbles   **B** Tiddlywinks   **C** Doctors and nurses

6 The Chinese performance artist Ou Zhihang is known for doing what in front of famous monuments?

    A Escapology   **B** Pillow fighting   **C** Nude push-ups

7 Canadian restaurant owner Sam Panopoulos claims to have invented which pizza style in 1962?

    A Four Seasons   **B** Hawaiian   **C** Margherita

8 Thanks to a long-standing tradition, the Glasgow statue of which duke is often seen wearing a traffic cone on his head?

    A Duke of Marlborough   **B** Duke of Edinburgh   **C** Duke of Wellington

9 What did the painter Vincent van Gogh allegedly give to a woman named Rachel, telling her, 'Guard this object carefully'?

A Part of his left ear   **B** His painting *Sunflowers*   **C** His little black book

10 In *The Office*, which character puts 'Eczema' under 'Weaknesses' in his staff appraisal?

A Keith Bishop   **B** Tim Canterbury   **C** Neil Godwin

11 Which of these is a two-letter word that is allowed in Scrabble?

A Hm   **B** Gr   **C** Ew

12 Sung in such hits as 'California Gurls' by Katy Perry, the 'Millennial Whoop' sound pattern uses which two syllables?

A Da-ba   **B** Eh-oo   **C** Wa-oh

13 In the sitcom *Peep Show*, which cereal did Mark describe as 'Cornflakes for people who can't face reality'?

A Rice Krispies   **B** Frosties   **C** Bran Flakes

14 In 1899, the Commissioner of what US agency allegedly claimed that 'everything that can be invented has been invented'?

A National Science Foundation   **B** Department of Energy
C Patent and Trademark Office

15 In a 1784 letter to his daughter, what did Benjamin Franklin describe as 'a bird of bad moral character'?

A Bald eagle   **B** Mountain bluebird   **C** Wild turkey

16 In 2008, the Russian city of Zheleznovodsk unveiled a monument to which medical procedure?

A Hair transplant   **B** Lumbar puncture   **C** Enema

OLAV'S FAVOURITE QUESTIONS

17 On *Desert Island Discs*, George Clooney chose which novel 'as there may not be toilet paper, and that's a huge book'?

A *Don Quixote*   **B** *Les Misérables*   **C** *War and Peace*

18 Looking like a 'hot dog with buck teeth and a tail', the famously ugly naked mole rat is native to which continent?

A Asia   **B** North America   **C** Africa

19 Which make of car is given a 'good thrashing' by Basil in an episode of *Fawlty Towers*?

A Austin   **B** Ford   **C** Vauxhall

20 Created the 1st Baron Brain in 1962, Walter Russell Brain was a specialist in what medical field?

A Cardiology   **B** Neurology   **C** Rheumatology

21 'Scuse me, while I kiss this guy' is a famously misheard lyric from which Jimi Hendrix song?

A 'Hey Joe'   **B** 'All Along the Watchtower'   **C** 'Purple Haze'

22 What did the computer engineer Ray Tomlinson invent in 1971, saying 'it seemed like a neat idea'?

A Email   **B** The Internet   **C** Video games

23 For whom did the Danish company Carlsberg create the beer Special Brew?

A Hans Christian Anderson   **B** Sigmund Freud   **C** Winston Churchill

24 At a 1992 State dinner, US President George Bush vomited into the lap of which country's Prime Minister?

A China   **B** India   **C** Japan

OLAV'S FAVOURITE QUESTIONS

25   Which of these statements about the subject of Frans Hals' painting *The Laughing Cavalier* is true?

A He is a cavalier   **B** He is laughing   **C** He is aged 26

26   In which Tom Clancy novel does Jack Ryan save the Prince and Princess of Wales from an IRA splinter group?

A *Clear and Present Danger*   **B** *Patriot Games*   **C** *The Sum of All Fears*

27   Linked to Yom Kippur, the Jewish custom of Kaparot involves whirling which item above your head while praying?

A A shawl   **B** A bunch of flowers   **C** A chicken

28   Who was the last private resident of 10 Downing Street?

A Mr Chicken   **B** Mr Hen   **C** Mr Duck

29   In 1999, which country became the last in the world to grant its citizens access to television?

A Bhutan   **B** Brunei   **C** Bahrain

30   What was the maiden name of the mother of Apollo 11 astronaut Buzz Aldrin?

A Armstrong   **B** Moon   **C** Lightyear

31   The OED claims that which 'notable initialism' first appeared in a 1917 letter from an admiral to Winston Churchill?

A FYI   **B** TTFN   **C** OMG

32   In a *Smash Hits* interview, which politician said their favourite record was 'How Much Is that Doggie in the Window?'

A Paddy Ashdown   **B** Tony Benn   **C** Margaret Thatcher

OLAV'S FAVOURITE QUESTIONS

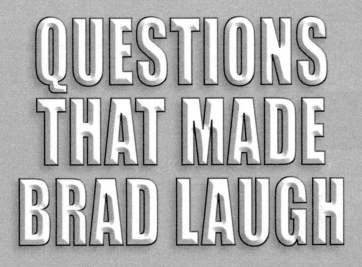

THE CHASE

QUESTIONS
THAT MADE
BRAD LAUGH

QUESTIONS THAT MADE BRAD LAUGH

When they're not off winning quizzing competitions around the globe, *The Chase* question-writing team like nothing better than trying to make Bradley Walsh laugh. He doesn't see the questions before he reads them to the contestants, so there's ample opportunity for the question setters to sneak in a cheeky question or two in the hope it will crack Brad up. To be fair, making Brad crack up, or 'corpse' to use the theatrical phrase, isn't the most difficult thing in the world, and once he gets going the Chaser usually finds it hard to keep a straight face too. The show can grind to a laughter-inflicted halt in no time at all. The most famous corpsing moment in *Chase* history concerned a perfectly innocent question about a German alpine skier who competed for her country at the 2010 Winter Olympics in Vancouver. So, let's start our selection of questions that made Brad laugh with this one. Ask yourself, what's so funny about Fanny Chmelar?

1 In what sport does Fanny Chmelar compete for Germany?

    A Swimming **B** Show jumping **C** Skiing

2 Used to make a variety of the alcoholic drink eau-de-vie, what are 'quetsch'?

    A Dalmatian nuts **B** Alsatian plums **C** Pyrenean grapes

3 What is the cartoon character Andy Capp known as in Germany?

    A Dick Tingeler **B** Helmut Schmacker **C** Willi Wakker

4 The giant cock that was placed on the fourth plinth in Trafalgar Square in 2013 is what colour?

    A Red **B** White **C** Blue

5 Dump, floater and wipe are terms used in which team sport?

    A Badminton **B** Volleyball **C** Water polo

6 In the 1990s, the character Chef from *South Park* had a Number One hit with which song?

    A 'Hot Spicy Sausage' **B** 'Fresh Juicy Melons' **C** 'Chocolate Salty Balls'

7 What was the first name of Mother Teresa at birth?

    A Agnes **B** Audrey **C** Alma

8 According to the lyrics of a '70s hit song by the group America, 'I've been through the desert on a horse with no...' what?

    A Name **B** Mane **C** Legs

9 In 2017, aerialist Erendira Wallenda set a record by dangling from a helicopter over the Niagara Falls by her what?

    A Teeth **B** Thumbs **C** Knicker elastic

10 Which of these represented the Seychelles in the 800 metres at the 2012 World Indoor Athletics Championships?

    A Gaylord Silly **B** Pansy Picker **C** Horace Mincy Walker

11 One-Handed Clean and Jerk was an Olympic event in what sport?

    A Gymnastics   **B** Shooting   **C** Weightlifting

12 What change was introduced by the ITF in 2002 to increase the number of rallies in tennis games?

    A Smaller racquets   **B** Slower courts   **C** Bigger balls

13 The rambutan fruit is also known by what other name?

    A Dirty lychee   **B** Hairy lychee   **C** Smelly lychee

14 According to the saying, what must you not 'let under the tent'?

    A The camel's hump   **B** The camel's nose   **C** The camel's toe

15 In the 1940s, which player scandalised the tennis world with her lacy knickers?

    A Doris Hart   **B** Nelly Landry   **C** Gussie Moran

16 19th-century composer William Crotch was also famous as a player of what instrument?

    A Oboe   **B** Bagpipes   **C** Organ

17 Van Morrison sang about which of these in his song of the same name?

    A 'Blue-Eyed Girl'   **B** 'Brown-Eyed Girl'   **C** 'Boss-Eyed Girl'

18 Complete the common saying: 'Softly, softly, catchee...' what?

    A Monkey   **B** Lion   **C** Crabs

19 In 2009, Sunderland scored against Liverpool when the football deflected in off what object?

    A Beach ball   **B** Ice-cream van   **C** Sunbathing German

20 'Cock shot' and 'beaver' are terms in what game?

    A Backgammon   **B** Ker-Plunk   **C** Twister

21 Which of these fruits has hairy drupelets?

    A Coconut   **B** Gooseberry   **C** Raspberry

QUESTIONS THAT MADE BRAD LAUGH

22 James Galway is nicknamed the 'Man with the Golden...' what?

A Gun   **B** Flute   **C** Balls

23 What is the correct term for a bird after it has hit an aircraft?

A Snarge   **B** Squab   **C** Splat

24 In mythology, what objects are associated with the deity Eros?

A Bow and arrow   **B** Ball and chain   **C** Bucket and spade

25 Neurologist Oliver Sacks's book of case studies is titled *The Man Who Mistook His Wife for a... what?*

A *Hat*   **B** *Tree*   **C** *Pork chop*

26 What 1993 film is concerned with activities around Gobbler's Knob?

A *Grumpy Old Men*   **B** *Jurassic Park*   **C** *Groundhog Day*

27 British rapper Tyrone Lindo is better known by what stage name?

A Big Narstie   **B** Massive Dirty   **C** Colossal Brown

28 What name is adopted by actors in the British theatre who wish to remain anonymous?

A Alan Smithee   **B** Roderick Jaynes   **C** Walter Plinge

29 What was the name of Theodore Roosevelt's second son?

A Fozzie   **B** Gonzo   **C** Kermit

30 According to A. A. Milne, what does Winnie-the-Pooh say every morning when he wakes up?

A What's for breakfast?   **B** Where am I?   **C** Who are you?

31 In 1948, who became Burma's first Prime Minister?

A U Nu   **B** I Nu   **C** We All Nu

32 Complete the title of the Frank Sinatra song: 'I've Got You Under My...' what?

A Thumb   **B** Skin   **C** Duvet

33 Which of these people could be seen regularly on '90s TV in a red swimsuit?

A Pamela Anderson **B** Pamela Stephenson **C** Pam St Clement

34 Aled Jones forgot the words to what song while singing at a Royal Variety Performance?

A 'Walking in the Air' **B** 'Land of My Fathers' **C** 'Memory'

35 What is unusual about a wombat's droppings?

A They are a delicacy **B** They are pink **C** They are cube-shaped

36 The Great Fire of London started in Pudding Lane and ended where?

A Pie Corner **B** Crumble Alley **C** Pastry Passage

37 Of what creature did Ozzy Osbourne say, 'It was like eating a Crunchie wrapped in chamois leather'?

A Bat **B** Badger **C** Beaver

38 What was the name of the section of the River Cherwell in Oxford formerly reserved for nude male bathing?

A Parson's Pleasure **B** Deacon's Delight **C** Rector's Relish

39 What is the name of Al Gore's wife of more than 40 years?

A Chipper **B** Tipper **C** Flipper

QUESTIONS THAT MADE BRAD LAUGH

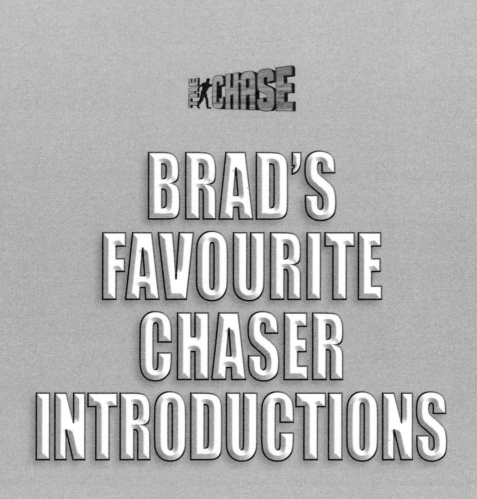

THE CHASE

BRAD'S FAVOURITE CHASER INTRODUCTIONS

BRAD'S FAVOURITE CHASER INTRODUCTIONS

One of Brad's favourite bits of the show is the Chaser intros, where he can make a joke about each of the Chasers before we find out who's coming over the bridge. The topics don't change much: the Beast likes his food, Paul is full of himself and wears a dodgy suit, the Vixen is hotter than the Sahara, Shaun is the most boring man on the planet, and never ask what goes on in Anne's cellar... But it's amazing how many gags you can get from that. Here, Chaser by Chaser, are some of the best.

THE GOVERNESS

When recording *The Chase*, Bradley and the Chasers are kept apart so he never has any idea which Chaser is coming across the bridge. This can sometimes cause him problems if his introductions are a little too cheeky! Anne, in particular, takes umbrage if she thinks Brad has overstepped the mark. Here are some of Bradley's favourite Governess lines…

BRAD'S FAVOURITE CHASER INTRODUCTIONS

She's a stunner – at least that was her job in the abbatoir…

Just looking at her face makes me think, is it Movember already?

She recently kicked a habit – unfortunately the nun was still wearing it.

She's the lollipop lady on the road to hell…

She's joined the Lords Taverners. They appreciate an old bat…

If she was Juliet, Romeo would have chucked himself off the balcony…

Looks like someone left the crypt open…

Not so much Lucy Lui, more Porta-loo…

Looks that make you think phwoar… out of ten. Or maybe three.

As pretty as a picture – the one in Dorian Gray's attic…

So cold, her washing machine has a defrost cycle…

She's been living with me ever since I went to the supermarket…
all I asked for was a bag for life…

316

Brad Pitt tried to pick her up once... I think he still has to wear a truss...

_____

She's got a personal nail technician... I say nail technician, actually, he's an arc welder...

_____

She has trouble getting up in the morning... I think the coffin lid needs oiling...

_____

She's the next leader of the SNP... after a Salmon and a Sturgeon, they're going for an old trout...

_____

She got mistaken for a movie star last week... I think it was Chuck Norris...

_____

The only person who puts anti-freeze on her cornflakes...

_____

She lost her job as the Tooth Fairy when they caught her carrying pliers...

_____

She was on the pull at the weekend... she's taken up tug-of-war...

_____

THE BEAST

The Beast, on the other hand, doesn't care what Bradley says about him. He's too busy thinking about catching the contestants and what he's having for tea. Here are Brad's favourite Beastly introductions…

Things that big normally eat krill…

He's eaten his laptop. A website told him there were cookies in it…

He's remaking the Hitchcock classic, 'Dial M for Murder'. Now it's Dial P for pizza…

It's like someone shaved a yeti…

The last time he gave up pasta, Italy went into recession…

He's been on holiday – two weeks at the Great Wall of China…
next year he's going to an Indian restaurant…

He accused me of swearing at him yesterday… all I said was 'small portion'…

The Queen asked him if he'd like a CBE or OBE, but he preferred a KFC…

Grumpy, overbearing, mean… yes, he's in a good mood today…

The last time I saw something that size, it was climbing up the Empire State Building holding Faye Wray…

The only man whose blood type is nutella…

He always has elevenses… and tensies and twelvsies and half past twosies…

The only man I know who puts ketchup on his cornflakes…

He's been on a stag weekend… next weekend he's going to eat a water buffalo…

Look at him… the original wide boy…

I tried to get on his good side, but it was going to take a train and two buses to get there…

I asked him what he wanted for breakfast and he said dinner…

The only man who supersizes his cornflakes…

He's got a bucket list… it starts with a bucket of chicken and a bucket of fries…

So big, his bath-tub has its own cruise line…

BRAD'S FAVOURITE CHASER INTRODUCTIONS

THE SINNERMAN

Bradley's intros sometimes suggest that the Sinnerman is a touch smug – then again, when you've been as high as the 11th best quizzer on the planet, you've got plenty to be smug about. Here are some of Bradley's favourite Paul Sinha introductions...

So smug, the make-up department have to wipe that grin off his face with Cillit Bang...

As sharp as a tack, as annoying as standing on one...

More lip than a Mick Jagger tribute act...

He's like a toddler's finger – he gets right up your nose...

He can deliver some lovely, charming compliments – just give him a mirror...

A head full of facts and a wardrobe full of horrors...

Everyone says he's unbeatable... my mistake, that says 'unbearable'...

So self-important, when he was born he wouldn't come out until the midwife put down a red carpet...

More irritating than Andrex's new sandpaper range...

More annoying than assembling flat-pack furniture without instructions...

Some people drink from the fountain of knowledge... he's been swimming in it...

A mind so fast, Mensa issued him with a speeding ticket...

How cocky is he? Imagine the love child of Simon Cowell and Piers Morgan…

He wanted to join the Marx Brothers… it would have been Harpo, Chico, Groucho and Sarko…

More little grey cells than the set of 'Porridge'…

IQ in the 170s… fashion sense in the 1970s…

More annoying than a bed and breakfast with nylon sheets…

He's so irritating, we issue all his contestants with calamine lotion…

He was voted Man of the Year by the British Polyester Industry…

So fast, he finishes the show at six and he's home by half past five…

THE VIXEN

What does Brad have to say about the feisty, fiery Vixen? Mainly that she's hotter than a very, very hot thing and nothing else too disparaging. After all, you don't want to upset a Bolton lass. Here are a few of Brad's favourite Jenny introductions...

The hottest thing in Bolton since Greggs left the oven on...

So hot, the last time she went to an aquarium it started selling fish suppers...

She's such an independent lady, she makes Beyoncé look like a stay-at-home housewife...

Hotter than tucking into a vindaloo in a sauna...

So hot, she could turn Peppa Pig into Kevin Bacon...

At Christmas, she can stuff the turkey and cook it at the same time...

So hot, when she's in panto she always plays Cinders...

I asked her what you give a man who has everything... she said a woman to show him how to work it...

Money vanishes when you play her... she's like the Bolton Bermuda Triangle...

So hot, if she was Princess Leah, Han Solo would have to shave his Wookiee...

You've heard politicians talk about a northern powerhouse... now you get to meet her...

She says blondes might have more fun but redheads catch more contestants...

So hot, her star sign is Scorchio…

The toughest thing to come out of Bolton since Amir Khan…

So hot, the last time she went to the zoo the penguins went on strike…

I'm not saying she's a man-eater, but she if she asks you what you weigh it's to work out the cooking time…

If she was Princess Jasmin, Aladdin would have got magic carpet burns…

So hot, she joined her local ice-hockey team and now they play water polo…

I call her the Vixen because she's foxy, sly and last week I caught her going through my dustbins…

So hot, she makes the Red Hot Chili Peppers look like Coldplay…

BRAD'S FAVOURITE CHASER INTRODUCTIONS

THE BARRISTER

Some people say that Shaun Wallace, our barrister and *Mastermind* Champion, is boring. But Bradley says he's nowhere near that interesting. What he definitely is, though, is a good sport who takes a lot of stick from our host – like in these favourite intros…

He's a qualified barrister and the reason some judges fall asleep during trials…

His head is a mobile computer – it's a slap-top…

The face of a halibut arriving at the Findus factory…

He got nits last week. It's all right now. They slid off…

Less Stormzy, more Drizzly…

Looks like a deflated space hopper getting bad news…

So wooden, the last time he went to the doctor it was for dry rot…

Fun fact – he isn't.

He went to a murder mystery party last night – he killed the atmosphere.

Gets the hump more often than a Dubai camel trainer…

He was in hospital last week after he accidentally cracked a smile…

He's a real party animal… unfortunately, it's a sloth.

I'm not saying he's got no friends but even his boomerang wouldn't come back…

So dull, even his highlighter pen is beige…

_____

As much fun as filing your VAT return online…

_____

He went wild last night… had a chocolate Hob-Nob with his cocoa…

_____

I've seen more life in a week-old kipper…

_____

He's so wooden, Health and Safety have declared him a fire risk…

_____

This is what happens if you have a full body botox…

_____

So dull, when he was a kid he didn't have an imaginary friend, he had an imaginary accountant…

_____

BRAD'S FAVOURITE CHASER INTRODUCTIONS

THE CHASE

THE CHASE AROUND THE WORLD

THE CHASE AROUND
THE WORLD

The Chase isn't just Britain's favourite tea-time quiz show; it's been a big hit all around the world. Apart from the USA and Australia, nine other countries have produced their own versions to date.

First up was **Germany**, back in July 2012, where it's known as *Grefragt-Gejagt*, which translates as 'Asked-Hunted'. It's been a big hit and is still running. It's presented by Alexander Bommes, a former professional handball player turned journalist and TV host. They have seven Chasers in rotation on the show, including the 2012 European Quiz Champion, Holger Waldenberger, known as the Giant, and Sebastian Klussmann, the founding chairman of the German Quizzing Association, who is called, quite accurately, Der Besserwisser – the 'Know-it-all' or 'Smart Aleck'. The others are Sebastian Jacoby, a former gold-medal winning curler, known as the Quiz God, Klaus Otto Nagorsnik, a quizzer and librarian known, unsurprisingly, as the Librarian, Manuel Hobiger, a seismologist known as the Quiz Volcano, and Thomas Kinne, a translator and film buff, nicknamed the Quiz Doctor. The only female Chaser is Grazyna Werner, a Polish language teacher who, apart from her native tongue, speaks German, Spanish, Italian, French, Russian and English. She's known as the Governess... though woe betide her when Anne Hegerty finds out!

Also starting back in 2012 was the **Russian** version, known as *Pursuit*. It was hosted by TV presenter and veteran of many different Russian quiz shows, Alexander Gurevich, and the four Chasers were Alexander Ediger, Olga Uspanova, Yuriy Hashimov and the Ukrainian journalist Boris Burda. Sadly, it's no longer running so we can't ask them what their Chaser names were.

As well as the **US** version of the show, 2013 saw *Potera* – literally meaning 'Chase'– start in **Serbia**, where it's still being screened. It's presented by sports journalist Jovan Memedovic, and the current Chasers are the well-known Serbian film director Milorad Milinkovic, lawyer and quiz champion Milica Jokanovic, and the boy genius, 25-year-old Zarko Stevanovic. They like a mixed bag of Chasers in Serbia as, until recently, the former punk-rock drummer and now conceptual artist Uros Duric was one of their number.

In the same year, the successful **Croatian** production started. Like the Serbians, the Croats use the literal translation of *The Chase* and call the show *Potjera*. The original presenter was the Bosnian actor Tarik Filipovic, but he left in 2019 and was replaced by Josko Lokas, a producer and presenter whose love life has long been a fascination of the Serbian red-top papers. The current roster of Chasers is Dean Kotiga, a professor of comparative literature, Morana Zibar, a writer and translator as well as a mum to young daughter Katja, Kresimir Sucevic-Mederal, a socio-linguistics scholar from the University of Zagreb (who was known as Rodney when he was young because he looked like Nicholas Lyndhurst), and electrical engineer and keen pub quizzer Mladen Vukorepa.

In 2014, the short-lived **Chinese** production aired. It was called *Tiaozhan Wenhua Mingren* or 'Challenge the Cultural Masters'– not the snappiest of titles, which may explain its short run. It was presented by Liu Wei and the Chasers were professor of history and culture Meng Man, history teacher Ji Lianhai, writer A Yi, arts professor Kang Zhen and Li Bo.

A more successful 2014 version of the show was in **Norway** where it was called *Jaget* ('Chased'). It was presented by stand-up comedian Sturla Berg-Johansen and ran until 2016. The Chasers were Trine Aalborg who, like Jenny Ryan, started out writing questions for quiz shows before appearing on them, professional quizmaster Jan Arild Breistein, who sadly passed away in 2019, and Thomas Kolasaeter, who claims modestly to be Norway's best quizzer!

Also starting in 2014 and running until 2015 was the **Turkish** version of the show. *Takip*, or 'Follow', was presented by Turkish actor Uraz Kaygilaroglu, well known in Turkey for playing Can in the comedy series *Pis Yedili*. The single Chaser was TV quiz-show veteran Muhsin Divan, who had the misfortune to be burgled while he was recording the show. The thieves got away with a valuable assortment of watches it had taken him over 30 years to collect.

After the **Australian** version premiered in 2015, the next country was **Israel** in 2017. *Hamirdaf* ('The Chase') is hosted by Ido Rosenblum, a TV presenter who wrote the successful Israeli film *The Debt*. The original Chaser is Itai Hermann, a TV professional who had written questions for quiz shows. Journalist Ron Kofman was a guest Chaser in 2017 and 2018, and sports reporter Nadav Jacobi guested in 2018. Biochemistry professor Michal Sharon joined as a full-time Chaser in 2018. She had been a contestant on the show and impressed everyone with a towering 12 correct answers in her Cash Builder!

The latest version of the show to hit TV screens is the **Finnish** *Jahti* – again a literal translation of 'The Chase'. It's hosted by actor and musician Mikko Leppilampi, who presented the Eurovision Song Contest in 2007. There are three Chasers – Eero Ylitalo, an information service manager known as Herra Arkisto (Mr Archive), Magnus Mali, a quiz writer who won €45,000 on *Who Wants to Be a Millionaire* when he was just 21 years old and is known as Sharp, and Markus Leikola, a political journalist, poet and novelist, who is known as Besserwisser or 'Know-it-all'… and you're right, that nickname is shamelessly lifted from the German version of the show!

So, that's the worldwide reach of *The Chase* so far. No doubt there will be more foreign productions, so next time you're on holiday, check out the tea-time TV!

THE CHASE AROUND THE WORLD

THE CHASE

CHASER TRIVIA

THE CHASE

CHASER TRIVIA

It's taken quite a while to assemble the formidable team of quizzers that are our Chasers. In the beginning, there were just two: Shaun Wallace and Mark Labbett. Soon the producers felt that a woman's touch was required, so the dynamic duo were joined by Anne Hegerty. This titanic trio soldiered on for two more series, when reinforcements arrived in the shape of the Sinnerman, Paul Sinha. With each addition, the Chasers became more and more intimidating. Surely the fantastic four were the strongest quizzing team in town? Maybe, but they got even stronger when a foxy young quizzer was signed up; with the Vixen, Jenny Ryan, on board, the fantastic four became the fabulous five – every one of them an amazing quizzer. But there's more to them than just quizzing, so here are a few Chaser facts you might not be aware of...

ANNE HEGERTY

Anne 'the Governess' Hegerty joined *The Chase* for Series 2 back in 2010 and, so far, she is the only Chaser to present an ITV quiz show as well as appear on one, hosting the successful *Britain's Brightest Family* since 2018. That year also saw her take part in *I'm a Celebrity... Get Me Out Of Here*, where she proved hugely popular, finishing seventh but extremely happy to leave at that point and glad to get back to civilisation.

Her quizzing pedigree is indisputable. In 2016, she was the second highest ranked female quizzer on the planet. She's also a regular Chaser on the Australian version of the show which, as she says, proves that she's big Down Under.

Anne's a big music fan, particularly fond of '50s and '60s doo-wop, and says she was a bit of a punk in her youth. She would like to make it clear though, that despite what Bradley Walsh says on the show, she has never worked as a professional wrestler!

She's become a firm favourite with pantomime audiences. In 2018, she came back from the jungle and went straight into a production of *Dick Whittington* in Windsor. She'd missed the first few weeks while her friend Anita Harris stood in for her.

And one final fact... Did you know that despite being born in London and living in Manchester, Anne quizzes internationally for Scotland? She did study at Edinburgh University and there's Scottish blood in her family.

JENNY RYAN

Jenny 'the Vixen' Ryan comes from a family with a passion for quizzing, so it's no surprise that our Bolton brainiac ended up as good as she did. Before she joined *The Chase* in 2015, she won the third series of *Only Connect*, reached the semi-finals of *University Challenge* with the University of Leeds and appeared on *Mastermind* answering questions on *Buffy the Vampire Slayer*.

Jenny is very musical and plays the ukulele with a band called Nanukes of the North (they're very big in Bolton!), who play all sorts of stuff, from 'Delilah' to punk classics. She also has a very good singing voice, as she demonstrated when the Chasers won *Let's Sing and Dance* for Comic Relief in 2017, with Jenny giving us her rendition of 'Somewhere Over the Rainbow'.

Proud of her Bolton roots, Jenny is a long-suffering supporter of the Trotters, Bolton Wanderers FC, but she's also a big cricket fan and can't think of anything better than a day in the sunshine at an Ashes test match. That is, apart from sampling her favourite bit of Bolton cuisine, a pasty barm – a pasty in a bread roll!

She describes herself as a professional cleverclogs, which is fitting as, before she was a Chaser, she actually wrote questions for the show!

And one final fact... Did you know that Jenny used to be a QI Elf?

CHASER TRIVIA

PAUL SINHA

Aside from being a formidable Chaser, Paul 'the Sinnerman' Sinha is a stand-up comedian and a qualified doctor. He regularly broadcasts on Radio 4, and one of his series won a prestigious Rose d'Or award for radio comedy in 2016.

Paul is highly respected on the international quizzing circuit. In 2018, he finished 11th in the World Quizzing Championship – that's 11th out of the entire population of the world!

Paul was educated at Dulwich College in South London; other famous old boys include writers P. G. Wodehouse and Raymond Chandler, *12 Years a Slave* actor Chiwetel Ejiofor, explorer Ernest Shackleton, cricketer and commentator Trevor Bailey... oh, and Nigel Farage.

A lover of all sport, when it comes to football Paul is a Liverpool fan. There's no long-standing family relationship with the club; it's just that when Paul was growing up in the '70s and '80s, they were rather good and he was a self-confessed glory hunter!

And one final fact... Did you know that Paul was born in Luton?

CHASER TRIVIA

MARK LABBETT

Mark 'the Beast' Labbett has, like Shaun Wallace, been on *The Chase* since Series 1. His nickname is doubly appropriate. Firstly he is an absolute Beast in a quiz, putting fear into contestants for the last 10 years; secondly, his name is the French for 'the Beast' – la Bête!

He's probably the most international quizzer in the world, as he has not only appeared on *The Chase* in the UK, but also in the USA and Australia. They say that travel broadens the mind and, judging by his quizzing, they're right. It also helps his air miles balance.

Appropriately for an ex-maths teacher, Mark spent a lot of time in education, attending not one but three separate universities! He was at Exeter College, Oxford, then the University of Exeter and finally the University of Glamorgan. He says he paid his way through university by winning on pub quiz machines!

His sports knowledge on *The Chase* is clear for all to see, but when he was younger Mark was a top-class rugby player (he was in the second row of the scrum) and a more-than-useful basketball player, not to mention putting the shot at university – all sports in which it helps to be six foot seven.

And one final fact… Did you know that despite his height, Mark's not the tallest in his family? He says his younger brother calls him Titch!

CHASER TRIVIA

SHAUN WALLACE

As well as his role on *The Chase*, Shaun 'the Barrister' Wallace is a practising barrister specialising in criminal law. He was one of the first Chasers, with Mark Labbett, in Series 1. He's also the only Chaser to have been a *Mastermind* Champion, winning in 2004. Sadly he no longer has his trophy – he was showing it to pupils during a school visit when he dropped it and it smashed to pieces!

Shaun is a real Renaissance man on *The Chase*, famed for his quizzing, obviously, but also for his singing and his poetry. There is no song he won't attempt to sing and as for his poetry, who can forget such classics as 'Joe, You've Got to Go'? Despite this talent, he is yet to release a record or a volume of verse. The world awaits eagerly.

He released the first volume of his autobiography, *Chasing the Dream*, in 2018 but *The Chase* fans will have to wait until Volume 2 to get the inside info on the show, as Volume 1 ends shortly before he was chosen as a Chaser.

Shaun is also the only Chaser to have stood for parliament. In the 2005 General Election, he was an Independent candidate for the Brent East constituency. Unfortunately he didn't win, but he did at least beat the Vote For Yourself Rainbow Dream Party!

And one final fact... Did you know that Paul Sinha isn't the only doctor amongst the Chasers? Shaun was awarded an Honorary Doctorate of Law by London Metropolitan University in 2015.

THE CHASE

ANSWERS

SOLO WINNERS

PETE

1 Fish
2 *East Is East*
3 Shakin' Stevens (also accept Shaky/Stevens)
4 Oedema (also accept fluid retention)
5 Six
6 Italy
7 Anthony Eden (also accept Eden/Robert Anthony Eden)
8 Prince Andrew (also accept Andrew/Duke of York)
9 Tiger Woods (also accept Woods)
10 New Mexico
11 Mike Leigh (also accept Leigh)
12 Rust
13 Hundred Years' War
14 Florence (also accept Firenze)
15 Peppermint (also accept mint)
16 *Oliver Twist* (not just *Oliver*)
17 A
18 Blake Edwards (also accept Edwards)
19 Gorilla
20 Norfolk
21 Charles II
22 Anita Brookner (also accept Brookner
23 Mineral water (also accept water)
24 Four
25 Louis Pasteur (also accept Pasteur)
26 Ottoman (also accept Turkish, Osman)
27 Tennis (also accept lawn tennis)
28 Shoes (also accept footwear)
29 Spanish

MAXINE

1 Brother-in-law
2 Himalayas
3 The Wanted
4 Fish
5 Boxing
6 Cheese
7 Christopher Eccleston
8 American Civil War (also accept US Civil War)
9 Rabbit (also accept bunny)
10 10
11 *Twilight*
12 Mount Pelée (also accept Pelée)
13 Beef
14 Bruce Forsyth
15 Anastacia
16 Nine
17 Dracula
18 Christmas
19 Mother and daughter
20 Candles (also accept soap)
21 Afghanistan
22 *Die Hard*
23 Ice cream (also accept dessert)
24 Ian McEwan (also accept McEwan)
25 Short Wave
26 Switzerland
27 JLS
28 Alexander the Great
29 Red (also accept scarlet)
30 Norwich
31 Windward
32 Ruth Watson (also accept Watson)
33 Liberal Democrats
34 Dictionaries
35 Boxing
36 Mekong
37 Pear
38 Radiation (also accept ionising radiation and particles)
39 Nancy Astor (also accept Astor)
40 Stephen Mangan (also accept Mangan)

HELEN

1 S'il vous plaît
2 Israel
3 18th (also accept 1700s)
4 Brain
5 David Beckham
6 Northern Ireland
7 Woodpecker
8 The Old Vic
9 (Guided) missile (also accept anti-ship missile)
10 Keith Chegwin (also accept Cheggers)
11 Four
12 Red
13 Newspaper (also accept he press/papers/journalism)
14 Icebreaker (also accept iceboat)
15 Texas
16 Alan Ayckbourn
17 Drink (also accept alcoholic drink/beverage/cocktail)
18 Cow (also accept cattle/dairy cow)
19 Greece
20 William Shakespeare (also accept Shakespeare)
21 Skin
22 1953
23 Four
24 James Herbert
25 Tonsils
26 Boat (also accept ship)
27 Pear
28 2000s (also accept Noughties)
29 Cricket
30 Referee (also accept umpire/judge)
31 Channel Islands
32 Reflex (also accept reflex angle)
33 Currants (also accept raisins/sultanas)
34 Saint Bernard
35 *Le Figaro* (also accept *Figaro*)
36 Nullarbor Plain (also accept Nullarbo)
37 Philosophy
38 Octagonal (also accept eight-sided)
39 World War Two (also accept Second World War)
40 United Russia

JOHN

1 Lb
2 German
3 Associated Press
4 Supergrass
5 Angling (also accept fishing)
6 Egyptian
7 Bird (also accept duck/water bird/sawbill)
8 Copper
9 Saturday
10 South Africa
11 Veins (also accept capillaries; not arteries)
12 Chicken (also accept hen/rooster/cock/fowl)
13 Onion
14 Ontario
15 Samoa (also accept Western Samoa)
16 Airspeed (also accept speed/velocity)
17 15
18 Oswald Mosley (also accept Mosley)
19 Edinburgh
20 Marian Keyes
21 Academy Awards
22 Medical profession (also accept doctor/medicine/surgeon/surgery)
23 West Ham United (also accept the Hammers/West Ham)
24 John F. Kennedy (also accept JFK/Kennedy/Jack Kennedy)
25 Milk
26 Beyoncé (also accept Beyoncé Knowles)
27 Richelieu (also accept Cardinal Richelieu)
28 Oesophagus (not windpipe)

DAVE

1 Romeo and Juliet
2 Beyoncé (also accept Beyoncé Knowles)
3 Dog
4 One million
5 Rugby union (also accept rugby)
6 Sagittarius
7 Rainier III (also accept Rainier)
8 Copper
9 Hip
10 Darts
11 Jools Holland
12 Pearl
13 Teachers
14 David (also accept Dave/Davy)
15 Denmark
16 T. Rex
17 Red
18 Leather (also accept animal hides)
19 Ferrari
20 Fairyhouse
21 Pot of gold (also accept gold)
22 Liberal Democrats (also accept Lib Dems)
23 The Navy (also accept Royal Navy)
24 Tiddlywinks
25 Blood

PIP

1 Green
2 One
3 Houston
4 1998
5 Army
6 Country (also accept Country and Western)
7 London
8 Felix Salten (also accept Salten/Siegmund Salzmann)
9 Exit
10 *QI* (also accept *QI XL*)
11 Macaroni
12 Chester
13 1970s (also accept 70s)
14 World War Two (also accept Second World War)
15 Red
16 Charles
17 *Batman*
18 Appletini
19 Persia
20 Brian De Palma
21 Africa
22 Nit
23 The Range
24 The Pennine Way
25 Blackwell
26 Atlantic
27 Aardwolf
28 Ivor Novello (also accept David Ivor Davies)
29 Film (also accept cinema)

RENEE

1 Eating (also accept tasting)
2 Naples (also accept Napoli)
3 Canada
4 Brendan Foster (also accept Foster)
5 Talkie
6 Jane Austen
7 Turtle (also accept Apalone)
8 Blue (also accept azure)
9 Cents
10 Ben Affleck
11 Exeter
12 Ruthenium
13 Limb
14 *Top of the Pops*
15 1880s
16 Bull
17 San Francisco
18 Heavyweight (also accept Heavy)
19 Pisces
20 Isaac Newton (also accept Sir Isaac Newton)
21 Cab (also accept taxi/taxicab)
22 Books (not sources or articles)
23 Malta
24 Jethro Tull
25 Horses
26 World War Two (also accept Second World War)
27 Goat
28 H
29 Sunshine Band
30 Air hostess (also accept flight attendant)
31 Triangle

SUSAN

1 English Channel (also accept the Channel/La Manche/the Thames)
2 Denominator
3 Stockholm
4 Armando Iannucci
5 Reggae (also accept ska)
6 Sunset Boulevard
7 Italian
8 Doe
9 Prince Philip (also accept the Duke of Edinburgh)
10 Nutmeg
11 *The Executioner's Song*
12 *Celebrity Juice*
13 Devonshire
14 China
15 A sunflower (also accept *Helianthus annuus*)
16 Wristwatches (also accept watches)
17 Eight
18 Dniepers (also accept Dnipro)
19 *Blue Peter*
20 Women's fashion (also accept fashion/clothes/clothing; not underwear)
21 Two
22 Cribbage (also accept crib)
23 Baghdad
24 Fish
25 Windsor (also accept House of Windsor)
26 1970s (also accept 70s)
27 Red and white

10ᵀᴴ ANNIVERSARY QUIZBOOK

HUW
1 Mediterranean (also accept the Med)
2 Artificial intelligence (also accept artificial)
3 *The Queen*
4 Russia (also accept Russian (Empire))
5 Basketball
6 Nepal
7 Simon Le Bon
8 Etihad (also accept Etihad Airways)
9 KFC
10 The Doges (also accept Doge)
11 Edgar Allan Poe
12 Judy Finnigan
13 20
14 White (also accept white with beige speckles)
15 Jacksonville (also accept Jacksonville Jaguars)
16 Male
17 Queen
18 Grace Kelly (also accept Princess Grace of Monaco)
19 Volvo (also accept the Volvo Group/Volvokoncernen/ Aktiebolaget Volvo/AB Volvo)
20 Ayatollah Khomeini
21 Judo
22 Ghost (also accept friendly ghost)
23 Scheherazade (also accept Shahrazad)
24 Rihanna
25 *The Pilgrim's Progress* (also accept *The Pilgrim's Progress from This World to That Which Is to Come*)
26 The Alamo (also accept Battle of the Alamo)
27 Pacific Ocean
28 *Fast and Furious* (also accept *The Fast and the Furious*)

CHRIS
1 Two
2 Pankhurst
3 Montréal
4 Commedia dell'arte
5 Gorilla
6 Maltese
7 Television (also accept TV)
8 17th (also accept 1600s)
9 Gunpowder (also accept black powder)
10 Half penny (also accept ha'penny/ha'pence)
11 *Nashville*
12 Showjumping (also accept stadium jumping/open jumping/jumpers)
13 Easter (also accept Easter Day/Easter Sunday)
14 Biggles
15 *Midnight Cowboy*
16 South Africa
17 64
18 Morris Minor
19 Eagle
20 Brazil
21 Spout
22 (Chanel) No. 5
23 Major League Baseball
24 Shanghai
25 Magnetic
26 Trees

JAMES
1 Asia
2 Foster's
3 Mata Hari (also accept Margaretha MacLeod)
4 17th (also accept 1600s)
5 Falklands War (also accept Falklands/South Atlantic War)
6 Albert Dock
7 AC Milan (also accept AC/ Associazone Calcio Milan)
8 12
9 Andy Warhol
10 *Minder*
11 Rugby league (not just rugby)
12 *The Archers*
13 *Escape to Victory* (also accept *Victory*)
14 Nellie (also accept Nellie the Elephant)
15 Iraq
16 Three
17 The Roman Empire (also accept Roman/Rome)
18 *Room*
19 French (also accept the French Revolution)
20 Atlantic (also accept South Atlantic)
21 Jessica
22 Heavy
23 Iain Banks
24 Greek
25 Letter (also accept mail/ post)
26 *Wicked*
27 Three
28 Trevor Baylis

ALISON
1 Chinese
2 Seven
3 Debra Messing
4 The Acropolis (not Parthenon)
5 The Sun (also accept star)
6 Steve Martin
7 Essex
8 Pompey the Great (also accept Pompey/Gnaeus Pompeius Magnus)
9 Thomas Hardy (also accept Hardy)
10 Duffy (also accept Aimee Ann Duffy)
11 Pre-Raphaelites (also accept Pre-Raphaelite Brotherhood)
12 Goalkeeper (also accept goalie/goal)
13 *Little House on the Prairie*
14 Hear (also accept detect/notice/sense)
15 Richard Strauss (not just Strauss)
16 Henry VIII (not Henry Tudor)
17 Frying (also accept fried)
18 *The Hurt Locker*
19 Rugby union (not just rugby)
20 Ash Wednesday
21 A
22 Lourdes
23 *Turandot*
24 Lederhosen

REBECCA
1 Golf
2 Graze
3 Unfinished
4 Skin
5 Cheese
6 Raft
7 Vishnu (not Rama/Krishna)
8 *Gardeners' World*
9 Champagne
10 Portishead
11 North Sea
12 Yellow
13 Rugby union (not rugby or rugby league)
14 Virginia Woolf
15 64
16 Chocolate
17 Light
18 Catherine Zeta-Jones
19 Treaty of Versailles (also accept Versailles)
20 GD
21 March
22 *A Bug's Life*
23 Russia (also accept Russian Empire; not USSR/Soviet Union)
24 Jarvis Cocker (also accept Cocker)
25 Vitamin A (also accept A)
26 Eucalyptus (also accept eucalypt/gum)

KEITH
1 Scotland
2 Guitar (also accept electric guitar/six string guitar)
3 13
4 Jeremy Hunt (also accept Hunt)
5 The BBC (also accept British Broadcasting Corporation/British Broadcasting Company)
6 Cadbury (also accept Cadbury's)
7 Mediterranean (also accept (the) Med)
8 *Appetite For Destruction*
9 Barbie
10 Mozart (also accept Wolfgang Mozart/Wolfgang Amadeus Mozart)
11 Alexander III (also accept Aleksandr Trety/Alexander Alexandrovich Romanov)
12 Maria Sharapova
13 Garfield
14 Cigar (not cigarette)
15 The Woodland Trust
16 Adult
17 Daughter
18 George V
19 Rice (also accept Oryza sativa)
20 Bay of Biscay
21 Optician (also accept optometrist/glasses retailer)
22 John Belushi (also accept John (Adam Belushi))
23 Tottenham Hotspur (also accept Spurs)
24 Louis XIV (also accept the Sun King/Louis Quatorze'
25 Gills
26 *Austin Powers*
27 Polish (also accept spit and polish)
28 Frying (also accept deep frying/shallow frying)

PETER

1 South America
2 Preston North End
3 (Dame) Agatha Christie
4 Tom Cruise (also accept Thomas Cruise Mapother (the fourth))
5 The House of Lords (also accept the Lords (Chamber)/Upper House/ Second Chamber)
6 Surrey
7 Bird
8 Light (also accept speed of light/electromagnetic waves)
9 Washington DC (also accept Washington)
10 Glastonbury
11 Golf
12 Ganges (also accept Ganga)
13 The Marines (also accept (the United States) Marine Corps/US Marines)
14 Acropolis
15 Jerome David
16 West Indies
17 Company
18 18th (also accept 1700s)
19 Diet
20 Ricky Martin (also accept Enrique Martin Morales)
21 50th (also accept 50th birthday/50 (years))
22 Ivan Lendl (also accept Lendl)
23 Archbishop of Canterbury (also accept Primate of All England)
24 Seven
25 *New Faces*

TOP 10 BIGGEST PRIZE WINNERS

JANICE, SARAH, KEVIN AND OVIE

1 Ice
2 Paracetamol (also accept Acetaminophen/N-Acetyl-paminophenol (APAP))
3 *Hollyoaks*
4 Kohlrabi (also accept German turnip)
5 Cat (also accept feline/ practical cat)
6 Green (also accept green light)
7 Arthur Daley
8 The Queen (also accept Elizabeth II)
9 12
10 Cricket
11 James Taylor
12 Germany
13 *Paradise Lost*
14 Shrewsbury Town (also accept Shrewsbury)
15 Ford
16 Checker (also accept Chubby Checker)
17 Land's End (also accept Dr Syntax's Head/Dr Johnson's Head)
18 Radon (not helium)
19 Wings
20 Quentin Blake
21 Africa
22 Shoe polish (also accept boot polish)
23 Burt Reynolds
24 Bulls (also accept Bradford Bulls)
25 1,000
26 Lee
27 England and Wales

JUDITH

1 Wood (also accept timber)
2 Boeing
3 *Coronation Street* (also accept *Corrie*)
4 Copper (not brass/bronze)
5 Islam (also accept Muslim religion)
6 *Magic Mike*
7 Polar bear (also accept *Ursus maritimus*)
8 *The Grapes of Wrath*
9 Statue of Liberty (also accept Liberty)
10 Odin
11 Sia (also accept Sia Furler)
12 Beirut
13 Manny Pacquiao
14 Summer solstice (also accept summer/Litha)
15 Herbert Asquith (also accept Asquith/ H. H. Asquith)
16 Vatican City (also accept the Vatican)
17 One Direction
18 *Ulysses*
19 Indiana Jones (also accept Henry Jones (Jr))
20 Bering Strait (also accept Bering)
21 *Oliver!*
22 Rigor mortis
23 Sister-in-law
24 *Top Gear*
25 *The Mill on the Floss*
26 Economics (also accept Economic Sciences)

ANSWERS

HONEY, DEB AND OLIVER

1 Colour (also accept wavelength/frequency)
2 *Call the Midwife*
3 Comet
4 William Hogarth (also accept Hogarth)
5 Iberian (also accept Iberia)
6 Spider-Man (also accept Peter Parker)
7 Greek (also accept Ancient Greek)
8 Edward IV
9 Oil (also accept rock oil/petroleum)
10 1970s (also accept 70s)
11 AC/DC
12 Northern Ireland (also accept Ulster; not Ireland)
13 Islam (also accept Muslim religion)
14 Ray-Ban
15 Strait of Malacca (also accept Malacca)
16 Knife
17 Fatima Whitbread (also accept Whitbread)
18 Cumbria
19 Butterfly
20 Uncle
21 New York City (also accept New York)
22 *Carry On Sergeant* (also accept *Sergeant*)
23 M6
24 Mafioso (also accept Mafiosa; not Mafiosi)

MATTHEW, CALUM AND JAN

1 Quidditch
2 *Top Gun*
3 Isis
4 Conservative (also accept Tory/Conservative and Unionist Party)
5 Archery
6 Bob Geldof (also accept (Robert Frederick Zenon) Geldof)
7 Four
8 Frida Kahlo (also accept Kahlo)
9 Casablanca
10 Ultra
11 Indian Ocean
12 Reindeer (also accept Santa's reindeer)
13 1930s (also accept 30s)
14 Wilson
15 *42nd Street*
16 Canada
17 Cheddar
18 *Blake's 7*
19 Charlotte Brontë
20 Southampton
21 Bird
22 *The Nutcracker*
23 17th (also accept 1600s)

ANTON, EMMA AND BONNY

1 Downing (Street)
2 Cheese
3 Samedi
4 John Betjeman
5 *The Godfather*
6 World War Two (also accept Second World War)
7 Water (also accept H2O)
8 Neneh Cherry (also accept Neneh Karlsson)
9 *Carry On* (also accept *Carry On* films)
10 Leg (also accept leg side)
11 Chatsworth House (also accept Chatsworth)
12 Two
13 Broccoli
14 *Aladdin*
15 Solute (not solvent)
16 Euro
17 Victoria (also accept Alexandrina Victoria/Queen Victoria)
18 Depeche Mode
19 Henry Ford (also accept Ford)
20 Brain (also accept cerebrum)
21 Bride (also accept bride-to-be)
22 Rhode Island
23 John Major (also accept Major)

10ᵀᴴ ANNIVERSARY QUIZBOOK

MICKEY, HELEN AND ROY

1 Mountain (also accept peak/mount)
2 German
3 *Blazing Saddles*
4 Porgy and Bess
5 Theresa May
6 Bird (also accept eagle/sea eagle/avian)
7 Wimpy (also accept Wimpy Bars)
8 The Saturdays
9 Israel
10 *The Matrix* (also accept the *Matrix* trilogy)
11 Prospero
12 Rome
13 HMS *Victory* (also accept the *Victory*)
14 Ice hockey
15 Methane (also accept CH$_4$)
16 Lungs
17 Toys 'R' Us
18 Louis XVI
19 Whisky (also accept whiskey)
20 Sandra Bullock
21 Football (also accept soccer)
22 Russia
23 5 Seconds of Summer (also accept 5SOS)

SANDRA, JONATHAN AND EAMMON

1 North Korea (also accept DPRK/Democratic People's Republic of Korea)
2 Anne
3 *Grease*
4 Actinium
5 Asia
6 Charlie Higson
7 Lactic acid
8 Basketball
9 November
10 MC Hammer (also accept Hammer)
11 Mario Testino
12 Mercury
13 Queen (also accept queen ant)
14 Horseracing (also accept racing/flat racing)
15 Jimmy Choo
16 Pride
17 1970s (also accept 70s)
18 Van Gogh (also accept Vincent van Gogh)
19 Cow
20 *We Will Rock You*
21 Eyes (also accept eye)
22 Japan
23 Adam Richman

DEBBIE AND DERRICK

1 Andy Murray
2 Palm
3 Disc jockey (also accept DJ)
4 Bones (also accept skeleton)
5 German
6 Kimono
7 Sarah, Duchess of York (also accept Sarah Ferguson/Duchess of York)
8 Crete (also accept Kriti)
9 Mediterranean
10 *Hi De Hi*
11 Bank of England
12 Gin
13 Labour
14 Grace Kelly (also accept Princess Grace (of Monaco))
15 Horse Guards Parade (also accept Horse Guards)
16 Centigram
17 Father
18 Pocahontas (also accept Matoaka/Amonute)
19 Cricket
20 Copper
21 Four
22 Barbra Streisand
23 Gulf of Mexico
24 18th (also accept 1700s)

CRAIG, RAKESH AND LAUREN

1 Autumn
2 Sugar
3 Mrs Doyle
4 Anwar Sadat (also accept Sadat/Muhammad Anwar-el Sadat)
5 Four
6 Catatonia
7 France
8 *Great British Menu*
9 Islam (also accept Muslim religion)
10 Cat
11 *Ender's Game*
12 Mediterranean
13 Pam Ayres
14 Jupiter (also accept Jove)
15 American Civil War (also accept US Civil War)
16 32
17 Brake light (also accept stop lamp/tail light/tail lamp)
18 The Streets (also accept Mike Skinner)
19 Athletics (also accept running/sprinting)
20 Peter Andre
21 Africa
22 Keep Britain Tidy
23 18th (also accept 1700s)
24 *Quantum Leap*
25 Monopoly

GAYNA, TIM, LUCA AND DIANE

1 Answer
2 Roman Republic (also accept Roman)
3 Sarah Jessica Parker
4 Kraftwerk
5 Electronic
6 North (also accept North Sea)
7 Copper (also accept cuprum)
8 Noah
9 Salt (also accept sea salt/ finishing salt)
10 Alison Moyet
11 Ice hockey (not just hockey)
12 Three
13 Nescafé
14 Piano
15 Bill (also accept draft bill; not white paper)
16 Its head (also accept head)
17 *Deeply*
18 Africa
19 Great Western Railway (also accept Great Western)
20 Heat (also accept hot weather/temperature)
21 Four
22 Car (also accept race car/ automobile/racing car)
23 Zagreb
24 Aphrodite

HIGHEST WINNING SCORES

TOM, MATT AND JOYCE

1 Greyhound racing (also accept whippet racing)
2 Red Square
3 *Will & Grace*
4 Punic Wars
5 Paper
6 *Aida*
7 Ferries (also accept ferry/ car ferries/passenger ferries/freight ferries)
8 *King Solomon's Mines*
9 Watt
10 *Avatar*
11 Kurt Waldheim (also accept Waldheim)
12 The skin
13 Chrissie Hynde (not the Pretenders)
14 Afrikaans
15 Catalan Dragons
16 Divorce (also accept annulment/decree absolute)
17 Essex
18 Neptune
19 Cadbury
20 Oslo
21 30
22 Myxomatosis (also accept infectious myxomatosis)
23 George Washington
24 *Live and Let Die*
25 Jamie Oliver

PAUL AND GARETH

1 Two
2 Russia
3 Celine Dion (also accept Dion)
4 Baltic
5 *TV Times*
6 Dog
7 Michelle McManus (also accept Michelle/McManus)
8 Antonio
9 Kilt
10 Tasmania
11 Fantastic Four
12 1930s (also accept 30s)
13 Four
14 Mushroom (also accept fungus)
15 Israel
16 Lepidoptera
17 Thank you (also accept thanks)
18 Hugh Grant (also accept Grant)
19 Wolves (also accept Wolverhampton/ Wolverhampton Wanderers)
20 George V
21 Italian
22 72
23 Coldplay
24 Michelle Ryan
25 Julius Caesar
26 Egypt
27 Lester Piggott (also accept Piggott)
28 Jennifer Beals
29 Red
30 India

10TH ANNIVERSARY QUIZBOOK

OLIVIA, GARETH, JO AND CHRIS

1 Lewis Hamilton
2 Meridian
3 Abu Dhabi
4 Chandler (also accept Bing/ Chandler Bing)
5 Red (also accept Little Red Book)
6 Hamburg
7 New York (also accept New York City)
8 Sleeve
9 Hugh Grant
10 Cambridge
11 Denise Welch (also accept Jacqueline Welch)
12 Nova Scotia
13 Victor
14 'Super Trouper'
15 *To Kill a Mockingbird*
16 Miss Piggy
17 Gabriel
18 *Sexy Beast*
19 Ravi Shankar (also accept Shankar)
20 Apple
21 Argentina (also accept the Argentine)
22 John Forsythe (also accept Forsythe)
23 Henrik Ibsen (also accept Ibsen)
24 Ryanair
25 Five

ANDREW, JOE AND MARIA

1 Biscuit (not cake)
2 *Tootsie*
3 North America
4 Methuselah
5 Ice hockey (not hockey)
6 easyJet
7 *The Lord of the Rings*
8 JLS
9 19th (also accept 1800s)
10 Chile
11 Monkey
12 Forsythia
13 *Emmerdale*
14 Indira Gandhi (also accept Gandhi)
15 Yugoslav (also accept Yugoslavian)
16 Hot water (also accept water/boiling water)
17 Three
18 Georges Seurat (also accept Seurat/Georges-Pierre Seurat)
19 Eddie Redmayne
20 Humerus
21 Train (also accept railway (train)/(steam) locomotive)
22 Henry VIII
23 *Cold Comfort Farm*
24 Wyclef Jean
25 Atlantic (also accept North Atlantic; not South Atlantic)
26 Omar Sharif

ROB, GRAHAM AND VERITY

1 Jason Donovan
2 Cricket
3 Debbie Reynolds
4 A window
5 1006
6 Anchovy (also accept anchovies)
7 Thomas Hardy (also accept Hardy)
8 Californium
9 Lion
10 Essex
11 Cher
12 Cambridge
13 Nappy
14 Writing (also accept penmanship/fine handwriting/decorative handwriting)
15 France
16 Boxing (also accept Middleweight boxing)
17 Spanish
18 Grape (also accept black grape)
19 1920s (also accept 20s)
20 Jason Derulo
21 Car
22 Nike
23 Ted Danson
24 Louis XIV
25 Swan
26 Milligram

ANSWERS

353

ANNA, DAVID AND ANGELA

1. Guitar (also accept electric guitar)
2. Radio 4
3. Jessica Alba (also accept Alba)
4. Iron
5. China
6. Eeyore
7. Backstreet Boys
8. Boston
9. The first
10. Bayeux Tapestry
11. Irish
12. Pink
13. Roll (also accept bread roll/bread/bun)
14. Bill Oddie (also accept Oddie)
15. Four
16. *Twelfth Night*
17. Furniture (also accept sofas)
18. Arabic
19. Hockey (also accept field hockey)
20. Flax (also accept Linum usitatissimum)
21. Gary Barlow
22. Italy
23. Rachel Weisz
24. Nickelback
25. Three
26. Cat
27. Thor Heyerdahl (also accept Heyerdahl)
28. Crete
29. *EastEnders*
30. Quills

SARAH, KIT AND CLARE

1. Basketball (also accept netball)
2. Gillian McKeith
3. Colin Firth (also accept Firth)
4. Unicorn
5. Port
6. Nine
7. Franz Ferdinand
8. *Despicable Me*
9. Babies (also accept baby)
10. Biscuit (also accept savoury biscuit)
11. Alex Kingston (also accept Kingston)
12. Nelly (also accept Cornell Haynes)
13. Tower Bridge
14. Boxing
15. Clint Eastwood (also accept Eastwood)
16. Dr Seuss
17. Italian
18. Atlantic Ocean
19. Scarlet fever
20. Kid Rock (also accept Robert James Ritchie)
21. Roman Catholic Church (also accept Catholic Church)
22. Jim
23. Tequila
24. Gloucestershire
25. 5 November (not Bonfire Night)
26. John Cleese (also accept Cleese)
27. Paula Abdul (also accept Abdul)
28. Spaniel
29. Poland

SARAH, VANESSA AND MARTIN

1. *Who Wants to be a Millionaire?* (also accept *Millionaire*)
2. Hilt (also accept grip)
3. 1997
4. 50
5. Owl
6. Euro
7. Gums
8. Vietnam
9. *Emmerdale*
10. Canada
11. Aldous Huxley (also accept Huxley)
12. 100
13. November
14. Spanish
15. The Beatles
16. Burt Kwouk (also accept Kwouk)
17. One point (also accept one)
18. Rome
19. John
20. Harriet Beecher Stowe (also accept Stowe)
21. Oak
22. Croupier
23. The Verve
24. Westminster
25. Three
26. Peterborough
27. Epsilon
28. Bird (also accept songbird/warbler)

10ᵀᴴ ANNIVERSARY QUIZBOOK

THERESA, GILL AND SHAHAB

1. Little Red Riding Hood (also accept Red Riding Hood)
2. Ian Hislop (also accept Hislop)
3. One
4. South America
5. Kylie Minogue (also accept Kylie)
6. Lenny Henry (also accept Henry)
7. 2000s (also accept Noughties)
8. Portugal
9. Nose
10. Peseta
11. Jean-Claude Van Damme (also accept Van Damme)
12. Louisiana
13. Vic Reeves (also accept Reeves/Jim Moir)
14. Bees
15. Dickens and Darwin
16. *Queen Mary*
17. Drum (also accept percussion)
18. Russia
19. Alexander the Great (also accept Alexander III of Macedon)
20. Wilkie Collins (also accept Collins/William Wilkie Collins)
21. 60 pence
22. Tomato
23. Terry Wogan (also accept Wogan)
24. Sandown Park (also accept Sandown)
25. India
26. Salman Rushdie (also accept Rushdie)
27. Museum of Modern Art

CALLUM, MARILYN, SARAH AND SEAN

1. France
2. *To the Manor Born*
3. John F. Kennedy (also accept Kennedy/JFK/John Fitzgerald Kennedy)
4. MOBOs (also accept MOBO Awards, Music of Black Origin)
5. William I (also accept William (of Normandy))
6. Washington DC (also accept Washington)
7. Standard variable rate
8. Mariah Carey
9. Monday
10. Australia
11. Annie Nightingale (also accept Anne Nightingale/Nightingale)
12. Harry Sidebottom
13. Rehabilitation
14. Esther Rantzen
15. Biscay (also accept Bay of Biscay)
16. Günter Grass (also accept Grass)
17. Three
18. Tulisa (also accept Tulisa (Tula) Constantavlos)
19. Maps (also accept charts)
20. Eleanor of Aquitaine
21. Japan
22. Jaw
23. Harvard
24. Jimi Hendrix (also accept The Jimi Hendrix Experience)
25. Linoleum
26. Oxygen
27. Elsa

SAM, JAMIE AND PHIL
CONTESTANT SET

1 Costa
2 Parker
3 *Lucky Jim*
4 Rome
5 Wire
6 Two
7 Grateful Dead
8 Ben Elton (also accept Elton)
9 Golf
10 Ear
11 Computers (also accept technology/IT/internet)
12 Managua
13 *Alice in Wonderland* (also accept *Alice's Adventures in Wonderland*)
14 Mercury
15 Cliff Richard (also accept Harry Rodger Webb/Richard)
16 Boxing
17 2000
18 Feet
19 Sydney Harbour Bridge
20 American
21 Eight
22 Airship (also accept dirigible)
23 1940
24 Vermont
25 Bread (also accept rye bread)
26 Disc

CHASER SET

1 Pig
2 Hinduism (also accept Hindu)
3 *Drop the Dead Donkey*
4 Bristol
5 Over the top
6 Seven
7 Profumo affair
8 Howard Webb (also accept Webb)
9 Yin
10 Owl
11 Florida
12 Gloucester
13 Heart
14 Silver
15 The White Stripes
16 Richmond
17 Green
18 Birmingham
19 Stars
20 Shelagh Delaney (also accept Delaney)
21 John Cleese (also accept Cleese)
22 Lion
23 Omar Sharif (also accept Sharif)
24 George IV
25 Milk
26 Australia
27 *Spirit*
28 Nuevo sol (also accept sol/new sol)
29 Gold
30 India

CELEBRITY CLEVER DICKS: 10 WHO GOT 10

SHAUN WILLIAMSON
1 Andrew Lloyd-Webber (also accept (Lord) Lloyd-Webber)
2 Mother-of-pearl (also accept nacre)
3 Haile Selassie (also accept Haile Selassie I)
4 Ice cream
5 Lenny Henry (also accept Lenworth Henry)
6 Brass
7 Norwich City (also accept Norwich)
8 Squeeze
9 *Excalibur*
10 The Blitz (also accept Blitzkrieg)
11 Stoke Mandeville (also accept Stoke Mandeville Stadium)

MATHEW WRIGHT
1 Pig
2 Mrs Robinson
3 Madonna
4 Argentina
5 Cricket
6 Charles Dickens (also accept Dickens)
7 Luton Airport
8 The Oscars (also accept Academy Awards)
9 Moriarty (also accept Jim Moriarty)
10 Kangaroo

10TH ANNIVERSARY QUIZBOOK

ALASTAIR STEWART
1 Scotland
2 Bottle
3 *The Sun* (not *Scottish Sun*)
4 Oaks
5 Time
6 Julius Caesar (also accept Caesar)
7 Ann Widdecombe
8 John F. Kennedy (also accept Kennedy/JFK)
9 Winnipeg
10 Prince Philip (also accept his father)
11 Hamlet

KEITH CHEGWIN
1 Monopoly
2 Tart
3 *True Lies*
4 Robin Cousins
5 Telescope (also accept refracting telescope/ Newtonian telescope/ Gregorian telescope, etc.)
6 Gloucestershire
7 Prime Minister
8 'Wandrin' Star' (also accept 'I Was Born Under a Wandrin' Star)
9 Pedals (also accept foot pedals)
10 At sea (also accept on the ocean/in (international) water)
11 Judaism (also accept Jewish/Reform Judaism)

JESSICA TAYLOR
1 One
2 Wicket keeper (also accept wickie)
3 *Les Misérables*
4 Venison
5 *Fireman Sam* (also accept *Sam Tam*)
6 Sagittarius
7 *An Officer and a Gentleman*
8 Brain
9 S Club 7 (also accept S Club)
10 Diamond
11 *Nineteen Eighty-Four*

RORY MCGRATH
1 24 (also accept four and twenty)
2 Lord's (also accept Lord's Cricket Ground)
3 'Get Back' (also accept 'Get Back to Where You Once Belonged')
4 Jacques Cousteau (also accept Cousteau/Jacques-Yves Cousteau)
5 Mayonnaise
6 Red Sea (also accept Red)
7 Gold
8 Orlando Bloom (not Dominic Scott Kay)
9 Stephen Hawking (also accept (Professor) Hawking)
10 Marie Antoinette (also accept Josèphe Jeanne Marie Antoinette)
11 *The Herbs*
12 Tokyo
13 *Roy of the Rovers*

JONATHAN ROSS
1 Three
2 Bubble gum (also accept gum/chewing gum)
3 *Sherlock*
4 Victoria
5 *The Scream*
6 Mark Wahlberg
7 Exorcism (also accept casting out)
8 Conchita Wurst (also accept Thomas Neuwirth)
9 Manga
10 Iceland
11 Johnny Marr

STEVE PEMBERTON

1 Wolf (also accept Big Bad Wolf)
2 Barcelona (also accept Barça)
3 'We Didn't Start the Fire'
4 Denis Thatcher
5 German
6 *South Park*
7 M1
8 The Grinch
9 Table Mountain
10 Dudley Moore
11 Samuel Pepys (also accept Pepys)

IAN LAVENDER

1 Indian
2 Cricket
3 David Cameron (also accept Cameron)
4 Alan Titchmarsh
5 Wales
6 Laurel and Hardy (also accept Stan Laurel and Oliver Hardy)
7 Ascot
8 Thief
9 Five
10 Golden Gate
11 Chicken

MATT ALLWRIGHT

1 Boat
2 Roses
3 Three
4 The Bible
5 Midge Ure
6 Terry Gilliam (also accept Gilliam)
7 Knife (knife edge)
8 Tate Modern
9 Greg Rutherford (also accept Rutherford)
10 Record
11 Transport
12 Grandfather (also accept grandfather clock)

CELEBRITIES GOING BIG

TIM VINE

1 **B** Performing clown
2 **C** Willi Wakker
3 **A** Fish
4 **B** Chelsea
5 **B** Alec Guinness
6 **A** Cat's pyjamas
7 **A** Tees
8 **A** Denmark

DENISE WELCH

1 **C** Wham!
2 **A** Wigan
3 **C** Jessie J
4 **C** Professor
5 **C** Chilli pepper

JIMMY CARR

1 **C** Sisley
2 **A** Ice Cube
3 **C** Easter Sunday
4 **B** French Open
5 **A** Dog's nose

JOEY ESSEX

1 **B** A woman
2 **C** Tyga
3 **A** Frogmore
4 **A** Mummy bag

ADE EDMONSON

1 **A** Backside
2 **C** *Wonder Woman*
3 **C** Market
4 **C** 1849
5 **B** *Happy Days*
6 **A** Accountants
7 **C** Redwood

ANSWERS

ED BYRNE
1 **A** Bicycle
2 **B** Grog
3 **C** Hank Wangford
4 **B** Rapier
5 **A** Alex James
6 **B** *Curb Your Enthusiasm*
7 **A** Horror

RACHEL RILEY
1 **C** Sliced bread
2 **C** *Shipping Forecast*
3 **B** Mark Lewis-Francis
4 **B** Antiseptic
5 **C** 24 hours
6 **A** Frank Sinatra
7 **C** Ecology
8 **B** Bentley

DUNCAN JAMES
1 **B** Drink it
2 **C** Temple
3 **C** Wrestling
4 **C** Kingfisher
5 **A** 90 minutes
6 **A** Forefinger and thumb
7 **B** Martina Navratilova
8 **A** Snake

BRITAIN'S BRAINIEST FAMILY

HATTIE (CASH BUILDER)
1 Moon landing (also accept Apollo 11 moon landing)
2 David Beckham
3 *The Catcher in the Rye*
4 Jesus Christ (also accept Jesus/Christ; not John the Baptist)
5 Fidel Castro (not just Castro)
6 Tivoli Gardens (also accept Tivoli)
7 Apple (also accept Apple Inc./Apple Incorporated)
8 Oscar
9 The Isle Of Fernando's (also accept Fernando's)
10 Lego

HATTIE (HEAD TO HEAD)
1 **C** *The 101 Dalmatians*
2 **A** Allo
3 **A** *La Bohème*
4 **A** Adam
5 **C** Wipe-turkey
6 **A** 1930s
7 **C** Take That
8 **A** Aunt

CHLOE (CASH BUILDER)
1 Bed
2 *Game of Thrones*
3 'Who Let the Dogs Out'
4 Joséphine (also accept Joséphine de Beauharnais)
5 Yuppie
6 Wasabi
7 Democratic Party (also accept Democrats)
8 Stephen King
9 *Vogue* (also accept US *Vogue*)
10 Atlantic (also accept South Atlantic)
11 Nina Conti

CHLOE (HEAD TO HEAD)
1 **A** Elbows
2 **C** Istanbul
3 **A** Ewok
4 **A** A crooked cat
5 **B** Mary Berry
6 **A** Blue

NED (CASH BUILDER)
1 Darts
2 KFC (also accept Kentucky Fried Chicken)
3 Jurassic
4 Tarmacadam (also accept Tarmac)
5 Baseball
6 *The Conjuring*
7 Francisco Franco (also accept Franco)
8 Laa-Laa
9 Mecca (not Medina)

ANSWERS

NED (HEAD TO HEAD)

1	**C** Box and whisker	4	**A** Kara	7	**A** On fleek
2	**B** Lawyer	5	**C** Beavers		
3	**C** USS *Missouri*	6	**B** Three		

PETER (CASH BUILDER)

1	G	6	Whitman	10	Royal Variety Performance (also accept Royal Variety/Royal Command Performance)
2	Adam Ant (also accept Stuart Goddard)	7	Lea and Perrins		
3	Brian Cox	8	*Under Milk Wood*	11	Wonder Woman (also accept Diana Prince)
4	Cat (also accept feline)	9	Lady Macbeth (not Macbeth)		
5	Liberty				

PETER (HEAD TO HEAD)

1	**C** Henry VIII	4	**C** MI6	7	**C** Foxtrot
2	**C** Vegetarian	5	**A** Sea urchin		
3	**B** Windermere	6	**A** Lightness		

THE FINAL CHASE – THE FRENCH FAMILY

1	The Beatles	10	Caesars Palace	18	Alan Sugar (also accept Sugar/Lord (Alan) Sugar/ Baron Sugar)
2	100 years old (also accept 100 years/one hundred)	11	Banksy		
3	Colombia	12	Star (not constellation)	19	Laura Trott (also accept Trott)
4	Maya Angelou	13	Terry Waite (also accept (Terence Hardy) Waite)	20	1918
5	The Police	14	Asia (also accept Asian)	21	Spring
6	Vodka	15	*Cabaret*	22	Karl Lagerfeld
7	Nile	16	Spider	23	Dido
8	John Paul II (also accept Karol Wojtyla)	17	*The Ring Cycle* (also accept *Der Ring des Nibelungen/ The Ring of the Nibelung/ The Ring*)		
9	*Going for Gold*				

THE FINAL CHASE – THE GOVERNESS

1	Four	11	Vice Admiral	22	Transylvania
2	*EastEnders*	12	Scotland	23	Hymen (also accept Hymenaeus; not Hera)
3	Polaris	13	Dick Francis		
4	Perth	14	Coca-Cola	24	*Groundhog Day*
5	Paint (also accept war-paint)	15	King John (also accept John)	25	Horse-racing (also accept flat racing)
6	Snapchat	16	Thames	26	Manhattan
7	Dogs (also accept dog/ canine)	17	South Africa	27	James Watt (also accept Watt)
8	Pakistan	18	Martina Cole	28	Pitbull (also accept Armando Pérez/Pit)
9	*Top Gear*	19	Suit		
10	Liver	20	*Psycho*		
		21	Cattle (also accept cow)		

ZERO CASH BUILDERS

CASH BUILDER QUIZ 1
1 Facebook
2 Royal Navy (also accept Navy)
3 Andy Murray (also accept Murray)
4 Ernest
5 Cumbria
6 *The Railway Children*
7 Dick van Dyke (also accept van Dyke)
8 Alexei Sayle (also accept Sayle)
9 MI6
10 16th (also accept 1500s)

CASH BUILDER QUIZ 2
1 Chalk
2 Jedward (also accept John and Edward Grimes)
3 Paul McCartney (also accept McCartney)
4 Canada
5 Father
6 *Sunday in the Park with George*
7 Krusty
8 Medway
9 Ashton Kutcher
10 Bearskin
11 Aristole Onassis (also accept Onassis)

CASH BUILDER QUIZ 3
1 *Blue Peter*
2 Gouda
3 Middlesbrough
4 *The Hurt Locker*
5 Deadheading
6 Guns N' Roses
7 English
8 (The) Caucasus
9 Bankrupt (also accept bankruptcy/bankrupted)
10 Ordnance Survey

CASH BUILDER QUIZ 4
1 Russell
2 Delta
3 Seve Ballesteros (also accept Ballesteros)
4 *Sex and the City*
5 Wheeler-dealer
6 Mo Mowlam
7 Rocking horse
8 Arctic Monkeys

CASH BUILDER QUIZ 5
1 Scotland
2 Revelations
3 Cat
4 Scrooge (also accept Ebenezer Scrooge)
5 Eurovision Song Contest (also accept Eurovision/ESC)
6 *Klute*
7 Chickens
8 *War and Peace*
9 Ethel Skinner (also accept Ethel)
10 France

CASH BUILDER QUIZ 6
1 Head (also accept head and neck)
2 Jeffrey Archer (also accept Baron Archer of Weston-super-Mare/Lord Archer)
3 Lesley Garrett
4 Ottoman
5 *Ice Age*
6 Liberty horse (also accept Liberty)
7 Butterflies
8 John Bull
9 *Calamity Jane*
10 Runway

CASH BUILDER QUIZ 7
1 Tarot
2 Grizzly (also accept Grizzlies)
3 Jools Oliver
4 Tralee
5 Peter Ustinov (also accept Ustinov)
6 Hampton Court (also accept Hampton Court Palace)
7 *Coronation Street*
8 Vesuvius
9 The Wanted

ANSWERS

CASH BUILDER QUIZ 8

1 'Careless Whisper'
2 Royal Navy (also accept Navy)
3 Sony
4 Great Sphinx (also accept the Sphinx)

5 Bradley Wiggins (also accept Wiggins)
6 Isaac Newton (also accept Newton)

7 Arnold Schwarzenegger (also accept Schwarzenegger)
8 Trojan Horse (also accept wooden Horse)
9 Green

CASH BUILDER QUIZ 9

1 Saturday
2 Hopalong
3 Micky Flanagan

4 Alphorn (also accept Alpenhorn/Alpine horn)
5 Scallop (also accept scallop shell/pecten (shell))

6 *Starlight Express*
7 Two
8 Quebec
9 *Despicable Me*

CASH BUILDER QUIZ 10

1 Africa
2 Lady
3 Kate Winslet
4 Baths (also accept public baths/bathhouse/thermae)

5 Edna Everage (also accept Dame Edna)
6 Labrador (also accept Labrador Current)
7 English

8 Henry VII
9 Ziegfeld (also accept Florenz Ziegfeld/Ziegfeld Follies)

CASH BUILDER QUIZ 11

1 Police
2 Driving test (also accept L-Test)
3 Jo Brand

4 Bourbon
5 Old Father Time (also accept Father Time)
6 Giselle

7 Celtic
8 New Forest
9 Stereophonics

CASH BUILDER QUIZ 12

1 Green
2 Frankie (not Frank)
3 Aphrodite
4 Hip (also accept hips)

5 *Sergeant Pepper's Lonely Hearts Club Band* (also accept *Sergeant Pepper*)
6 Three
7 Dame

8 Mornington Crescent
9 The wipers (also accept windscreen wipers/bus wipers/the wipers on the bus)

CASH BUILDER QUIZ 13

1 England
2 Domestos
3 Kitt (also accept Knight Industries Two Thousand)

4 Marie Antoinette
5 Chicken (also accept hen/cock)
6 Robin Thicke

7 Diving (also accept dive/flop/flopping)

CASH BUILDER QUIZ 14

1 *Friday the 13th* (not *Halloween*)
2 Bounty
3 The Rolling Stones

4 Lego
5 John Smith
6 Old Trafford (also accept Emirates Old Trafford)

7 Madonna
8 Myopia (also accept myopic)

CASH BUILDER QUIZ 15

1 One
2 Paris
3 *3rd Rock from the Sun*
4 Midas

5 January
6 George Gershwin (also accept Gershwin/Jacob Gershvin)

7 Pineapple
8 *Shrek* (also accept *Shrek II*)
9 Ulysses

CASH BUILDER QUIZ 16

1 *Life of Brian* (also accept *Monty Python's Life of Brian*)
2 Fret
3 Reagan (also accept Nancy Reagan)
4 10 (also accept three score years and 10)
5 *Neighbours*
6 Josiah Wedgwood (also accept Wedgwood)
7 David Attenborough
8 *Bend It Like Beckham*

CASH BUILDER QUIZ 17

1 Scotch egg
2 Semi-final (also accept third place play-off)
3 Julius Caesar (also accept Caesar)
4 Spaghetti Westerns (also accept Italian Western)
5 Angel of the North
6 Rockall
7 Scorpio (also accept Scorpius/the Scorpion)
8 World War One (also accept First World War/Great War)
9 Boyzone

CASH BUILDER QUIZ 18

1 Tennis
2 Arnold Schwarzenegger (also accept Schwarzenegger)
3 Hall of Mirrors
4 Justin Bieber
5 Canterbury Cathedral (not just Canterbury)
6 *Up*
7 Amazon
8 Mill (also accept the Mill on the Floss/water mill)
9 Duct (also accept tear duct)

CASH BUILDER QUIZ 19

1 CID
2 Two
3 Janet Jackson
4 Flares
5 Billy Bunter (also accept Billy/William George Bunter)
6 Baked Alaska (also accept Norwegian omelette)
7 Worzel Gummidge (also accept Gummidge)
8 Hudson
9 Henry Cooper

CASH BUILDER QUIZ 20

1 Horses
2 Asia
3 Salvador Dalí
4 Algarve
5 Nicki Minaj
6 Russell Grant
7 Loadsamoney

CASH BUILDER QUIZ 21

1 Country and Western (also accept Country/C&W)
2 Cotton
3 Siegfried Line (also accept Siegfried)
4 Linford Christie (also accept Christie)
5 May (also accept (Louisa) May Alcott)
6 Laura Dern
7 Fish (also accept white fish)
8 Dragon

CASH BUILDER QUIZ 22

1 Queen
2 *Star Wars*
3 Dizzee Rascal (also accept Dylan Mills)
4 Just William
5 Weebles
6 Algebra
7 Mercury
8 *The Ring* (also accept *Ring Cycle/The Ring of the Nibelung*)
9 Stephen Fry

ANSWERS

CASH BUILDER QUIZ 23

1 Hangman
2 Missile
3 Toronto
4 Egg
5 Fish (also accept herring)

6 (General) Galtieri (also accept Lieutenant General Leopoldo Galtieri)
7 Mickey Mouse (also accept Mickey)

8 Bill Bryson
9 Paloma Faith (also accept Paloma Faith Blomfield)

CASH BUILDER QUIZ 24

1 China (also accept People's Republic of China)
2 Nose (also accept Roman nose)
3 The Smiths

4 Karl Lagerfeld (also accept Lagerfeld)
5 Constable (also accept John Constable/not Sergeant)

6 Grits (also accept hominy grits)
7 Clubs
8 Ben Haenow
9 *A Tale of Two Cities*

CASH BUILDER QUIZ 25

1 Scrabble
2 Toxic
3 Turner

4 Chris Evert (also accept Chris Evert-Lloyd/Chris Lloyd)

5 Manchester
6 George VI
7 *The Full Monty*

CASH BUILDER QUIZ 26

1 Pingu
2 Ribcage
3 *Carry On* (also accept the *Carry On* films)

4 Scotland
5 Oven
6 Jimmy Hill

7 Uncle Albert (also accept Albert)
8 Chile
9 10

CASH BUILDER QUIZ 27

1 National Theatre
2 Blue
3 Anthony Eden (also accept Eden)

4 Sausages
5 Tottenham Hotspur (also accept Spurs/Tottenham)
6 Raymond Burr

7 'Sing a Song of Sixpence'
8 Carisbrooke (also accept Carisbrooke Castle)
9 Pronto

CASH BUILDER QUIZ 28

1 YouTube
2 Saddam Hussein (also accept Saddam)
3 Pig (also accept swine)

4 McVities
5 Football
6 *Pitch Perfect* (also accept *Pitch Perfect 2*)

7 New York (also accept New York City)

CASH BUILDER QUIZ 29

1 Zero (also accept zero pounds/zero pence/nought/nothing)
2 North America (not just America)

3 Conservative (also accept Tory)
4 Mind the gap
5 H & M (also accept Hennes and Mauritz)
6 Simone Biles

7 Five hundred thousand pounds (also accept half a million (pounds))
8 Himalayas
9 Lira

CASH BUILDER QUIZ 30

1 Barbie (also accept Barbie doll)
2 Aero
3 Pam Ayres

4 Argentina
5 *The Good Life*
6 Cubism (also accept Cubist)

7 Parthenon
8 Elton John
9 Martin Luther King Jr (also accept Martin Luther King)

CASH BUILDER QUIZ 31

1 Queen Victoria (also accept Victoria)
2 SEAT
3 The Moon
4 England

5 Magnus Magnusson
6 Abraham (also accept Abram/Avram)
7 Balmoral (also accept Balmoral Castle)

8 Hungary
9 Plinth
10 Dodo

CASH BUILDER QUIZ 32

1 Nook (also accept nook and cranny)
2 Mo Harris (also accept Mo/Big Mo/Big Mo Harris)
3 Atlético Madrid (also accept Atlético/Club Atlético de Madrid)

4 Holly Willoughby
5 The *Titanic* (also accept R(oyal) (Mail) S(hip) *Titanic*)
6 House of Lords (also accept the Lords/the Upper House)
7 Mountain

8 *Matilda*
9 Tess of the d'Urbervilles (also accept Tess Durbeyfield/Tess)

CASH BUILDER QUIZ 33

1 Scotland
2 Dashboard (also accept dash/instrument panel/fascia)

3 Jack Ryan
4 Patience (also accept solitaire)
5 Sap

6 Winston Churchill (also accept Churchill)
7 *Star Wars*
8 Mike Tyson

CASH BUILDER QUIZ 34

1 (Great) Sphinx (also accept Great Sphinx of Giza)
2 'Addicted to Love'
3 Norse (also accept Viking)

4 Donald Trump (also accept Trump)
5 Ten
6 Kara Tointon

7 Johanna Konta (also accept Jo Konta)
8 Bran

CASH BUILDER QUIZ 35

1 Manicure
2 Stuart Little
3 Louis Pasteur (also accept Pasteur)

4 Female
5 Purple
6 *Hollyoaks*
7 An ill wind (also accept ill)

8 'Que Sera Sera' (also accept 'Whatever Will Be Will Be')
9 Victoria's Secret

LAZARUS WINS

JOHN VS. PAUL

JOHN

1 Fish
2 London
3 Mediterranean
4 *Léon* (also accept *The Professional*)
5 Boxing
6 Dog
7 Rabbi
8 The Curragh
9 One per cent (also accept one)
10 Pasta
11 Ming (also accept Ming dynasty)
12 Javan (also accept Javanese)
13 Hot liquid (also accept steam/boiling water)
14 Hercule Poirot (also accept Poirot)
15 Antoni Gaudí (also accept Gaudí/Antonio Gaudí)
16 *Tombstone*
17 Japan
18 Punch
19 Microbes (also accept micro-organisms/bacteria/viruses/microscopic ones)
20 Sophocles
21 Ireland (also accept Republic of Ireland/Eire)
22 Jane Austen (also accept Austen)
23 Texas
24 Antigua
25 Earth
26 E. M. Forster (also accept Forster)
27 1950s (also accept 50s)
28 Cotton

PAUL

1 Dog (also accept canine)
2 Nova Scotia
3 Australia
4 Mark Thompson
5 Tennis
6 Land Rover
7 John Mortimer
8 Tali
9 Gold
10 British Library
11 Newquay
12 Robert Harris
13 Janet Jackson
14 Poland
15 Shark (also accept hammerhead shark/shovelhead shark)
16 Primal Scream
17 Travel (also accept travelling/journeys/holidays/vacations/going away)
18 Antarctica
19 Switzerland
20 *The Trumpet-Major*
21 Hedgehog
22 Hertfordshire
23 Caraway
24 Romania
25 Red (also accept pink)
26 Rik Mayall
27 South America (not just America)
28 Sean Connery (also accept Connery)
29 Beef

PHIL VS. PAUL

PHIL

1. London
2. Snoop Dogg (also accept Snoop Doggy Dogg/Calvin Cordozar Broadus, Jr)
3. Medicine
4. Amen
5. Five
6. Bounds
7. Winston Churchill (also accept Churchill)
8. Northamptonshire (also accept Northants)
9. Water (also accept fluids/liquids)
10. *Saturday Night Fever*
11. Cat (also accept old female cat)
12. C. S. Lewis (also accept Clive Staples Lewis)
13. Substitute
14. Skull (also accept head/cranium/forehead)
15. Arizona
16. Jordan
17. ABBA
18. Mary (also accept the Virgin Mary/Jesus's mother/BVM, etc.)
19. Thailand
20. Boxing (also accept pugilism)
21. March
22. Leg
23. Golf
24. Fred Goodwin
25. Atlantic
26. World War Two (also accept Second World War)
27. Horses
28. Greece

PAUL

1. *EastEnders*
2. *Private Eye*
3. Square (also accept rectangular/quadrangle)
4. X
5. Nelson Mandela (also accept Nelson Rolihlahla Mandela/Madiba)
6. Gorillas
7. Italy
8. Daniel Craig
9. Spanish
10. Oxygen
11. Columbo
12. Wembley
13. Noddy
14. Two
15. WOMAD (also accept World of Music, Arts and Dance)
16. Wool
17. Iraq
18. *The Help*
19. Football (also accept soccer)
20. Ostrich
21. Rovers Return (also accept the Rovers)
22. Conservative (also accept Tory)
23. Jacqueline Kennedy (also accept Jackie Kennedy/Jackie Onassis/Jackie O/Jacqueline Bouvier)
24. Head (also accept on top of the head)
25. 20th (also accept 1900s)
26. Radio Four (also accept BBC Radio 4)
27. Jack the Hat (also accept Jack 'The Hat' McVitie)
28. United States (also accept USA/America)

MATT VS. ANNE

MATT

1. Mustard
2. Monster Raving Loony (also accept Official Monster Raving Loony)
3. Ireland (also accept Republic of Ireland/Eire)
4. One (also accept one (troy) ounce)
5. Jaw (also accept mandible/lower jaw/jawbone
6. White
7. *Basic Instinct*
8. Serbia
9. ECG (not EKG – US term)
10. House of Commons (also accept Commons)
11. Guitar (also accept acoustic guitar, electric guitar)
12. Butterfly
13. Bow
14. George Harrison
15. The Crystal Palace
16. Liver
17. 3,000
18. J. Edgar Hoover (also Hoover; not Herbert Hoover)
19. Charlie Brown (also accept Charlie)
20. Bellagio
21. Asia
22. Karl Lagerfeld (also accept Lagerfeld)
23. Zulu
24. New York
25. G

ANSWERS

ANSWERS

ANNE

1 Clean
2 Cardiff
3 William Wordsworth (also accept Wordsworth)
4 Richard Gere
5 Rug
6 California
7 Tastes (also accept flavours)
8 Judaism (also accept Jewish religion/Hebrew religions/Jews)
9 Vision (also accept sight)
10 Calais
11 Brian Potter
12 Nottinghamshire
13 Africa
14 Italian
15 Prince Charles (also accept Prince of Wales)
16 Bertrand (also accept Bertrand Russell)
17 Four
18 Blue
19 Victoria (also accept Queen Victoria)
20 *Dombey and Son*
21 Lemon (also accept slice of lemon)
22 Clutch
23 London
24 Thomas (also accept Tom)
25 Navy (also accept Royal Navy)
26 Pies

SCOTT VS. JENNY

SCOTT

1 *Harry Potter*
2 French
3 *Footballers' Wives*
4 Habsburg (also accept Hapsburg)
5 Three
6 Kristen Stewart
7 Germany
8 Giuseppe Verdi (also accept Verdi)
9 Book
10 Skin
11 Rizzle Kicks (also accept Jordan 'Rizzle' Stephens/ Harley 'Sylvester' Alexander-Sule)
12 Vladimir Putin (also accept Putin)
13 Lord Greystoke (also accept (Viscount) Greystoke/Earl of Greystoke/Lord of the Apes)
14 Umpires
15 Norway
16 Red (also accept (dark) pink)
17 Roman (also accept Rome)
18 *How I Met Your Mother*
19 Asia (also accept Southeast Asia)
20 Olivia Newton-John
21 Bread
22 Edward VIII (also accept Duke of Windsor)

JENNY

1 Supermarket
2 Fungus (also accept fungi/ spore bearing)
3 George Clooney
4 Volkswagen (also accept VW)
5 Cross-shaped (also accept cross/cruciform/cruciate)
6 *Merlin*
7 Gallstone
8 Son
9 Wimbledon
10 Switzerland
11 The Script
12 Nine
13 Bird
14 Bath
15 Philip Pullman
16 Islam (also accept Muslim religion)
17 White
18 *Two and a Half Men*
19 Francisco Franco (also accept Franco/General Franco)
20 George Lazenby
21 WD
22 Brain (also accept cerebrum)
23 Pixie Lott

CHRIS VS. PAUL

CHRIS

1 Chicken (also accept rooster/turkey)
2 Mediterranean (also accept the Med)
3 Dragon
4 Kimi Raikkonen (also accept Raikkonnen)
5 Whisky (also accept single malt (whisky/Scotch))
6 *From Russia with Love*
7 Blue
8 Assad (also accept al-Assad)
9 Natural History Museum
10 Four
11 Gavrilo Princip (also accept Princip)
12 Light bulb
13 Hogwarts
14 Gwyneth Paltrow (also accept Gwyneth Kate Paltrow)
15 *Guernica*
16 Humber Bridge (also accept Humber)
17 28
18 Geena Davis
19 The Bible (also accept The New Testament)
20 Elephant
21 *Oliver!*
22 'Barbie Girl'
23 Pre-Raphaelite Brotherhood (also accept Pre-Raphaelite(s)/PRB)
24 Stuart
25 Leaf
26 Las Vegas (also accept Vegas)

PAUL

1 Aeroplane
2 To market
3 Wookiees
4 Edward I
5 Coffee (also accept espresso/black coffee)
6 *Family Guy*
7 Hercule Poirot (also accept Poirot)
8 Grigor Dimitrov (also accept Dimitrov)
9 Glass
10 'Barcelona'
11 Alexander Selkirk (also accept Selkirk; not Robinson Crusoe)
12 Yellow
13 Sheep (also accept ewe/lamb/ram)
14 Harris
15 Machu Picchu (also accept Machupijchu)
16 Princess Diana (also accept Diana, Princess of Wales/Princess Di/Diana Spencer)
17 108
18 *Mad Max*
19 Rome (also accept Ancient Rome/Roman Empire)
20 Lee Child (also accept Child/James)
21 Beard
22 Glasgow
23 Hydrogen
24 Oracle (not Teletext on 3/ITV-text)
25 Bacardi

BIGGEST CELEBRITY WINS

CAROL VORDERMAN, PAUL ROSS, SUE CLEAVER AND JOHN THOMSON

1 *Family Fortunes* (also accept *All Star Family Fortunes*)
2 Rugby (also accept rugby union)
3 Dappy
4 Norway
5 125
6 Sausage (also accept hot dog/Frankfurter)
7 Tyrone (also accept Tyrone Dobbs)
8 *Man of La Mancha*
9 Figure skating (also accept ice skating/men's figure skating)
10 Asia
11 Ryan Reynolds (also accept Reynolds)
12 Uffizi
13 London Bridge (also accept London)
14 Beef
15 Jerusalem
16 *The 39 Steps*
17 London
18 Chihuahua
19 Dean Martin (also accept Martin)
20 Eyes (also accept eye)
21 Delaware
22 500
23 Amy (also accept Amy March)

ANSWERS

HILARY JONES, TINA MALONE, CHARLOTTE JACKSON AND JON CULSHAW

1 Coca-Cola
2 Shedding (also accept moulting/shed/slough/sloughing)
3 *The Wombles*
4 *Emma*
5 Baseball (not rounders)
6 Air Force (also accept Royal Air Force)
7 Michael McIntyre
8 Fashion (also accept clothes/fashion design)
9 Water (also accept distilled water/filtered water/tap water)
10 Gas
11 Martin Shaw
12 Anosmia (also accept anosmic)
13 Bunting
14 Two
15 Maiden (also accept maiden voyage)
16 John Sullivan
17 Feet
18 Oxford
19 Bayern Munich (also accept FC Bayern München)
20 Mesrine (also accept Jacques Mesrine)
21 Whisky (also accept Scotch whisky/Scotch/Irish whiskey)
22 Arden
23 John Prescott
24 John the Baptist (not just John)
25 Cherry blossoms (also accept cherry)
26 Karachi (also accept Rawalpindi)

SAMIA GHADIE, ALEX BROOKER, ANNABEL GILES AND JULIAN CLARY

1 French
2 *Priscilla, Queen of the Desert* (the Musical) (also accept *Priscilla*)
3 Ajax (also accept Ajax Amsterdam)
4 Carmela
5 Gloves
6 *Gentlemen's Quarterly*
7 China
8 *Labyrinth*
9 Europe
10 Throat
11 Balmoral
12 New Zealand
13 Justin
14 Bedfordshire
15 Charles De Gaulle
16 Frank Sinatra (also accept Sinatra)
17 Victoria
18 Liberty Bell
19 Nintendo
20 1860s
21 Go
22 Norway
23 Inverness

FIONA BRUCE, RICK EDWARDS, KATE HUMBLE AND JOE SWASH

1 One
2 Cat (also accept feline/hairless cat)
3 Hugh Grant
4 Boris Johnson
5 Butter
6 Shirley Conran (also accept Shirley)
7 Eminem (also accept Marshall Mathers)
8 J. M. Coetzee (also accept John Maxwell Coetzee)
9 Piper (also accept bagpiper)
10 Matthew
11 Cacciatore
12 Anna Friel
13 Vacuum cleaner (also accept Dyson)
14 Republican
15 Henry VIII
16 Stanislas (not Stanislav)
17 History
18 Greece
19 Soap
20 Wu-Tang Clan
21 Crossed (also accept folded/feet on the opposite thighs)
22 IKEA
23 Sumo (also accept sumo wrestling)
24 Fish

ANSWERS

NADIA SAWALHA, JAMES COSMO, GEMMA ATKINSON AND JIMI MISTRY

1 France
2 Two
3 Mao Zedong (also accept Chairman Mao/Mao Tse-Tung)
4 Suranne Jones
5 Brown
6 Head (also accept over the hair)
7 Humes (also accept Rochelle Humes)
8 *The Hunger Games*
9 USA
10 Worcestershire Sauce (also accept Worcester Sauce)
11 Millennium Stadium
12 Genesis
13 Pottery (also accept ceramics/making pots/throwing pots)
14 Red
15 Sharon Osbourne
16 Bury
17 Death (also accept Black Death)
18 Norway
19 Four
20 *Serena*
21 Bread

NIGEL HAVERS, MELINDA MESSENGER, MICHELLE HARDWICK AND DAVE GORMAN

1 Train (also accept railway)
2 Chilli con carne
3 Three
4 Phil Taylor (also accept Phil 'The Power' Taylor)
5 Hair (also accept head)
6 *Jason Bourne*
7 Tennessee Williams
8 Mumford and Sons
9 Lattice (also accept lattice pie topping/lattice pastry/lattice crust)
10 Julius Caesar (also accept Caesar/Gaius Julius Caesar)
11 Merida
12 Tesco
13 Jacket
14 Instagram
15 Terry Hall (also accept Hall)
16 Chinese
17 Falklands War (also accept Falkland Islands War/Malvinas/Falklands (Conflict))
18 *Happy Valley*
19 Tennis
20 Grayson Perry
21 Liverpool
22 World War One (also accept Great War/First World War)

JAY RAYNER, LUCY PORTER, KRISHNAN GURU-MURTHY AND STEVE DAVIS

1 Ice (also accept snow/hail/ice pellet)
2 France
3 Gareth Bale (also accept (Gareth Frank) Bale)
4 Julia Gillard (also accept Gillard)
5 Scientology (also accept Church of Scientology)
6 Scar
7 24
8 Cherry
9 Shirley Williams (also accept Baroness Williams)
10 Styx (also accept Acheron)
11 *Love Me or Leave Me*
12 Latin
13 Missing Out
14 Five
15 Julian May
16 Tunnel
17 Swan
18 *A Passage to India*
19 Pupils (also accept pupil/iris)
20 Steam engine (also accept steam)
21 San Francisco

ANN WIDDECOMBE, SAM NIXON, MARK RHODES AND JIMMY CARR

1 Heart
2 Dark
3 Snake
4 Charles II
5 Bicycle (also accept bike/cycle)
6 Melons
7 The Edge (also accept Dave (Howell) Evans)
8 John Selwyn Gummer (also accept (John) Gummer)
9 God
10 Mortgage
11 Dick Francis (also accept Richard Francis)
12 Parliament Square (Garden)
13 Ship (also accept steamship/boat/cargo ship)
14 Tea(bags)
15 Hebrew
16 *Into the Woods*
17 TFL
18 Synthesiser
19 Choux pastry
20 Oxford
21 Goalkeeper (also accept in goal)
22 (Sir) Michael Parkinson
23 Basil

CHASER PERFECT RUNS

ANDREW, EMMA, CHRISTINA AND DAVE VS. MARK

1 Tennessee
2 Baldwin
3 Afghanistan
4 Five
5 Atlantic
6 MSG
7 Meatballs
8 Joyce Grenfell (also accept Grenfell)
9 Parthenon
10 Amanda Holden (also accept Holden)
11 United Nations (also accept UN)
12 Boris Karloff
13 Lennox Lewis (also accept Lewis)
14 Apple
15 Pianissimo
16 John Dillinger (also accept Dillinger)
17 Rook
18 *Emmerdale*
19 Rwanda
20 West Germany (also accept Germany)
21 North Sea
22 Venus
23 Charles I
24 Acronym
25 Balearic Islands (also accept Pitiusas)
26 Dalmatian

ALAN, DAVE, KATE AND GILL VS. PAUL

1 One
2 Cousin (also accept first cousin)
3 Lynda Carter
4 *Moby-Dick*
5 Roman Empire (also accept Roman/Rome)
6 Barrels (also accept beer barrels/casks/buckets/tubs)
7 C-3PO
8 Austrian
9 Breakfast
10 Six
11 *Nevermind*
12 Italy
13 Belladonna
14 Thumb (also accept pollex)
15 Dr Strangelove (also accept *Dr Strangelove, Or: How I Learned To Stop Worrying and Love the Bomb*)
16 Chalk (also accept gypsum/French chalk/calcium sulphate)
17 Cardiff City (also accept Cardiff (City FC))
18 17th (also accept 1600s)
19 Cat
20 Vanessa Paradis

REGGIE, GRAHAM, LUCY AND PAULINE VS. SHAUN

1 Summer
2 Ronnie Corbett
3 Heavyweight
4 George IV
5 Lily
6 Victoria (also accept Lake Victoria/Victoria Nyanza)
7 Elton John
8 Persian (also accept Persia/Achaemenid Empire
9 Horse
10 Will Smith
11 Mary Shelley (also accept Mary Wollstonecraft Godwin)
12 Krone (also accept Norwegian krone/crown)
13 11th
14 Gin (also accept Hollands/Dutch gin/Schiedam)
15 Liberal (also accept Liberals/Liberal Party; not Liberal Democrat)
16 Grandmother (also accept granny/gran)
17 Spock (also accept Mr Spock/(First) Officer Spock/Science Officer Spock)
18 Joel Garner
19 Aniseed (also accept anise/mastic/liquorice)
20 Village People
21 Sulphur

ANSWERS

PHILIP AND GAYNOR VS. PAUL

1 Gold
2 Vienna
3 *Whistle Stop Café*
4 Richard II
5 J. K. Rowling
6 Womb
7 United Arab Emirates
8 *The Italian Job*
9 Pan
10 1920s (also accept 20s)
11 Marcel Duchamp (also accept Duchamp)
12 Dog (also accept canine)
13 Cape Town
14 Spain
15 Skull (also accept head/ between parietal bones and occipital bone)
16 The wool (also accept wool)
17 A hand
18 Hebrew

SHAUNA AND MATT VS. ANNE

1 One
2 Table tennis (also accept ping pong)
3 Liesl von Trapp (also accept Liesl)
4 Robert F. Kennedy (also accept Bobby Kennedy/ Robert Kennedy/RFK)
5 Brain (also accept encephalon)
6 Jenna Coleman (also accept Jenna Louise Coleman)
7 Michael Faraday (also accept Faraday)
8 Herodotus
9 Asia
10 C'est la guerre
11 Gene Vincent (also accept Gene Vincent and the Blue Caps)
12 Russian
13 Moth (not butterfly)
14 Krypton
15 David Copperfield
16 Horses (also accept humans/racehorses)
17 Selenium

JOHN, CAIA AND DAVID VS. ANNE

1 Princess
2 Whales (also accept dolphins)
3 *South Park*
4 Styx
5 Mediterranean (also accept the Med)
6 Nicole Kidman
7 Chemist (also accept pharmacy)
8 Morocco (also accept Kingdom of Morocco)
9 Crab
10 U2
11 Three
12 Eurostar (not Eurotunnel)
13 Betty Ford (also accept Elizabeth Ford)
14 Hair loss (also accept baldness/balding/hair thinning)
15 Tennis (also accept lawn tennis)
16 White (also accept cream)
17 Florida
18 Al Pacino
19 World War Two (also accept Second World War)
20 'American Pie'

NICK AND JOSEPH VS. PAUL

1 English
2 Ballet (also accept classical ballet)
3 Paul O'Grady
4 Daphne du Maurier (also accept Du Maurier)
5 Right-hand drive
6 Mark Zuckerberg (also accept Zuckerberg/ (Eduardo) Saverin/(Dustin) Moskovitz/(Chris) Hughes/ (Andrew) McCollum)
7 Cricket
8 *The Silence of the Lambs*
9 Prosecco
10 *Nighthawks*
11 Winston Graham (also accept Graham)
12 *Thunderbirds*
13 Pablo Picasso (also accept Picasso)
14 Leopard
15 Potato
16 Money

ANSWERS

KAREN, GARETH AND MIKE VS. JENNY

1 Tom
2 Wales
3 Boba Fett
4 Proscenium arch (also accept proscenium/pros (arch))
5 Boston Red Sox (also accept Red Sox)
6 Eagle (also accept golden eagle)
7 Tomato
8 Dave Lister (also accept Lister/David Lister)
9 World War Two (also accept Second World War)
10 BS
11 Mars
12 BBC
13 Pineapple
14 Prosecutions
15 River Ouse (also accept Ouse)
16 Colours (also accept wavelength/frequencies)
17 Brothers (also accept siblings)

CHASE ODDITIES

HIGHEST SCORE IN A CASH BUILDER

1 Eagle
2 Choux
3 Guy Ritchie (also accept Ritchie)
4 Wiltshire
5 John Peel (also accept Peel)
6 Sn
7 Satellite navigation
8 Abraham Lincoln (also accept Lincoln)
9 Life of Brian (also accept Monty Python's Life of Brian)
10 Samuel Pepys (also accept Pepys)
11 France
12 A Streetcar Named Desire
13 Venus
14 Clint Eastwood (also accept Eastwood)

HIGHEST SCORE IN A CASH BUILDER BY A TEENAGER

1 Chopsticks
2 The Godfather
3 Three
4 Point
5 Harry Houdini
6 Private Eye
7 (Sir) Alex Ferguson
8 Niger
9 The Imitation Game
10 Dog
11 Chicago

BIGGEST LOW OFFER EVER ACCEPTED

1 C Your dad
2 C Stromboli
3 B Cheese Grater
4 A Hades

BIGGEST COMBINED HIGH OFFERS

JONATHAN

1 C Holidays
2 C Spain
3 B Richard II
4 C J. R. R. Tolkien
5 C Ships
6 B Helium

IONA

1 A Brazil
2 A Two
3 C Daily Mail
4 B Chicken
5 C A ballet dancer
6 A Dumbfuggle
7 A Her bum
8 B Ozzy Osbourne

STEPH

1 C Macaroni
2 B Stern John
3 B Moth
4 C Fire
5 B Leg
6 A Salvador Dalí
7 A Facebook

MICHAEL

1 C Sex and the City
2 A Four
3 A Holly Golightly
4 B Pyramid scheme
5 A Worms
6 B Uranus
7 B Hair salon

HIGHEST SCORE BY A SOLO PLAYER IN A FINAL CHASE THAT DIDN'T WIN

PAT

1 Japanese
2 Hawaii
3 Gilbert and Sullivan (also accept William S. Gilbert and Arthur Sullivan)
4 Jana Novotna (also accept Novotna)
5 RAF (also accept Royal Air Force / Air Force)
6 Boris Johnson (also accept Johnson)
7 Madeira (also accept Madeira Islands)
8 Minimum Lending Rate (also accept Minimum Lending)

9 Romance
10 Model making (also accept modelling/models/model planes)
11 *The Wrestler*
12 Lake Michigan (also accept Michigan)
13 366
14 Military Intelligence
15 Apple
16 Georgia
17 Eric and Ernie (also accept Eric and Ern/John and Ernest)
18 Thailand
19 *Aspects of Love*

20 Beaver
21 Sonic
22 Hair
23 *Twilight*
24 South Africa
25 Asia
26 Frequency Modulation
27 1926
28 Clare Francis (also accept Francis)
29 *Home and Away*
30 Lira

ANNE

1 Ireland
2 Rust
3 Ernest Hemingway (also accept Hemingway)
4 South Korea
5 31
6 Judaism (also accept Jewish)
7 Buddy Holly (also accept Holly)
8 Ruminants
9 Tango

10 Leonardo DiCaprio (also accept DiCaprio)
11 Alamo
12 Belgium
13 Pinocchio
14 Wallet (also accept Purse)
15 Heracles (also accept Hercules)
16 Netherlands (also accept Holland)
17 Euro
18 Red Sea

19 1940s
20 Banjo
21 Technology
22 Mary, Queen of Scots (also accept Mary)
23 Smorgasbord
24 Richard Dunwoody (also accept Dunwoody)
25 Australia
26 Hydrogen

TIM

1 Fun
2 36
3 *Jersey Shore*
4 Saddle
5 Lancashire (also accept Lancs)
6 Mordor
7 1936
8 Cheese
9 Harry Redknapp (also accept Harry)
10 Justin Bieber (also accept Bieber)
11 Comet I (also accept Comet)
12 Eye

13 Joey (also accept Joey Tribbiani)
14 Sioux (also accept Oglala)
15 Africa
16 Six
17 German
18 *Grey's Anatomy*
19 Maine
20 United Nations
21 Mushroom (also accept wild mushroom/fungus)
22 Kenny Logan (also accept Logan)
23 *Financial Times* (also accept FT)

24 Playing cards (also accept cards)
25 Himalayas
26 Duffy (also accept Aimee Anne)
27 16th (also accept 1500s)
28 Ireland (also accept Republic of Ireland/Eire)
29 Cleanliness
30 Edelweiss
31 Judaism (also accept Jewish)
32 William the Conqueror (also accept William I)
33 Eugene O'Neill (also accept O'Neill)

ANSWERS

MARK

1 Football
2 Nothing
3 Pauline Quirke
4 Ken Loach (also accept Loach)
5 28
6 Pacific (also accept South Pacific)
7 David Gray (also accept Gray)
8 Bertolt Brecht (also accept Brecht)
9 Bear (also accept teddy bear)
10 January
11 *Happy Days*
12 Shetland Islands (also accept Shetland(s))
13 Six
14 Pandas (also accept giant pandas)
15 Honey
16 Larry Hagman
17 Portugal
18 Labour
19 Nicole Scherzinger (also accept Scherzinger)
20 1960s (also accept 60s)
21 Fred Flintstone
22 Ivan the Terrible (also accept the Terrible)
23 Wasps (also accept hornets)
24 USA (also accept America)
25 Chinese (also accept Chinese lunar)
26 Matt Lucas (also accept Lucas)
27 1973
28 Brachiosaurus
29 *I'm a Celebrity...Get Me Out of Here* (also accept *I'm a Celebrity*)

HIGHEST AMOUNT EVER PLAYED FOR IN A FINAL CHASE

RONNIE

1 Massage
2 Pasta
3 IOU
4 Red
5 Shoes
6 Rasputin
7 *The History Boys*
8 Italy
9 Bird
10 Vanessa Williams
11 *The BFG*
12 Thomas Edison
13 *The Sound of Music*
14 Detective
15 Magazine
16 Fertilisation
17 Wes Anderson
18 Jesus
19 Pablo Picasso
20 Cat
21 Euston

MARK

1 Leonardo da Vinci
2 16
3 *Charlotte's Web*
4 Asia
5 Grand National
6 Grape
7 *Dragons' Den*
8 Mars
9 Leonard Nimoy

LOWEST EVER SCORE IN A FINAL CHASE

CONTESTANT

1 Glastonbury
2 *Lord of the Rings*
3 Russia
4 Ganymede
5 *The Sound of Music*
6 Hockey
7 25
8 Aaron
9 Owl
10 Sylvester Stallone
11 Jacob Zuma
12 The king
13 Europe
14 Mile
15 Viola
16 Donkey Kong
17 *Dad's Army*
18 Newton
19 Two
20 Mao Zedong (also accept Chairman Mao/Mao Tsetung)

CHASER

1 H
2 Petrograd
3 Baseball

MOST PUSHBACKS IN A FINAL CHASE

1. Snake
2. Irish
3. Spandau
4. Tom Conti
5. Dog
6. Hinduism (also accept Hindu)
7. Contributions
8. 1930s
9. Kylie Minogue
10. Kent
11. Revelation
12. Japanese cuisine
13. Christmas Day
14. Records
15. *George's Marvellous Medicine*
16. Charles
17. Poker
18. 2Pac
19. Camelot
20. Amazon
21. Martial
22. Walkers
23. 'Lose Yourself'
24. Agatha Christie
25. Candles

OLDEST MALE CONTESTANT

1. Dog
2. 'Livin' on a Prayer'
3. Cleopatra
4. *The Big Bang Theory*
5. Five
6. Everton FC
7. Orange
8. *Zoolander*

OLDEST CONTESTANT EVER

1. One
2. World War Two (also accept Second World War)
3. Hovercraft
4. Haw
5. Shredder
6. Tigger

GUESS THE CONNECTION

CONNECTIONS QUIZ 1

1. **C** Winston Churchill (features on the £5 polymer note)
2. Adam Smith (features on the paper £20 note, to be replaced by J.M.W. Turner)
3. **A** Jane Austen (features on the polymer £10 note)
4. J. M. W. Turner (will feature on the £20 polymer note from 2020)
5. The Queen (the first monarch to appear on a UK banknote)
6. Alan Turing (announced 2019 to appear on the new £50 polymer note)

Connection: People on UK banknotes

CONNECTIONS QUIZ 2

1. Bounty
2. Dime
3. Mars
4. Milky Way
5. Double decker

Connection: Chocolate bars

CONNECTIONS QUIZ 3

1. Hamilton
2. Camelot
3. Chess
4. Hair
5. Chicago

Connection: Musicals

CONNECTIONS QUIZ 4

1. Macmillan
2. Cameron Mackintosh
3. **A** Baldwin
4. Wilson Phillips
5. Eden
6. Churchill

Connection: UK Prime Ministers

CONNECTIONS QUIZ 5

1 Submarine   **3** Walrus   **5** Norwegian
2 Jude Law   **4** Diamonds
Connection: Beatles songs ('Yellow Submarine'/ 'Hey Jude' / 'I am the Walrus' /
'Lucy in the Sky with Diamonds' / 'Norwegian Wood')

CONNECTIONS QUIZ 6

1 Peach   **3** Sunshine   **5** Granite
2 Golden   **4** Beavers
Connection: US state nicknames (Peach State = Georgia, Golden State = California,
Sunshine State = Florida, Beaver State = Oregon, Granite State = New Hampshire)

CONNECTIONS QUIZ 7

1 Joan Bakewell   **3** *Gypsy*   **5** Apple
2 Manchester   **4** Custard
Connection: Tarts

CONNECTIONS QUIZ 8

1 **A** Luna 1   **3** **C** Minerva   **5** Hermione
2 Dudley   **4** Draco   **6** Sirius
Connection: Harry Potter characters (Luna Lovegood / Dudley Durdsley / Minerva McGonagall /
Draco Malfoy / Hermione Granger / Sirius Black)

CONNECTIONS QUIZ 9

1 Rupert Murdoch   **3** Heath Ledger   **5** Kylie Minogue
2 Germaine Greer   **4** Shane Warne   (also accept Kylie)
Connection: Famous Australians

CONNECTIONS QUIZ 10

1 Beehive   **3** **A** Armadilla   **5** **B** Birds'-Nest
2 Walkie-talkie   **4** Gherkin
Connection: Buildings (New Zealand's parliament building / 20 Fenchurch Street, London / The SEC
Centre Glasgow / 30 St Mary Axe, London / Beijing National Stadium)

CONNECTIONS QUIZ 11

1 Lulu   **3** Katrina   **5** Bucks Fizz
2 Euphoria   **4** Waterloo
Connection: Eurovision Song Contest Winners

CONNECTIONS QUIZ 12

1 **C** Constable   **3** Columbus   **5** **A** Screaming
2 Matron   **4** Jack   **6** Cowboy
Connection: *Carry On* films

CONNECTIONS QUIZ 13

1 Ruby   **5** Apples   **9** Tea
2 Murray   **6** Pears   **10** Leaf
3 Whistle   **7** Dog   **11** Frog
4 Flute   **8** Bone   **12** Toad
Connection: Cockney rhyming slang (Ruby Murray = curry / Whistle and flute = suit /
Apples and pears = stairs / Dog and bone = phone / Tea-leaf = thief / Frog and toad = road)

ANSWERS

CONNECTIONS QUIZ 14
1 Harry Potter
2 Catherine the Great
Connection: Royal family

3 Meghan Trainor
4 *Just William*

5 George

CONNECTIONS QUIZ 15
1 Desmond Morris
2 Lotus position
Connection: Car companies

3 Jaguar
4 Yamaha

5 Harrison Ford

THE CHASE DOWN UNDER

CASH BUILDER
1 Ned Kelly
2 Odie
3 White
4 Hammer (also accept Mjölnir)
5 *Forrest Gump*

6 Nicaragua
7 Vegemite
8 Pitcher
9 Copper
10 Kirribilli House
11 Manila

12 Siri
13 Giraffe
14 *The X-Files*
15 The *Pequod*

FINAL CHASE
1 Rubik's Cube
2 Brain
3 Fiji
4 Iago
5 (Qantas) Wallabies

6 Jupiter
7 (Mister/Mastro) Geppetto
8 Tame Impala
9 Tina Fey
10 Ear

11 *Live and Let Die*
12 Dog
13 (King) George VI
14 Capital (Hill)
15 Anubis (also accept Anpu)

MULTIPLE CHOICE
1 B Neutral
2 C 38 minutes
3 A Bus
4 B Facepick
5 C Bishop
6 A Eyes
7 A A-league

8 B Tim Minchin
9 C Divine wind
10 B spoons
11 B AK
12 C Star Wars
13 C Russ Le Roq
14 A Polynesia

15 B 15
16 A Blundstone
17 A Incus
18 C Haircut
19 B Croque madame

ANSWERS

QUESTIONS CHASERS COULDN'T GET

1 Golf
(Chaser said cricket)

2 B Richard III
(Chaser said C Henry II)

3 John Lennon
(Chaser said Amundsen)

4 B Hammer
(Chaser said A Chisel)

5 Harry Potter
(Chaser passed)

6 Blue
(Chaser said yellow)

7 C Swallow
(Chaser said B Seagull)

8 B Clam juice
(Chaser said C Bat spit)

9 Yellow
(Chaser said green)

10 Vaseline
(Chaser said KY jelly)

11 A Mark
(Chaser said B Matt)

12 A The bleachers
(Chaser said C The whiteners)

13 Alexander Fleming
(Chaser passed)

14 Star
(Chaser said car wash)

15 A Ballroom dancing
(Chaser said B Billiards)

16 C Abba
(Chaser said B Slade)

17 Hydrogen
(Chaser said oxygen)

18 A Atlantic Highway
(Chaser said B Road to Hell)

19 Boxing Day
(Chaser said New Years' Day)

20 Two
(Chaser said one)

21 A Drive it
(Chaser said B Eat it)

22 Great-niece
(Chaser said cousin)

23 A LeBron James
(Chaser said C Lionel Messi)

24 A Fluffy duck
(Chaser said B Fluffy dice)

25 He-Man
(Chaser said SpongeBob SquarePants)

26 Homeboy
(Chaser passed)

27 Alan Titchmarsh
(Chaser said Germaine Greer)

28 Green
(Chaser said yellow)

29 B Siegfried and Roy
(Chaser said A Penn and Teller)

30 B Talking mongoose
(Chaser said A Singing spider)

31 B Royal Burpee
(Chaser said A King Plank)

32 Pinkerton
(Chaser said FBI)

33 Paris
(Chaser said Peking)

34 Toecap
(Chaser said heel)

35 Chips
(Chaser said fruit)

36 A Cygnet
(Chaser said B Gosling)

37 Private
(Chaser said corporal)

38 C Formula One
(Chaser said B Sailing)

39 Marks and Spencer
(Chaser said Spar)

40 A The Danish flag
(Chaser said C The Danish king)

41 'Polly Put the Kettle On'
(Chaser said 'Ring-a-Ring o'Roses')

42 Machine guns
(Chaser said guns)

43 Four
(Chaser said three)

44 Stevie Nicks
(Chaser said Adele)

45 Bed
(Chaser said sofa)

46 The devil
(Chaser said Father Time)

47 Termites
(Chaser said ants)

48 RSPB
(Chaser said RSPCB)

49 B Wedding ring
(Chaser said C Piece of haggis)

50 A Arthur Conan Doyle
(Chaser said C Anton Chekhov)

51 C Dickie Brickie
(Chaser said A Willy Nilly)

52 Ear
(Chaser said finger)

53 Highlighter
(Chaser passed)

54 B Venus
(Chaser said A Saturn)

55 *Mork and Mindy*
(Chaser said *Metal Mickey*)

56 *EastEnders*
(Chaser said *Coronation Street*)

57 The T-Birds
(Chaser said The Jets)

58 Ten
(Chaser said one)

59 Tango
(Chaser said foxtrot)

60 Buckingham Palace
(Chaser said Buckingham House)

61 Dominoes
(Chaser said Scrabble)

62 **C** Rectangular
(Chaser said **A** Triangular)

63 **A** Head guards
(Chaser said **C** Underwear)

64 Tom
(Chaser said Robert)

65 Spain
(Chaser said Mexico)

66 Victoria Beckham
(Chaser said Geri Halliwell)

67 The spleen
(Chaser said bone)

68 **A** Seed money
(Chaser said **B** Root payments)

69 Popcorn
(Chaser said biscuits)

70 Champagne
(Chaser said water)

71 Wall
(Chaser said window)

72 Trousers
(Chaser said shoes)

73 Cupid
(Chaser said Apollo)

74 Buckaroo!
(Chaser passed)

75 **A** Convent
(Chaser said **B** Castle)

76 Aquarius
(Chaser said Gemini)

77 Black
(Chaser said red)

78 Yen
(Chaser said shekel)

79 Watch
(Chaser said bike)

80 **B** Merman
(Chaser said **C** Dragon)

81 **B** A mile
(Chaser said **C** Two miles)

82 **B** Putter
(Chaser said **A** Driver)

83 **C** Javelin
(Chaser said **B** Shot put)

84 **A** Live
(Chaser said **C** Earth)

85 **A** Love
(Chaser said **C** Desire)

86 **A** Brenda Blethyn
(Chaser said **B** Pauline Quirke)

87 **B** Stuart
(Chaser said **A** York)

88 Autumn
(Chaser said summer)

89 **B** Crepe Suzette
(Chaser said **C** Rum Baba)

90 Gelignite
(Chaser said gelatine)

91 **C** Toad
(Chaser said **A** Newt)

92 Yellow
(Chaser said blue)

93 **B** Eat it
(Chaser said **C** Wear it)

94 **B** *Goodness Gracious Me*
(Chaser said **A** *The Fast Show*)

95 **B** Shoulder blades
(Chaser said **C** Ribs)

96 **A** Wedding dresses
(Chaser said **C** Handbags)

97 **A** Rheumatism
(Chaser said **B** Heartburn)

98 **C** Pearl
(Chaser said **A** Amethyst)

99 **C** Silly Sausage
(Chaser said **A** Crazy Cucumber)

100 Tea
(Chaser said wine)

101 **B** Gala pie
(Chaser said **A** Homity pie)

102 Bobby
(Chaser said JR)

103 Three
(Chaser said two)

104 **A** 'Everywhere'
(Chaser said **B** 'Nowhere')

105 **B** Tennis ball in a sock
(Chaser said **A** Marble in a balloon)

106 **B** His hair
(Chaser said **A** His feet)

107 **B** International orange
(Chaser said **A** Worldwide white)

ANSWERS

OLAV'S FAVOURITE QUESTIONS

1 A Bob Holness
2 A Cricket
3 A Football
4 A 'No Limit'
5 A Marbles
6 C Nude push-ups
7 B Hawaiian
8 C Duke of Wellington
9 A Part of his left ear
10 A Keith Bishop
11 A Hm

12 C Wa-oh
13 B Frosties
14 C Patent and Trademark Office
15 A Bald eagle
16 C Enema
17 C *War and Peace*
18 C Africa
19 A Austin
20 B Neurology
21 C 'Purple Haze'

22 A Email
23 C Winston Churchill
24 C Japan
25 C He is aged 26
26 B *Patriot Games*
27 C A chicken
28 A Mr Chicken
29 A Bhutan
30 B Moon
31 C OMG
32 C Margaret Thatcher

QUESTIONS THAT MADE BRAD LAUGH

1 C Skiing
2 B Alsatian plums
3 C Willi Wakker
4 C Blue
5 C Water polo
6 C Chocolate Salty Balls
7 A Agnes
8 A Name
9 A Teeth
10 A Gaylord Silly
11 C Weightlifting
12 C Bigger balls
13 B Hairy lychee
14 B The camel's nose

15 C Gussie Moran
16 C Organ
17 B 'Brown-Eyed Girl'
18 A Monkey
19 A Beach ball
20 A Backgammon
21 C Raspberry
22 B Flute
23 A Snarge
24 A Bow and arrow
25 A *Hat*
26 C Groundhog Day
27 A Big Narstie
28 C Walter Plinge

29 C Kermit
30 A What's for breakfast?
31 A U Nu
32 B Skin
33 A Pamela Anderson
34 C 'Memory'
35 C They are cube-shaped
36 A Pie Corner
37 A Bat
38 C Rector's Relish
39 B Tipper

ACKNOWLEDGEMENTS

Thank you to Michael Kelpie, Martin Scott, Helen Tumbridge, Ian Cross, James Bovington, Lisa Milestone, Emily Pentecost-Daley and Caroline Sale of Potato for all their hard work and good humour during the production of this book, and to Chas Newkey-Burden for his development of the book structure and spadework on the manuscript. Thanks also to Shirley Patton of ITV Global Entertainment for making this book happen in the first place and to Sonya Newland for her editorial skills. Finally, thanks to the Chase question team and, of course, to Bradley Walsh and the Chasers for providing us with 10 years of fantastic teatime fun!